Praise for
Target Opportunity Selling

"Nic Read's book reminds us that large, complex sales are different in kind from transactional sales and therefore require a different approach. An interesting concept at the core of this book is of a 'looping' process, in which the sales opportunity changes as the relationship with the customer develops. These opportunities can take months or years to land, so his insight into the longitudinal progression of a complex sale is a welcome addition."

—Professor Lynette Ryals, Professor of Strategic Sales and
Account Management, Director of the KAM
Best Practice Research Club, Pro Vice Chancellor,
Cranfield School of Management

"As curriculum head of a leading university's sales center, I am constantly scanning for conceptual frameworks that better capture today's value-creation process. Since we teach and develop the Next Generation of sales professionals, we cannot use dated 'Sales 1.0/2.0' materials from past decades. So it's a pleasure to see that in this book Nic Read provides a research-based, forward-looking, and incredibly useful framework for 21st-century sales force value creation."

—Andrea L. Dixon, PhD, Executive Director of the Center for
Professional Selling and Keller Center for Research,
Hankamer School of Business, Baylor University

"A lot of books offer tips from an author's glory days as a salesperson. But it's difficult for readers to duplicate the same situations, so results are hit-and-miss. *Target Opportunity Selling* offers an alternative that's better suited to the corporate world. It's researched on best practices and offers a scalable play-by-play guide any professional can follow to achieve predictable results. Highly recommended."

—Carl Farrell, Executive Vice President, SAS Americas

"Nic Read has created a sales bible littered with the confronting insights of new research, lessons from established leaders, and his own observations as a recognized sales process leader operating around the globe. He's woven this amalgam into a clear process and a good read. It's recommended for any existing sales leader, and all who would become so."

—Hugh Macfarlane, Founder & CEO, MathMarketing
and author of *The Leaky Funnel*

"Don't even think of not studying this book in minute detail if you are in B2B sales. You have never seen 'selling-on' discussed in such detail and with such depth. When I started my consultancy two decades ago there was nothing like this on the market. There is still nothing like it. Get it!"

—Bertie du Plessis, CEO, MindPilot (Pty) Ltd
and Naspers Head of Training and Development

"Insightful and one of the most practical manuals on the science of selling yet written. Not only does it reveal an alternative to the sales funnel more suited to solution selling, but by mapping proven techniques to today's buyer behaviours, Nic shows how to create the type of value that fuels growth beyond single transactions. If you're into the Challenger sale model, this book will take you to the next level."

—Joe Ringer, Sales & Market Strategist, CSC,
Australia, Asia, Middle East & Africa

"An exceptional 'box of tools' on how to win over and over in the complex sales environment. If you've been in the sales game all your life or are just starting out, *Target Opportunity Selling* is an essential foundation for every professional. This book is sure to become an industry-defining work of timeless importance."

—Lindsay Lyon, Executive Chairman, Shark Shield Pty Ltd
and former Partner, Siebel Systems

"I have read almost every book on professional sales. *Target Opportunity Selling* tops them all. It is highly recommended as a practical guide for anyone with the conviction and will to succeed. Best buy ever."

—Ingrid Kast, Chairman, Kast & Partners
International Executive Search

"Excellent. *Target Opportunity Selling* is enriched with many best practices, dos and don'ts. A must-read for sales management and account executives selling high-level products with complex sales cycles."

—Thomas Emmerich, Sales Operations Director,
SAS Institute GmbH

"Nic's original *Selling to the C-Suite* is a classic for engaging senior decision makers. Now *Target Opportunity Selling* offers us a step-by-step road map to create new sales opportunities, with real strategy and winning tactics. This book's 300 pages are packed with sage advice for winning complex B2B sales. Outstanding. There's no padding here!"

—Patrick Boucousis, CEO, Traxor

"*Target Opportunity Selling* is a great combination of solid fundamentals and new approaches that are essential in today's selling environment. Nic shows us how the best salespeople use research to 'open' the sale and a perfectly executed selling process to 'close' the sale and build lasting business relationships."

—Duane Sparks, Creator of Action Selling
and Chairman, The Sales Board

"Nic has used a wealth of research and real-life experiences to create the most comprehensive sales book of modern times. Highly entertaining and readable, this can improve the productivity of your salespeople immediately."

—Paul Cooper, VP EMEA Sales, CallidusCloud

"*Target Opportunity Selling* clearly outlines how top sellers consistently expand and win business with today's Ideas Buyers. If you're going after big accounts, this book is filled with fresh strategies that you can immediately use."

—Jill Konrath, author of *Selling to Big Companies*
and *SNAP Selling*

"Every page will open your eyes, challenge you, even make you squirm. Nic Read pulls no punches making a case for change in the sales game. Then he shows how with a practical toolbox and conversational style that's as smooth as a great coffee shop coaching session. *Target Opportunity Selling* is this generation's bible for strategic selling."

—Yoke Barrish, *Entrepreneur* Magazine

"If you've ever lost a sale you were sure was in the bag, seen decision criteria change to favour a competitor, or had customers stop taking your calls, it's because someone else is outselling you. Would you like to turn the tables? This is the sales book for you."

—Andy Sim, General Manager, Enterprise & SMB,
Samsung Electronics

TARGET OPPORTUNITY SELLING

TOP SALES PERFORMERS REVEAL
WHAT REALLY WORKS

NICHOLAS A.C. READ

New York Chicago San Francisco Athens London Madrid Mexico City
Milan New Delhi Singapore Sydney Toronto

1 2 3 4 5 6 7 8 9 0   DOC/DOC   1 9 8 7 6 5 4 3

ISBN 978-0-07-177307-2
MHID 0-07-177307-X

e-ISBN 978-0-07-177323-2
e-MHID 0-07-177323-1

Library of Congress Cataloging-in-Publication Data

Read, Nicholas A.C.
  Target opportunity selling : top sales performers reveal what really works / Nicholas A.C. Read.
     pages cm
  ISBN-13: 978-0-07-177307-2 (hardback : alk. paper)
  ISBN-10: 0-07-177307-X
  1. Selling. 2. Sales management. 3. Marketing. I. Title.
  HF5438.25.R43 2013
  658.85—dc23

                                        2013023063

McGraw-Hill Education books are available at special quantity discounts to use as premiums and sales promotions or for use in corporate training programs. To contact a representative, please visit the Contact Us pages at www.mhprofessional.com.

For every salesperson who aspires to greatness,
and every sales manager who embraces progress,
this road map is for you.
—NR

Contents

CONTENTS

Foreword

The modern sales approach was born in the rise of postwar industrialism nearly a century ago as factories retooled to crank out new products in fabric, plastic, and chromium steel. Competitors with similar products sent salespeople door-to-door, and their telephone-based equivalents were given territories, demo kits, and rich incentives to hit the bricks and bring home the bacon.

Those who had the right features, price, network, or personality to "sell the sizzle" raked in the orders and pocketed the commissions. Advertising executives created slogans, marketing departments offered incentives, and engineering teams developed new widgets. But it was always the salespeople on the front lines whose task it was to outpace, outtalk, and outsell the competition. As depicted by *Mad Men*'s Don Draper or sales booster Blake in the film *Glengarry Glen Ross*, persuasion and coercion went with the territory.

This was a raw merchant culture, and we still see vestiges of it today in the BRICS economies,[1] market bazaars, and low-end transactional sales. But there's no room for it in the high-end business-to-business solution sales that go down in the boardroom. Today, strategic opportunity management is not about dropping boxes, pushing tin, or looking for ways to trap the buyer. It's about facilitating an exchange of ideas that adds the type of commercial or personal value a customer cannot produce on their own and is willing to pay someone else to do for them.

This is consultative by nature and richly rewarding in practice.

Selling in this environment means you have to build relationships with multiple decision influencers across the customer's organization, all of whom have unique needs. You're the ringmaster for virtual team members that might include peers, managers, partners, or specialists from the next cubicle or across the world. You keep everyone on the same page. Selling is a team sport.

It's impossible to "wing it" and be successful in such a setting. You need a common sales language so the team members can talk about what's happening in a sale and decide if they're winning or losing—and what to do about it. Sales plans need to be written down and shared. After all, you can't execute what you don't plan. You can't improve what you don't measure.

We at SAS know this better than anyone. Corporations and government agencies in more than 50,000 sites around the world use SAS solutions to anticipate opportunity, empower action, and drive impact. As the accumulation of data increases exponentially, SAS provides the capabilities to not only answer "What happens next?" but also to make decisions on how to transform the way they do business. This insight, foresight, and action is what we call "the power to know." It's such a valuable resource that SAS has seen steady growth every year since our 1976 inception to become the largest privately owned software company in the world.

But as good as our products, services, and people are, our culture is one of innovation—we never rest on our laurels. With that in mind we work hard to win, delight, and retain our customers. There are many ways we do this. Most relevant to readers of *Target Opportunity Selling* is that the ideas you'll explore in this book are what SAS and other industry leaders actually use.

Back in 2008 we retained the services of author Nic Read and his company SalesLabs to help us improve the effectiveness of our sales and sales management personnel around the world. Through embedding their consulting, training, tools, and coaching into our sales culture, we've seen results that buck the trends of the global financial crisis. For example, SAS worldwide revenue continues to grow—new sales are up in the United States, as well as in Latin America and Europe. This has allowed our company to continue to invest in our workforce, while others in our industry have been cutting back.

So you see, this book isn't about *theory*. It's about *what really moves the needle*. Like Nic's previous book *Selling to the C-Suite*, this one is based on real research, science, and field experience. It pulls no punches in challenging the status quo, and importantly it has the teeth to do so.

At a time when corporate and government leaders in the United States and around the world are calling for jobs growth and greater economic stability, there's a school of thought that says you can't have jobs growth without top-line revenue growth.

If selling is the solution to this malady, then this book is the medicine.

Read it, execute, and prosper.

Nick Lisi
Vice President, SAS Americas

Acknowledgments

There are some very clever people around the world working on breakthroughs that I believe will revolutionize the sales profession and raise the bar on how companies achieve revenue growth. Their task is difficult because they're attempting to bring about change in a profession that lacks a central governance body and has no global standard for sales education at the tertiary level. As a result, change will come one company at a time—an exercise in herding cats. But with the world economy bearing witness to the need for change, I suspect we're about to see at least some of their ideas take root and spread like wildfire.

I'm thrilled to call these pioneers my colleagues and collaborators. All were generous in sharing their time, data, insights, and experience. They helped shape this book materially and directionally through their input or inspiration.

Russell Ward of Silent Edge, David Thomson of the Blueprint Growth Institute, Jim Dickie of CSO Insights, and Dr. Jim Loehr and Dr. Jack Groppel of the Human Performance Institute all stand out as visionaries who learned how top performers do what others only dream of, found a way to measure these secrets, and made them available to the world. Their ongoing work turns "voodoo" into "how to."

Executives who volunteered their insights into what works in the real world, who vested their faith and enthusiasm in this work or by their example inspired me to dig deep, include Steve Leonard and Craig Steel of EMC; Calvin Schmidt and Dwayne Wright of Johnson & Johnson's Wellness & Prevention, Inc.; Carl Farrell, Nick Lisi, Werner Deumens, Riad Gydien, Jamie Robbins, and many more at SAS; Owen Hill and Kathryn Thomas at Life Technologies; Donald "Duck" Payen and Carla DaSilva at Air Mauritius; Andy Lang and Matt Lovegrove with Ernst & Young; Mervyn Myers, Steve Hollis, and Andrew Dinsdale at KPMG; Hugh Macfarlane at MathMarketing; Patrick Boucousis at Traxor; and Brad Milner at TechCSO. Not all their insights made it into the final manuscript, but their spirit imbues each page.

Of equal value were the sales professionals on six continents who allowed my team and me to observe how they sell over a period of four years. They provided candid opinions about the tools they use (both internally developed and purchased from training and software vendors), what works, what doesn't, and why. Then they allowed us to ride along on their customer calls; watch how they prepare and debrief; listen to their telesales approaches; and experience how managers run their sales meetings, deal reviews, and coaching sessions.

By seeing what top, middle, and low performers do on a daily basis and then graphing this to the revenue they produced, clear trends emerged that turned some traditional wisdom about how selling *really* works on its ear. While they are not cited by name in this work, lessons from the collective made this book what it is.

Academicians whose passion for sales research ignited a deep interest and rich source of collegial insight include Professor Andrea L. Dixon of the Hankamer School of Business at Baylor University; Professor Lynette Ryals of Cranfield University School of Management; Dr.

Terry Loe of the Center for Professional Selling at Kennesaw State University; Professor David Roberts of the Kenan-Flagler Business School at the University of North Carolina; and Professor Adrian Payne of the Australian School of Business at the University of New South Wales.

Colleagues whose encouragement, humor, and generosity of spirit energized me while writing include Richard Owers, Mark Lindsay, Ingrid Kast, Dr. Anthony Mahler, Betty Catchpole, Maibritt Thoft-Christensen, Jason Huls, Mike Gersten, the artistic Stanley VonMedvey, the irrepressible Jillian Upton, and the "action wrangler" Chad Burns.

McGraw-Hill Education executive editor Donya Dickerson and editing manager Jane Palmieri are highly prized for their support, prudence, and patience. Thanks also to Amy Lynn Lee, Jamie Salisbury, Tori Amos, and Hans Zimmer for anthems that jump-started the narrow hours. And of course, I'd be handicapped without the amazing people at the Wikimedia Foundation, Apple, and Adobe, whose hardware, apps, and information helped a project of this magnitude find form.

Of course my ultimate thanks go to the most supportive team of all: my polar stars Cassandra, Jonathan, Ashleigh, and James, who relocate to foreign lands and do breakfast-by-Skype in their stride, and my bonny wife Heather who not only keeps all the wheels in motion but makes it look easy.

Chapter 1

Beyond the Sales Funnel

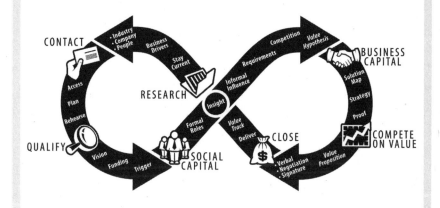

The Sales Expansion Loop

My preceding book, *Selling to the C-Suite* (McGraw-Hill, 2009), demystified why executive buyers single out some salespeople to be Trusted Advisors but give others the ejector seat. The book was based on a decade of research in bull and bear markets, and it reported what leaders across industries and cultures said about how, why, and when they get involved in their company's large purchasing projects.

And with so many people struggling through a financial crisis at the time of *C-Suite*'s publication, it hit a chord. I was invited to keynote at sales conferences across North America, Latin America, Asia, Europe, and Africa. Morning and nightly television news shows wanted to hear these tips, as did newspapers, magazines, and drive-time radio. The appetite for certainty in a time of uncertainty was palpable. People put the book to the test. Its lessons helped them. I cherish every tale of success.

Then as the economies of the world continued to wobble, a recurring question was raised by the hundreds of CEOs and vice presidents of sales who drew me aside in boardrooms, airport lounges, and conference mixers.

Their question was this:

You've shown us how executives buy today. Can you show us how top salespeople sell today?

It was the "today" part that caught my attention. Have the rules of selling changed? Are they different from how we sold yesterday or during the last decade or the last century? It's an intriguing question.

If we hypothesize that selling is only about skills, then with the hundreds of published works produced in the past two centuries by Carnegie, Ziglar, Hopkins, Tracy, Rackham, Bosworth, Page, Gitomer, and other contributors, surely we already have the academic foundation—in books and training courses—to sell effectively. If we only reread and practice their lessons, wouldn't we all perform better? Of course we would. On an individual level we can always sharpen the saw. Covey taught us that.

And that might be enough . . . if improving our win rate in complex and strategic sales opportunities was a matter of skills execution alone. But few sales directors think it's that simple anymore.

Buyers are more risk averse; they seldom make decisions without involving other stakeholders, advisors, or opinion leaders. It's no longer good enough to find and pitch to one economic buyer, fox, or grand poobah in the inner circle. The customers expect you to network with all the players, to make it easy for them to buy by your getting everyone on the same page. To do this, the customers take it as a given that you will do your homework and be curious enough to learn the issues that may affect multiple personas in different ways; to build supporters in these ranks; and to make a case for change and navigate the minefield of competing biases that may cause people in the same company to hold polarized views on whether there's a need to buy, buy now, or buy from you.

The role of business-to-business salespeople today is to provoke people with new ideas so they become dissatisfied with the status quo through gaining a vision of tomorrow. Customers expect us to add value in every meeting, to propose solutions that give the most bang for the buck, and to remain accountable to deliver our promises long after the close.

Your company expects you to convert name lists, networking lunches, and marketing leads into sales opportunities; to keep your pipeline stacked with enough revenue to offset the deals that don't pan out; to qualify out of low-probability deals as fast as possible; to orchestrate the profitable deployment of presales subject matter specialists; to maintain sales records and reporting systems; to coordinate with third-party solution vendors who partner today and compete tomorrow; and to work miracles at the end of each quarter and especially at the end of each fiscal year.

A salesperson's job description is seldom written in these terms, but there's no doubt about it, that when you accept a role in the business-to-business sales profession today, it's certainly not for the fainthearted nor the enthusiastic amateur. It's one of the toughest (yet most rewarding) gigs in the world. It's a complex, high-stakes, demanding profession.

Does this sound like your world?

Good, that means this book is written just for you.

The best practices you'll read here answer the questions executives and sales professionals are asking everywhere. They are drawn from nearly 20,000 hours of interviews, coaching sessions, and field accompaniments with business-to-business salespeople who exceed their targets year after year. To keep the headhunters at bay, you won't read anyone's personal names. Their lessons are grouped collectively and listed in this book as being from "top sellers" or "stars." These legends are out there right now, seeding ideas, nurturing contacts, inking fresh deals, and hitting their quotas early in challenging markets. With this book, you will join them.

Let's begin.

Have you noticed that no matter how great your offering, there are times when some prospects just don't value what you're selling? They won't engage in consultative discussions, and they only want you to send an e-mail or provide factual information to fill a supplier comparison table while they hide behind blind tenders and tight lips. Let's call these prospects *Product Buyers*. By the time they invite suppliers to talk, they can be two-thirds of the way through their buying process,[1] and now they are looking to narrow their options by comparing suppliers against the criteria they have already collated.

At other times you find yourself talking to prospects who *know* they don't have all the answers yet, and so they are looking to you for advice and insight. After all, you're someone who talks to their peers at other companies. You see what issues their peers are facing and what they're doing to solve their challenges. This makes you a valuable source of knowledge about what others are doing to achieve reductions in cost, time, and risk or to gain increases in productivity, efficiency, and profit. These prospects welcome you to the table if you bring these insights. They're prepared to invest time in you to diagnose their real needs and explore options they didn't know existed. Let's call these *Ideas Buyers*.

Both types of prospects buy differently, from the depth of conversation they're prepared to have and the number of people you end up meeting with, to the time it takes to get a signature on the order form.

The skills needed to sell to each type of buyer are identical, but selling to Ideas Buyers requires a broader range of capabilities and the dance steps (i.e. the milestones in your sales cycle) are more complicated.

So let's look at these two sales cycles a little closer.

One is relatively short. It is based on clearly defined or easily influenced decision criteria, where competitors have no great advantage over you, and the decision to buy is held by a small number of Product Buyers (such as those purchasing officers or consultants who tell you to deal only with them and warn you not to go over their head). This type of sale might be declared "simple," and the traditional sales funnel is a relatively good model for navigating it. The goal is to move "*from Hi to Buy*" as quickly as possible.

When sales stars come across these types of opportunities, they do a "preflight check" to test whether the premeeting research and first-meeting conversation (whether by phone or face-to-face) are designed to tease out where deeper issues exist and whether the needs and opinions of additional stakeholders can be canvassed to build wider interest and support. They look at how big the iceberg is below the waterline. Their goal is to find topics that allow them to lift the conversation to a poignant issue they can use as a game changer. Theirs is an attempt at *reengineering* the decision criteria.

Where attempts at reengineering fail, top sellers waste no time declaring the opportunity to be a simple sale. They don't manage the deal using the depth of project plan that's applied to complex solution sales, and they don't report simple sales on the same pipeline as complex sales. They maintain *separate* pipelines that measure sales effectiveness by different steps, different velocities, and different conversion rates. Some companies even mandate that if their solution sellers are flooded with more opportunities than they can easily handle, they should qualify which ones are simple and flick those to a different sales team, channel, or partner.

Where you identify you're competing in a high-stakes conceptual sale to Ideas Buyers, you need to manage the opportunity with different steps more appropriate to an environment where the decision process will be longer, where multiple players will be involved in shaping the buying criteria and timeline by formal and informal means, and where competition is rife and ruthless. The goal is to move these larger opportunities *from first contact to closed contract* with as much certainty as possible. By necessity this approach involves a lot of plan-do-plan-do in successive waves throughout the sales cycle.

Sales organizations know complex sales don't close as quickly as simple sales, nor do these sales travel through identical steps in the sales cycle. So these companies create two funnels in their *customer relationship marketing* (CRM) software—each one tuned with different milestones and different lengths of time and conversion ratios between each of these steps.

However, even with the logic of this being recognized, most sales reps are still faced with a daily diet of looking at the visual iconography of a traditional sales funnel. That's a problem for several reasons, some subliminal, some overt. Think for a moment about the messages the funnel sends to any seller today.

The funnel implies that customer engagement is a linear process that has a start and an end (Figure 1.1). The underlying message is that you should get to the close, then jump to the next deal. In promoting the sales funnel as an image at the heart of their forecast and performance reviews, sales directors are unwittingly reinforcing the linear, transactional, coin-operated mindset that the funnel represents. It's understandable. They've grown up with the funnel as a staple part of the sales vernacular their whole career. Let's take a look at the funnel.

The funnel starts wide with many good intentions and ends narrow with only a few opportunities becoming signed contracts. It's a con-

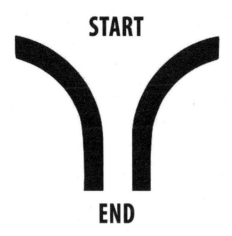

Figure 1.1: The Traditional Sales Funnel

cept from the days when product was king and selling was a numbers game of making enough telephone calls to get enough appointments to pitch enough proposals to win enough deals. The funnel is a purely transactional artifact.

What self-respecting solution seller can accept the awful ratios of attrition displayed in the funnel? When you sell the vision, help customers develop their business case for funding, and write the project spec, conversion rates are nearly 80 percent—not a fraction of a fraction, receding at each step. The funnel promotes a mediocre mindset that expects and then accepts failure.

The funnel also leads sales managers to form erroneous conclusions about their pipeline, which get reported to the finance director as forecasts. Have you ever seen a funnel with a numbered gauge on the side? Sure you have. It usually starts with "10 percent" at the top and "100 percent" at the bottom.

The original intent for this segmentation was to show how far through the sales cycle each opportunity was. By knowing how long it took for a healthy sale to advance between stages, and by knowing what percentage made it through each stage, managers could do a rough calculation of how many wins would be coming down the proipeline. They would then immediately see if any shortfall of leads high up in the funnel was statistically likely to create a shortfall of revenue months into the future. With this foresight they could act to head off any emerging problem while there was still time to impact the outcome.

But they couldn't estimate the actual revenue that would be won.

In an attempt to improve on that, at some point in our collective past an unknown manager started to think those percentages down the side of the funnel would be a pretty neat way of factoring the revenue at each stage. Without a better model to use, this logic started to catch on, and nobody questioned if it actually made any sense in a world of complex sales.

But those percentages down the side of the funnel do not equal the customers' probability of buying, nor do they predict how much revenue from each sale will be on the table after the final negotiation.

So when you see a salesperson who believes a $1 million deal sitting at the "50 percent" mark should be forecast as $500,000, you're looking at a rep who probably flunked math. In the real world, the deal is worth the whole million at every step. It's not the stage in the funnel that determines how much revenue comes into your coffers. It's the *win probability* of each individual opportunity. You'll read about a more reliable way to qualify if you're winning or losing later in the book.

So if the funnel is culturally and commercially wrong for selling complex solutions over a longer, more competitive sales cycle, what have top sellers replaced it with?

There's a clue on the cover of this book. Instead of a linear funnel, the shape of these solution sales looks more like a cyclical "figure eight." This model is called the *Sales Expansion Loop* (SEL) (Figure 1.2).

The Loop follows a stepwise progression, but unlike the funnel it does not promote an endpoint to the selling process. Instead, the close of each sale primes the pump for the next opportunity. It is a perpetual process of creating and improving relationships and revenue

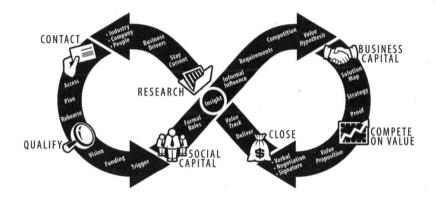

Figure 1.2: The Sales Expansion Loop (SEL)

streams. Its icon is based on the symbol for "infinity" because this is what a relationship looks like to the Ideas Buyers.

Navigating the Loop begins right in the center. You see that ring around Insight? This is where you start. You actually pass through the Insight junction three times when selling to the Ideas Buyers.

The first time is where you're seeking insight on their industry, company, and people, which takes you to the top left of the Loop into what's called the *Research* step.

Follow the arrows, and the second time is in the middle of the sale where you test if you are adding insight to the customers and they are giving you insight that can help you win.

Follow the arrows, and the third time is after you've won the sale and delivered your solution: you track the extent to which your value proposition is being enjoyed by the customers as promised by you, and you give insight to them on additional ways to leverage their investment or improve their business, as only an insider can do. This sets the ball in motion for additional opportunities, and so you cross back to the Research stage for the next deal in the same account.

In this book we'll explore how you can master this new model.

Turn the page, and we'll get started.

Chapter 2

Research

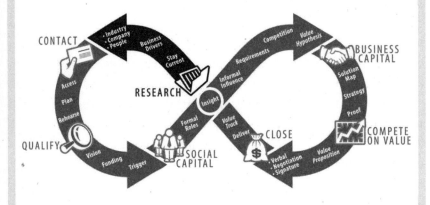

The Sales Expansion Loop: Research

The word *research* comes from the French word *rechercher*, which means "to go about seeking knowledge."[1] It is a "harnessing of curiosity" to establish facts and solve new or existing problems.

With a little bit of homework and preparation, you can understand the customers' world, see through their eyes, and walk in their shoes. But why would you want to bother? Because if you want to pitch an idea to a prospect that they're not already considering, you must be conversant with the issues that are going on in their industry, company, or personal roles, and you must extrapolate how your offering can improve the metrics they're assessed on—their reputation, personal power, or other contribution. Research is a fundamental exercise if you want to bait the hook correctly. In this chapter we're going to look at *industry research*, *company research*, and *people research*.

The need for research applies when you're selling a deal that you didn't engineer but were invited to bid for (as in responding to a tender). Some people somewhere came up with the idea that talking to you and your competitors was a good idea. How did that happen? Where did they get their information? What were the reasons that prompted them to wake up one morning and see the need to do this? You must dig behind the tender to the events and people that triggered it if you're going to have any hope of controlling that sale.

If you can backtrack and see the before-and-after picture in their head, including the reasons they have to change, the genesis of the opportunity, and seeing who owns it as a personal project or business imperative, you can start to arm yourself with information that you can use in your meetings with them.

Some salespeople ask: "But why shouldn't I just respond to the criteria they listed in the tender documents?" Well, certainly those are a given. But your competitors will be responding to exactly the same items. There's no differentiation in doing that. But by understanding the context of *why* the customer is taking action and by showing them you understand it, you are painted as someone who's talking the language of the very people who gave their instructions to the procurement manager in the first place. Maybe you can turn what would otherwise be a simple sale into one more worthy of your time.

There's a saying: "How you talk is where you'll walk." It means you end up selling to the people you speak like. If you want to deal with the purchasing department, talk only about your features, service levels, terms, and price. If you want to deal with the people whose business needs are at the core of the buying decision, learn their issues and talk about them. It can give you a tremendous advantage over competing sales reps.

As Billy Joel sings in his song *An Innocent Man*, it helps to go back to the start to find out where a problem began. "The Piano Man" would make an excellent salesperson. He sees the value in understanding *yesterday* to make sense of *today*.

If you don't commit to conducting research on your customer's world, let's face it, you'll be unarmed when an Ideas Buyer asks what you understand about their business—being able to quote only what you skimmed from their website is like going to a gunfight armed with a penknife.

So how do you understand the business drivers and triggers for action that shape a buyer's decision process? *Selling to the C-Suite* (McGraw-Hill, 2009) contains a 22-page chapter titled "Understanding What Executives Want" as well as an 18-page Appendix titled "Guide to Customer Research" written by Dr. Stephen Bistritz, my coauthor on that book. Those combined 40 pages serve as a master class on how to conduct customer research. I won't replay that information here, but there are a few tenets top sellers reveal they use most often, and I feel they're important to touch on now.

If, like most sales professionals, you are time poor, then customer research may become a casualty of other activities. That's why the top 20 percent of sellers block a sacrosanct time every month to stay up-to-date on existing customers and target prospects. They do their homework, and they connect the dots to figure out the best point of entry, to decide what to talk about and how to show their solution as a relevant part of the conversation. They choose a time in the week that they're unlikely to find customers interested in having a meeting, and they conduct their research in those hours so it's not dead time.

Salespeople in the United Arab Emirates and Indonesia know every Friday the majority of their customers attend prayers in their mosques. Some countries observe a break in the hot afternoon hours, like the *Mittagspause* that closes shops and clears out offices in some southern German regions. Enterprising account managers use these times to catch up on their customer research. There's no excuse to say: "I don't have time." Put it in your calendar as if it were an important customer meeting, and don't overwrite it for anything— not even for a real customer meeting. Once you lose the rhythm, it's difficult to get it back.

Having a regular routine for conducting customer research is like performing periodic automotive maintenance: "An ounce of prevention is worth a pound of cure." There are few moments in a sale as cringeworthy as winging it with no research and then having the customer ask your opinion about something you know nothing about but which is so significant that everyone in their industry is talking about it. Ouch. Don't let the door hit you on the way out.

We live in an age of wonders when it comes to customer research. Websites provide rich information on your customers' industry, their business, and their people . . . if you know where to look. And armed with the right information, you can ask the right questions when you're face-to-face. There's no information as relevant and fresh as that which comes directly from the customers themselves. Of course, you must still validate one person's opinion across two or three other contacts to make sure it's an accurate reflection of the situation and not just one person's skewed view.

At the time of writing this book, a top seller in our research sample was profiling a company called Aqua Sciences, based in the state of Florida. Let's follow the seller's approach for conducting research on this prospect (if you're reading this book many years after its first publication and the Aqua Sciences website is no longer active, don't worry, the principles of research will still be valid).

This seller opened a search engine, typed in the company name and its home city, and set the search engine parameters to look for hits from only the past year so that the search results would be current.

Open up a browser on your phone, laptop, or tablet as you read this chapter, and follow along.

COMPANY RESEARCH

A Google search immediately returns links to news media about Aqua Sciences at sites like *Bloomberg Businessweek*. There's a *PR Newswire* article. From these first articles we learn that the company builds machines that extract moisture from the air using salts, to distill clean potable water for drinking, cooking, or medical use. Their machines are the size of cargo containers, and the machines operate 24 hours a day on solar, geothermal, or diesel power where normal power and water infrastructure may not be available. Each unit creates up to 600 gallons of water a day for about 30 cents a gallon. That's cheaper than most bottled water. We see their emergency water stations have been shipped to hot spots (the Federal Emergency Management Agency used these water stations in Haiti), and they have been used by the U.S. military in the Middle East to create water for U.S. personnel in the desert to avoid the cost and risk of shipping water using tankers. To an insurgent, a tanker of water in a convoy looks a lot like a tanker of fuel—an easy target. So it's much better to simply place portable water-making machines in each camp.

Clicking on the Aqua Sciences website, we see the company has won awards from *TIME* magazine and the *Wall Street Journal*, and it has been featured in stories published or broadcast by Fox, CNN, *WIRED*, *Fast Company*, and other media. The company's "News" tab hasn't been fed regularly, suggesting that the company may have been too busy to keep its news page current. We need to know more.

With a little more clicking on the computer, we see that the name of the company's CEO is Abe Sher. Typing his name into the search engine opens a new line of inquiry. In a 13-minute YouTube video, we see Sher speaking at the 2011 Global Competitiveness Forum in Riyadh, Saudi Arabia, on a speakers' panel that included former U.S. president Bill Clinton, former U.K. prime minister Tony Blair, and business guru Michael Porter. That video sheds a lot of light on Sher's priorities, where he's been focusing his efforts the last few years, and why maintaining his website hasn't been a priority. He's working on big projects in Saudi Arabia with oil giant Arenco to prove that the technology can work in the toughest deserts with near-zero humidity. He calls it their "Frank Sinatra strategy": if they can make water there, they can make it anywhere. The company doesn't seem to employ a lot of people, but it has titans as partners.

A *Who's Who* listing reveals that Sher is a lawyer turned serial investor, with global interests from mining to microelectronics. Not an engineer or inventor, but someone skilled at bringing ideas to life, a visionary. The seller concluded that Sher was quite likely an Ideas Buyer, open to having a discussion about ways he can tame the tiger he's holding by the tail.

It is a private company, so there are no online filings on the stock exchange, annual reports, or quarterly analyst commentaries. No earnings call transcripts from sites like *Seeking Alpha*. No *Wikinvest* company profile, and only scant information on *Hoovers*.

However, these are all sites that top sellers recommend checking for key prospects and accounts that *are* public companies. You can find a treasure trove of information in these places. It's particularly insightful to read the transcripts of a company's quarterly earnings calls four times a year. For example, go to the *Seeking Alpha* home page, type in the name of any public company you know, and see what you get. Always read the "Q&A" section where the analysts get to ask all the tough questions that aren't scripted. It tells you much about the way the executives think, their plans, their tone, and style. Students of neurolinguistics can use these word clues to decode whether those executives digest information visually, aurally, or kinesthetically, so that they can tailor their prospecting e-mails, letters, or presentations accordingly.

Don't forget to read to the end of the presentation section on the earnings call transcripts, and browse through the comments and blogs there. While not an official part of the earnings call, you can stumble across valid third-party viewpoints from shareholders, journalists, and other people who know the business. These add to your knowledge about current affairs, unresolved problems, and public sentiment.

Recruitment websites will tell you if a company is growing and hiring, and in which roles and locations. You can deduce something about where a company is planning to grow by where it's investing in its people. Glassdoor.com is a different type of recruitment site in that it allows people who have recently left a company to sound off about what it's really like to work there. Ostensibly a resource for candidates doing their homework before applying to work in a different place, it gives salespeople the inside scoop on what past staff members have to say about the management culture, specific executives, their strategies, strengths, and weaknesses, the company's products, office environment, layoffs, growth plans, and so forth. If you tap your inner voyeur and sift gossip from fact, it's amazing what people will reveal once they're outside a company, things that they might never have said openly when they were employed there.

All this information is gold if you have curiosity about what makes the customers tick and an appetite for using that knowledge to find ways to help them. The more you mean to them, the more they will mean to you.

INDUSTRY RESEARCH

No business is an island, so it's helpful to know something about the industry in which your prospect operates. Then you can put their business issues in context with events in their environment. In our Aqua Sciences example, we've been introduced to the "atmospheric water" industry. I type this term into my search engine. There are many competitors that show up. A fast click-through reveals that companies such as Air2Water, AWS, and EcoloBlue make domestic units nowhere near the same industrial scale as Aqua Sciences' units. But it looks like Aqua Sciences competes directly with firms such as Watermaker India and Atlantis Solar. Within seconds I am on their competitors' websites, repeating the same exercise as above, to see how the market is treating them and what issues they all have in common. As you do this with your customers, you should write down anything that reveals the goals, challenges, or other pressing issues these companies all seem to be dealing with in their industry.

As I read these links, I uncover industry magazines, news articles, and other sources that tell me the size of the water market worldwide, how pressing the problems of water shortages are in poor and developed nations alike, and how more than one government is saying that water is the next oil—a currency worth trillions, a commodity that will bring wealth and power to those who can make it out of thin air.

So we've been scouring the Internet for about 30 minutes now (*including* skimming that 13-minute YouTube clip), and we've found out quite a lot about the company, its industry, and its CEO. Despite this being a private company about which information is more difficult to find than for public companies, you can see how such a small investment of time can be a major education. Would we now be better prepared to have a conversation with Sher and his representatives about their business, and—in discussing the current affairs and opportunities in their industry—would we be able to build enough basic credibility to earn the right to a meeting? Certainly.

I wonder if you repeated this process right now on one of your biggest prospects, what could you turn up in the next half hour? It might surprise you.

This type of curiosity is all too often missing in the rank and file of salespeople who never learned it in their first job and whose subsequent sales managers never coached them to acquire the skill. But "detective work" is familiar territory to the world's best. If you are prepared this way, it stands to reason that you'll start having discussions with customers about the right issues and with the right people. Speaking of which . . .

PEOPLE RESEARCH

No customer research is complete until you've found out all you can about the people you need to sell to. It's fascinating to see where people turn up outside the company they work for. Often on their LinkedIn page, you'll see logos of the forums or organizations they're plugged into. Maybe it's worthwhile joining these for a while and see if your prospect is commenting there. If so, what are they talking about? What's important to them? What are their likes and dislikes?

Try typing a prospect's name connected to a suffix like .pdf, .ppt, or .doc or connected to a term like "strategy," "challenge," "problem," or "opportunity." Add the current year, next year, or the year after that. If this person has been in the press or on a blog discussing the business and its future, this is a good way to find those articles.

If you search the prospect's name and add "press release" and the names of your competitors, it can be handy to discover if the prospect has shown a preference for your rivals in the past.

To manage this process automatically, you can enter your search parameters into Google Alerts (http://www.google.com/alerts) if you have a free Google account. Specify how often you want to be pinged with news about the prospect's appearances on the Internet and what keywords you want trawled, and the system will accordingly monitor the Internet, and then it will alert you to its findings. Many newspapers and online trade magazines offer similar clipping services. If you're not using these tools already, sign up for them today. They could be paying off as fast as next week.

Ultimately, the purpose of the Research phase is to identify emerging needs, isolate where your offerings can make a difference, and spot which of the customer's officers are the most likely points of entry to talk about these issues. By investigating the company, industry, and key people, you will find clues for what's topical, and you'll see what winds are blowing the customer's business. The more educated you are on these trends, the better your conversations will be regardless of whether you're responding to a tender or having conversations with Ideas Buyers to create new demand.

Let's jump ahead in the sales cycle by several weeks and assume we've successfully made contact.

Once you're talking to people about their issues, it's worth keeping in mind that they might not be as schooled as you are about their own company. You might see trends that they cannot from inside their business silo. By taking time to understand these things, you may find yourself serving as *their* guide, giving context to how their business works and how issues in another department ricochet into theirs.

This can help you draw what's called a *Trigger Map*.

A Trigger Map shows how issues that impact one department ripple into others. It seeks to establish cause and effect, the links in the chain, and to find the root cause or weakest link. The better this map is prepared, the more issues it will bring to the surface and the more people you will find to call on.

For example, let's say a call center manager is having the problem that too many inbound calls are hitting her switchboard simultaneously. She has no way to predict volumes, so can't roster the right number of people to each shift. Customers are complaining of long wait times, her workers are stressed, and morale is low. Any number of solutions might be prescribed for this isolated problem.

But on closer examination, it is learned that the reason for the jump in call volumes is an escalation in dissatisfied customers who ordered products from this company, were promised particular delivery dates, and were then left waiting. Now it looks like the call center problem may be downstream from some inefficiency in the delivery department.

Asked why customers aren't receiving their orders, the delivery manager reveals that the sales team is promising products that aren't in stock. Back orders are placed, and old model units are installed to pacify the customers until the new model is in stock (at additional cost to the vendor), but the problem is getting larger every week.

The delivery manager's vans are crisscrossing the city, his drivers are fatigued, and fuel costs are up.

The sales manager is concerned about the number of orders getting canceled because of this situation, the effect on his forecast accuracy, and the threat of his top reps leaving because the sales they have closed are being bungled by the company's inefficiencies. He discloses that the reason his salespeople promise products that aren't in stock is because the warehousing report is several days behind and nobody really knows what they have in the warehouse.

The warehouse manager logs products in and out by checking serial numbers against a printed manifest. This information is typed into a spreadsheet at the end of each day by a shared temp. Sometimes they get called to work in other departments and can be out of the warehouse for days, which means information is always lagging.

The financial controller is troubled by sales commissions being paid out on orders that are later reversed and the impact of the increasing number of credits and discounts on cash flow.

The questions you must ask to extract this information aren't particularly challenging. In fact, Rudyard Kipling's poem "The Elephant's Child" in his *Just So Stories*[2] explains how to frame such questions:

> *I keep six honest serving men*
> *(They taught me all I knew);*
> *Their names are "What" and "Why" and "When"*
> *And "How" and "Where" and "Who."*

In talking to the call center manager, we might divine if the problem is isolated to her department alone or if her department is a victim of problems upstream in the business ecosystem. We might also learn whether her department's inefficiencies are in turn hurting yet other functions downstream. Such questions might look like these:

- "*What* changed in your department or elsewhere to cause this?"
- "*Why* do you think it is happening?"

- "*When* was this first noticed?"
- "*How* specifically is the problem manifest?"
- "*Where* do you think the cause is coming from?"
- "*Who* should we speak with there?"

A Trigger Map for this situation might look like the diagram in Figure 2.1. As you can see, one department's issues impact other departments' issues. There's a causal chain at play.

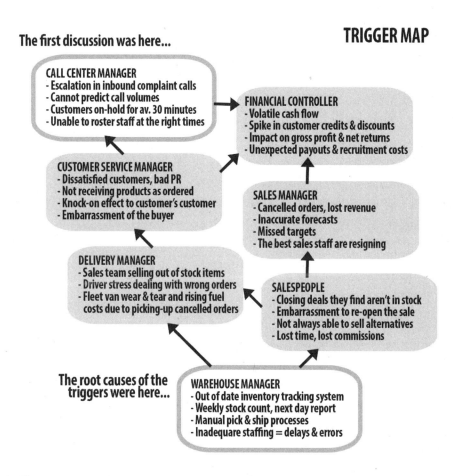

The first discussion was here...

TRIGGER MAP

CALL CENTER MANAGER
- Escalation in inbound complaint calls
- Cannot predict call volumes
- Customers on-hold for av. 30 minutes
- Unable to roster staff at the right times

FINANCIAL CONTROLLER
- Volatile cash flow
- Spike in customer credits & discounts
- Impact on gross profit & net returns
- Unexpected payouts & recruitment costs

CUSTOMER SERVICE MANAGER
- Dissatisfied customers, bad PR
- Not receiving products as ordered
- Knock-on effect to customer's customer
- Embarrassment of the buyer

SALES MANAGER
- Cancelled orders, lost revenue
- Inaccurate forecasts
- Missed targets
- The best sales staff are resigning

DELIVERY MANAGER
- Sales team selling out of stock items
- Driver stress dealing with wrong orders
- Fleet van wear & tear and rising fuel costs due to picking-up cancelled orders

SALESPEOPLE
- Closing deals they find aren't in stock
- Embarrassment to re-open the sale
- Not always able to sell alternatives
- Lost time, lost commissions

The root causes of the triggers were here...

WAREHOUSE MANAGER
- Out of date inventory tracking system
- Weekly stock count, next day report
- Manual pick & ship processes
- Inadequare staffing = delays & errors

Figure 2.1: A Trigger Map

Let's say the salesperson talking to the call center manager did a great job probing her concerns, and he pitched a computerized voice response solution that would give customers a way to resolve their issues on hold, in half the time it would take them to connect to a live person. The manager's need for additional staff would be resolved in the short term, and the salesperson would be justified in feeling he had sold a great solution.

And yet in this example the *real* cause of the complaints remains unresolved. Customers are still angry, and absenteeism in the call center is still on the rise. Workers in the warehouse, delivery vans, sales office, and finance department are still struggling with their individual problems.

The salesperson succeeded in selling to a symptom, but not to the cause.

If only he had been more curious about *why* things were happening and less compliant in answering the immediate request of one department, he might have asked questions sufficient to create a Trigger Map, and he might have found the root cause that actually existed back in the warehouse—where he could have sold a larger software solution.

For example, if a computerized inventory control system were installed to track deliveries and dispatches, a live data feed could keep the salesforce informed on inventory levels in real time as they placed orders. Replacement product could be forecast and ordered from the factory well in advance of running low. Customers wouldn't place orders that couldn't be filled. Delivery and call center staff wouldn't have to put out as many fires.

By identifying that the warehouse's problem was the real trigger behind all this pain in the business, a myriad of direct and indirect costs could have been alleviated. Chances are that software, hardware, and services would have been sold into multiple departments instead of into just one. For this salesperson, identifying the warehouse's problem could have led to a sale several times larger, secured his quota several months earlier, and created customer loyalty several times stronger.

There's no hard rule for how to draw a Trigger Map—use Visio, PowerPoint, a flipchart, or sketch it on a restaurant napkin. The important thing is to use a visual medium to draw your best guess at where your customer's issues come from and how these impact their own department, people, and processes. Then put the page and a pen in front of them. Stars know that the sooner they can get the customer engaged in sharing a mutual task, the sooner the customer will feel a connection with them—no more strangers or combatants, but allies.

Show how you've given thought to the customer's situation before meeting them. Your intent is to help. Demonstrate that you've put in unpaid effort on their behalf. Customers like this. Next, explain the Trigger Map, point out how you think issues connect, and ask the customers what they think.

As soon as the customer starts putting lines through your guess-work, saying "That's not right," and then draw in lines and words of their own, they own what's on that paper. It has become a joint effort. Now they're invested in the conversation, and you're no longer seen as someone on the other side of the desk trying to push something at them. Now you're on *their* side.

Stars tell us that relationships are built with many small gestures and moments. Using a Trigger Map is one of them. The same applies when you present your idea of what the *customer's evaluation process* should look like, you invite them to modify it, and then they put pen to paper for you. Or when you show them your idea of what the *organization chart* and *decision process* look like, you leave it incomplete, and then they have an excuse to draw additional lines and boxes.

Drawing the components of *your solution* on a flipchart serves the same purpose: you create a list of bullet points and connect these with arrows to the names of stakeholders who will receive the most value. You leave empty bullet points for the customer to fill in with additional ideas—and by doing so they own that picture.

People connect with the things they touch. When people help others, they invest part of themselves with those people. This is why stars never reject something as simple as a customer's offer of a glass of water or cup of coffee. They know it's not about the drink (they may leave it sitting untouched). It's about achieving a connection. So they say "Yes, please" and accept any investment of effort from the customer instead of rejecting it. The same can be achieved by asking your customer for street directions, for an opinion of what's good on the lunch menu, or simply for advice of any kind. Powerful emotions are waiting to be tapped when you do this.

The paper "The State of Psychological Ownership: Integrating and Extending a Century of Research," by J. Pierce, T. Kostova, and K. Dirks (*Review of General Psychology*, 2003), explains this dynamic:

> *People come to find themselves psychologically tied to things as a result of their active participation or association with those things. The most obvious and perhaps the most powerful means by which an individual invests him/herself into an object is to create it. Feelings of ownership are accompanied by a sense of efficacy and competence, and are pleasure producing. Exploration of, and the ability to control, one's environment gives rise to [such] feelings.*

As top sellers know, when you give your customers the opportunity to put their thumbprint on something as simple as your drawing of an incomplete Trigger Map, evaluation plan, or organization chart, the very act of correcting it instills in them that sense of competence, control, pleasure, and ownership mentioned above.

This all begins with your being curious about your customer and researching them on a regular basis. Remember, nobody else will conduct this research to win the sale—except maybe your competitors!

Chapter 3

Contact

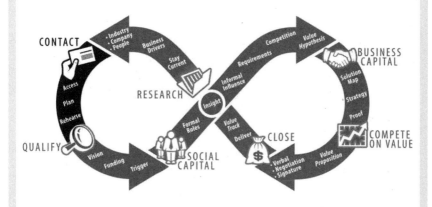

The Sales Expansion Loop: Contact

One point every top performer agrees with is that before making your first call or going to your first meeting, you must be prepared. But how prepared do you need to be?

PREPARING AND REHEARSING

If you ever saw an Apple product launch by the late and greatly missed Steve Jobs, you saw a consummate professional at work. Almost every word, inflection, emphasis, and gesture was choreographed to perfection and delivered with good humor. The word on the street from Apple's campus was that before any big presentation, Jobs would invest two to three days rehearsing it.

It's worth surfing YouTube to revisit Jobs unveiling the iPhone for the very first time at MacWorld 2007. Watch closely what he does. He has a conversation. He teases and baits. He uses simple graphics. He embraces the power of silence to build suspense and focus. He's not in a hurry. He knows exactly where he is at every moment, and because of that, he is in complete control of his material and the audience.

There isn't a single bullet point in the whole slide deck. Jobs built rapture with words, pauses, and pictures. In anyone else's hands, it could easily have been a text-heavy, must-read-each-line affair—the eponymous "Death by PowerPoint." Instead, he always delivered a compelling keynote that blew the audience's collective mind. It's still impressive today (even after the iPhone's first features are no longer new) because of the way he *sold* it. Like a good episode of *Mad Men*, it stands up to repeat viewings. Watch it for yourself. Listen to the hype words and emotional cues Jobs applies. This is a sales master at the top of his game.

But not all of us can rehearse for three days, and not everyone is naturally "smooth." The good news is that not all top sellers have these gifts either. They work at it by taking a *written plan* into their meetings as a guide to ensure that they achieve what they intended to.

This way they don't have to remember so much, and they can focus on getting their execution right.

This is important because, as the nineteenth-century German field marshal Moltke the Elder observed: "No plan survives contact with the enemy."[1] A century later when former U.S. president Dwight D. Eisenhower was serving as the supreme commander of the Allied forces in Europe during World War II, he clarified this by saying: "Plans are worthless, but *planning* is everything."[2]

These leaders knew that when people internalize where they want to end up and how to get there, they can face surprises and tangents in the course of duty and still get back on track to complete their objective because the very act of writing, agreeing with, rehearsing, or reading a plan places it into the amygdala—that part of the brain where instinct and "mental muscle memory" reside.[3] That's why you should always have a plan, even if you're selling alone and don't need to share information with anyone outside your own skin. It's a ritual that programs your brain with structure. Once that's in place, it's easier to be adaptive and spontaneous on the fly.

I've met salespeople who believe if they go in to a customer meeting with a written plan in front of them, they'll somehow look manipulative or like "a rookie with a script." Ego tells them they're experienced enough to not need a plan. Some worry that if they're writing notes down or glancing at a printed page, it limits important eye contact with the customer, which can "break the spell." Some even quote the military leaders mentioned above and say that as soon as you start talking, your plan is already out of date so why bother writing a plan in the first place? They're missing the point.

If you don't want to write things down and break eye contact, use the voice recorder in your smartphone when you have a meeting. You're allowed by law to do this, just as students are permitted to record their university professors for learning purposes.[4] But always, *always* go in with a written call plan.

FACE-TO-FACE MEETING PLANS

When we ask buyers for their view on this, they say they prefer to have salespeople come prepared to meet with them, and they like to see the salespeople writing down or recording what they say. In fact, they get nervous about how much the salespeople will remember after the meeting if they fail to take notes.

Who else uses checklists, procedural documents, and meeting minutes? Doctors, counselors, lawyers, accountants—*professionals.* Who doesn't do any of this? Plumbers, electricians, painters—*tradespeople.* You decide in which category your sales career belongs. If you don't have a meeting template, Figure 3.1 contains a sample Face-to-Face (F2F) Meeting Planner (or Prospect Call Plan), so you can see how top sellers structure their first encounter with a new contact.

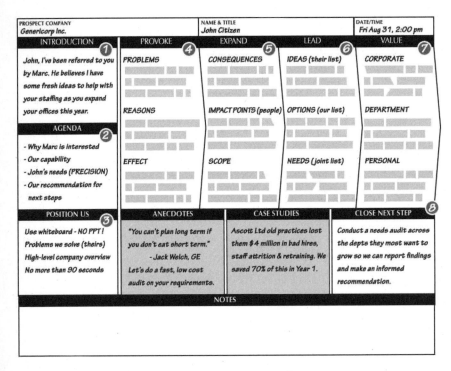

Figure 3.1: Sample Face-to-Face (F2F) Meeting Planner (or Prospect Call Plan)

Let's take a tour of this one-page planner so you understand the logic and flow.

Step 1. Introduction

This should never be a long monologue about you, your company, your history, or how many awards you've won. Instead, it serves as a bridge between your initial contact (e-mail, phone call, or referral) and the conversation you're about to have. A brief introduction is important because it sets the tone and establishes your personality. Summarize whatever it was that caused your prospects to want to meet. Remind them of those reasons.

It helps to be the first one at the table to introduce yourself. Set the bar by stating: "Hello, I am . . . My role is . . . The reason I'm attending today is . . . The value I hope to add to this meeting is . . . What I'd like to achieve from this meeting is . . ." Write these introduction points on a printed agenda, and give the customers a copy. Invite them to introduce themselves the same way. Imagine what insight this will give you, especially if it's one of those meetings where people turn up you didn't expect, and you want to know who they are and why they're there. This approach is your ticket to those answers.

Step 2. Agenda

As stated above, always give them a printed agenda. A simple three-part structure usually suffices: (a) to discuss their *current state*, what's working and what's not based on your research and their input, (b) to explore their *desired state* and the prospect's personal view of their needs, and (c) to mutually agree on the basis for further discussion or *action*. Share this with them in advance so they can contribute to the subtopics under these headings—let it be *their* meeting too!

As you finish explaining the agenda for the meeting, confirm how long you have, and make sure the prospects will commit to that time. Then launch into the meeting without skipping a beat.

If they're nodding their head in the meeting (and you already gave them a chance to add points before the meeting), don't interrupt your own flow by asking if they now want to add anything to the agenda. It sends a record scratch across the whole soundtrack. Have confidence in your preparation, and show you're a guide who knows where to go. They'll follow.

Step 3. Position Us

True to your word, the first part of your agenda is to *briefly* explain your capabilities. This is the "get to know you" step where you establish your credentials. There's a school of thought that "you should start by talking about them, before you talk about you." You've probably heard such sayings before, and top sellers agree with them in principle because so many sales presentations can be blabfests about the seller that completely exclude the buyers' issues.

But here in the opening of a call, sales stars appreciate that the prospect has absolutely no idea if you and your company are the real deal or not. Overcoming that unstated concern and establishing yourself on a firm foundation are worth spending a minute on. You *must* talk about you, but only briefly. Put your PowerPoint away. Don't touch your company brochure. Those props slow you down. Keep it light, and sell without them. Start by saying something along these lines:

You mentioned when we spoke that you had an interest in *W*. You know, that issue is one of the primary reasons my company was founded *Y* years ago. It's an area we throw so much of our research and development at because getting that right is key to the *X* number of customers we support. I don't have to tell you how important it is! In fact, if I had to say what attracted me to work for this company when I joined *Z* years ago, this would be one of the main draws for me because . . . [insert a story that reveals your passion for what you sell].

See what happened here? You started by referring to a fact they already agree with (*W*). In this case it's a statement of need from their own lips. This places you both on the same side of an opinion, which is where you want them to see you, not on the other side of the figurative table.

You then established how that topic is important to your company and to you personally—an area you *specialize in* and understand well. You even slipped in how many customers you have (*X*). This builds credibility, as does the reference to how many years you've been in business (*Y*). You included how long you've worked at this company (*Z*) so they know you're not a newbie.

You ended by sharing something personal so they see you as a real person and not just another suit. People remember stories, pictures, and feelings long after they've forgotten specific words.

Jim Collins and Jerry Porrass, authors of *Built to Last* (Collins Business, 2002), say, "Some managers are uncomfortable with expressing emotion about their dreams, but it's the passion and emotion that will attract and motivate others."

Why is this? John Medina, a molecular biologist with a fascination for how the mind reacts to information, wrote the *New York Times* bestseller *Brain Rules* (Pear Press, 2009). He points out that the brain doesn't pay attention to boring things, but when it detects an emotionally charged event (like a *good* opening, presentation, or closing in a sales call), the amygdala releases a spurt of the chemical dopamine (which gives a jolt to the buyer's motivation and pleasure centers), which aids involvement, memory, and retention.

In the time it took to read that last sentence, your own brain has given you a shot of this juice. The science sounds interesting and new, so you're curious, right? Well, you should be. It's a massive scientific validation to the sales axiom "People decide with emotion, then justify with logic." This knowledge is what governs the design of the Sales Expansion Loop: building social capital serves as a primer[5] before building business capital.

Achieving this dopamine hit early is why you should always pepper your opening with something personal and passionate. It's not really about conveying information at all. It's to fill the buyers' brain with these chemicals that tell them they like you, believe you, and trust you, all within the few minutes it takes to go from shaking their hand to wrapping up the *Position Us* stage of your first call.

Steps 4 to 6. Provoke, Expand, and Lead

After they're addicted, your job is to keep them on a natural high for the rest of the meeting. Top sellers do this by stimulating the customer with a thought-provoking dialogue. There's a very specific cadence to doing this right, and there's a deep psychological connection waiting to be forged if the steps are followed in the correct sequence.

In describing how they do this, many stars told us that they didn't consciously follow a framework. For many it was intuitive. But by having the stars break down the types of things they say and the effects of those words on the buyers they meet, we were able to replicate a model the rest of us can follow. I call this model the "PRECISION Questions," and it is the subject of the next chapter.

Step 7. Value

Column 7 in the Face-to-Face Meeting Planner template (Figure 3.1) holds a place to write down anything you hear in the meeting that might be a breadcrumb that could lead you to a strong value proposition later in the sales cycle. Some salespeople wait till the end of their sale and then hit the prospect with a company-to-company value pitch. But you're not selling to a company. You're selling to the people inside that company. So in every call it pays to have your ears open, listening for clues about what the individuals within the group believe the value needs to look like. They may express this at the *corporate*, *department*, or *personal* level. Capture that and save it for later in the sale when it's your turn to sell.

Across the bottom of the F2F Meeting Planner, you'll see resources that are helpful to fill out in anticipation of the call.

Resource 1. Anecdotes

In this field you prepare notes to tell the prospects an interesting true story or parable that reveals a self-evident truth or strikes a flash of insight to support a point you want to drive home. For example, pharmaceutical company sales reps whose competitors have issued recent product recalls because they rushed their drugs to market might want to boast about their own company's slow-but-steady track record by using an anecdote about "The Tortoise and the Hare."

Or to help a customer embrace the concept of change being difficult but necessary, they might tell the anecdote of Aron Ralston,[6] the climber who endured five days of agony after being trapped by a fallen boulder, who had to amputate his crushed arm with a pen knife in order to survive, and point out their challenges are just as urgent to resolve.

Anecdotes vicariously place you or the customer in the shoes of the story's hero, or they invoke the business, sporting, or life wisdom of others, no matter if it is Shakespeare, Oprah, or Yoda. If you think ahead to your meeting, find a point you want your prospect to remember, then turn it into a memorable anecdote and write it on your call plan so it serves as a prompt. You may not remember to use it otherwise.

Resource 2. Case Studies

In this field you give yourself bullet points about customer success stories you feel are relevant to the prospect you're calling on. Use bullet points to write down whatever factual statistics you want to recall, not the whole story. Remember you're writing on this plan only to help you be more fluid and conversational in the call, so keep it simple enough to read at a glance.

Step 8. Close Next Steps

In this field you write down the specific commitment to which you want the prospect to agree. Your destination must be clear before you start the meeting so you know when you've reached it. Never make the infraction of asking the customer at the end of your meeting where *they* want to take things. It's *your* responsibility to advance the sale, to lead the customer to activities and deadlines, and to ask for the order.

Buyers express disappointment when salespeople don't ask them to open doors or take action. This was one of the surprise findings in our research into this topic. According to senior executives, failure to ask for a commitment of any kind leaves them feeling like they were "spending" their time rather than "investing" their time. Investments are always forward looking—and so should be your first meeting. When salespeople hesitate to "push their luck" to ask for small commitments in each meeting, they seldom get the chance to ask for big commitments later. If you took five minutes to write a list of the sort of commitments you could ask the customer to keep as a result of any meeting, you may be surprised how many opportunities reveal themselves. It's all about training the customer to say "Yes."

During the research for this book, my team went out on whole-day accompaniments with a cross-section of salespeople to observe what they actually did before, during, and after their sales calls. We saw some reps reach the end of the first meeting and then go into a "mental holding pattern" as they considered what to do next. But at that point, it was too late to ask themselves what to do next. It's much easier to glance down at your call plan and ask them to commit to the thing you already wrote down. And if the discussion has revealed that a different outcome is more appropriate, shift to that. But for goodness sake, ask for something!

It could be as simple as asking them to convene another meeting for you with people whose names came up in the discussion. Maybe you want to volunteer to be sent to other departments on a fact-finding mission. You could ask for a personal referral to key stakeholders. Perhaps you could invite them to be videotaped for your website or magazine talking about the needs of people in their role, or you could capture their opinion about an issue that's topical and important to them. If you have a VIP breakfast or other public event coming up, maybe they'll agree to be panelists or attendees. Perhaps the next step is for you to present your solution, or for you to take them to a "customer reference site" where you can show how a company that already bought from you is using and enjoying the benefits of your solution. Maybe the commitment you ask for is to run a billable needs analysis workshop with their peers. It might even be for them to read an excerpt from a company publication or case study and commit to give you feedback.

Whatever commitment you extend, prospects get another dopamine hit when you ask for it with passion and directness, and explain how it will help them as well as you.

Some top sellers end first meetings by presenting a preformatted sheet that lists in sequence the typical steps a customer would go through when deciding to buy the sellers' solutions and the typical time it would take to complete each step. The sellers show this to the customer and explain that it's a road map they'd like each party to follow so there are no surprises and so that dates can be agreed to in advance to make sure appropriate people and resources are available for key meetings (like group presentations, site visits, demonstrations, and even signing the contract). A column for assigning responsibilities in both companies is usually included.

In large sales for which your team needs to invest time and money to scope, design, or validate the prospect's needs, list those activities as billable. Including these billable activities serves as a litmus test for the prospect's resolve. The fee may be full freight, or it may be cost recovery, or it may be reimbursable after they sign an order, but never give resources away for free. People rarely respect the commercial value of your efforts if you don't charge for them. Giving them away doesn't increase your chances of winning, and worse, it drives up your cost of sale!

With the time frames listed, if your customer has a critical date by which a solution needs to be purchased or installed, it's helpful to work back from that deadline and set the dates on which your buying steps need to be completed for the customer to hit their launch on target. Seeing the prospect review this list and suggest changes gives you a powerful buying signal at the end of the first call. The same goes for when they pencil in the people who should be responsible for certain activities. With these changes, additions, and deletions, the document becomes *their* buying plan. They now own it. But you have controlled it.

It gives you a level of competitive immunity when they agree to these dates and steps, because they've started to follow your advice (a habit you want them to grow into). You've established a peerlike rapport early. The steps in their buying process now map directly to your selling process, and they're marching to the beat of your drum. Any competitors that start circling the deal will find your process, your language, and your criteria embedded in the fabric of the buying process. Also, you already know all the key dates and events the buyer will undertake, and you can make sure their calendar is kept so busy with you and your team members that there is little room left for others to stick their nose in.

Top sellers call this a *Close Plan* internally and a *Mutual Project Plan* with customers (Figure 3.2). They report that this approach can collapse the time it takes to complete a deal because it embeds mutually agreed upon dates into the decision process.

Like passengers on an aircraft or hikers in the wilderness, customers like to know they have a competent guide who can take them out and bring them safely home again. Showing them you know the path to follow for projects of the nature they're considering and then suggesting they follow your plan will build belief and confidence in you and your company.

Now ask yourself: Do I present Close Plans in my *first* calls? Do I ask for mini-commitments that advance the sale at the end of *every* customer meeting? What would be the effect if all of my team members started doing so tomorrow?

Invest half an hour to create a Close Plan as a template in Excel, print it out, and then use it at the end of every first meeting with new

MUTUAL PROJECT PLAN

Draft # __1__   Date: __4__ / __6__ /20__14__   Company: _Genericorp_   Contact Person: _John Citizen_   Title: _Database Mgr_

Task	BILL (✓)	Date	ASSIGN (initials)
Poll stakeholders		5/6	JC
Agree on draft plan		5/20	RW
NDA/contract review		6/18	MT
Needs assessment	✓	6/11	RW
Review findings		6/18	JC
Solution design	✓	7/7	RW
Prototyping	✓	7/31	TW
Test/pilot on-site		7/31	TW
Review results		8/14	JC
Plan implementation		8/28	RW
SOW & SOP		8/28	MT
Agree to contract		9/10	MT
Deliver		★10/1	RW

WEEK 0 2 4 6 8 10 12 14 16 18 20 22 24 26 28 30 32 34 36 38 40 42 44 46 48 50 52

Figure 3.2: Sample Mutual Project Plan (or Close Plan)

prospects for the next 30 days. At the end of the month, review in your mind the extent to which customers picked up a pen and added ideas to what you had already written. How many put key dates in their diary? How much bolder have you become in asking people to make commitments?

Big things have small beginnings.

Chapter 4

PRECISION
Questions

The PRECISION Questioning Framework

While talking to a group of several hundred salespeople at a conference, I asked which professions they regarded as great questioners.
Some replied "reporters and consultants," and this led to a spirited
debate on the basis that reporters "only extract information" whereas
consultants "have a way of asking questions that make you think you
came up with the ideas they planted."

In asking consultants from KPMG, Ernst & Young (EY), and
Deloitte how they ask questions in such a way that they plant ideas at
the same time, their responses were consistent. They said they don't
go into many sales pursuits planning to sell any specific product. To
do so would be to abandon being consultative. They know their
companies offer a broad range of services to match any scenario, so
in their initial meetings, they like to get the customer talking about
themselves, their issues, and their ideas.

When the customer asks what they should buy, these consultants
smile wanly and say: "It depends. Let's explore that a little more."
And they continue drilling for deeper insights.

Sometimes weeks or months pass after the first meeting, and
still nothing has been pitched. What they're doing is a thorough
assessment of the customer's situation, their people's attitudes and
shopping lists, and their ability to support from the inside what the
consultant will eventually bring from the outside. Selling a widget
is not their primary concern at all. Setting up a successful project is.
They keep their product in their pocket, talk less, and learn more. And
the more they learn, the more they earn.

They report that by the time they actually get around to proposing
something, the customer is already using their language to describe
it and is motivated to get started. Handled properly, concerns about
price change from "How can we afford to do this?" to "How can we
afford *not* to do this?"

While researching this book, I observed these sellers meeting with
senior and middle managers, and patterns emerged consistent with how
top stars sell at telecom, energy, biotech, legal, finance, technology,

manufacturing, distribution, and many other types of businesses. There's a specific pattern of questioning and discussion that high performers follow. There are variations, but the core steps are consistent every time. And so are the results they get. This model unfolds in three strings of questions.

In the first string your intent is to *provoke* a reaction to those issues you believe the customer faces for which you have a solution. You don't mention the solution. You talk about their world. There are three steps in this string: Problems, Risks, and Effect (Figure 4.1).

Figure 4.1: The P-R-E String

STEP 1. PROBLEMS

Stars begin by focusing on a business driver or trigger they know the customer has, as a result of their research and Trigger Map and as confirmed by their initial e-mail, phone call, or referral. Once face-to-face the stars test for further reaction to these problems so they can be sure the people they are calling on understand the business issues and that these people are indeed the right people to meet.

These top sellers ask open-ended questions to get buyers talking about their current state and their desired state. Where a gap can be seen between the two, a problem or unfulfilled need emerges.

We call this the *Problems* step. It looks like this:

- *"What* steps are you considering to address [insert the triggers you know exist]?"
- *"Where* is this problem the most acute? Where else?"
- *"When* did these ideas first start to be discussed here?"
- *"Who* was the first person you remember talking about it? Who else?"
- *"Why* was it important to them?"
- *"How* did you get involved?"
- "As we see other companies in your industry facing pressure to take action on the same problems, we see a level of urgency to put solutions in place. How would you describe the importance of doing so here? To what extent is this on your radar at the moment?"
- "If improvements were possible, what are the first things you'd like to see change? Why those?"
- "How do you do these things today? What do you like most about the way this is achieved? What has to improve soon?"

STEP 2. RISKS

A logical extension of the preceding dialogue is for the customer to ask if the seller has any ideas to fill that gap. Here the seller resists the urge to pitch their solution. It's premature to do so. They instead talk about the "typical things" people try and why these can be disappointing when they're not thought through fully (here the features of their competitors' offerings are contrasted with their own, but without labeling either company).

For example:

- "In the urgency to get started, we find some companies needlessly make sacrifices because they don't know all the options available. Typical trade-offs they make include getting things done on time, with the right quality, and having the job finished right instead of needing to be reworked."
- "A common mistake in projects like this occurs when people believe [insert something customers easily get wrong without the right advice]. The consequences of this can be [insert metrics from any failed projects in your industry that have become cautionary tales]."
- "This project of yours is a logical response to [describe the business trigger behind the project]. But if it's run without all the information or resources it needs, cracks can appear."
- "For example, a company I know wanted speed [from an unnamed competitor], and it ended up sacrificing efficiency [like you can deliver]. Another company wanted the latest technology [from an unnamed competitor], but it sacrificed the stability of a well-established support team [like you can deliver]."

You see what we're doing?

This *Risks* step shows the customer you've been around the block and know the mistakes people can make using obvious or traditional solutions. It also starts to lay mines around your competitors, without naming them. The expertise you begin to show in this step is very appealing to any buyer but especially to risk-averse buyers.

One intriguing trend we have observed is that the Risks step is often managed by presales technical experts, solution specialists, or product managers who attend the customer meeting with the salesperson. I call them *techxperts*. They let the salesperson open the discussion in the Problems step; then these specialists take over in the Risks step by telling the customer about challenges and wrong choices they may not know to look for. This provides invaluable food for thought to the prospect, while establishing the seller's brand as a leader. As they say, knowledge is power. When the Risks step is complete, the techxperts hand back to the salesperson.

STEP 3. EFFECT

The visual in the P-R-E string in Figure 4.1 shows the Effect step as a padlock. It serves as a summary and mini-close where you lock the customers into agreeing that, so far, you're both on the same page.

What do you say in this step? Top sellers summarize what's just been discussed about how they've been able to solve these problems for past customers, without the attendant risks occurring. They offer the opinion that they can do so again for *this* customer. They confirm that the customer wants to explore how the supplier could have this same effect on their business. This is how it goes:

- "My team has a solid track record helping companies like [insert reference names] handle complex projects like this."
- "We've done this without [insert the risks] occurring. In fact, we consistently produce results in the range of [insert a typical performance metric you have in a case study]."
- "Based on what we know of your company, I'd *hypothesize* that once our approach is in place, you could expect results in the same range, possibly better. Is this the type of effect you'd like a partner to have on this project?"

Now you see the end-to-end logic of the P-R-E string. It literally seeks to achieve a state of awareness where Problems + Risks = Effect.

It ensures that the conversation is founded on the customer's issues, not on your product. It serves to provoke the buyer to confront their problems, establish a vision for change, and recognize that you have specialist expertise they can benefit from. Top sellers use this as the basis for all further discussion.

If you thumb back to the Face-to-Face (F2F) Meeting Planner in the previous chapter (Figure 3.1), you'll see Step 4 is a column labeled "Provoke" that contains headings for the P-R-E string. This is where you use it as part of a first meeting agenda. See how the dots connect?

Sometimes if the conversation is pushing up against the 60-minute mark, this is as far as stars will go in a first meeting. They might end by saying something like this:

> That's all we have time for today, John. Now based on what you've shared with me, I'm very certain we can help you. I'd like to collect some ideas and continue this discussion in a couple of days. In the meantime, I'm curious. Let's say I come back and show you an approach that you fall in love with: what would be our next steps? For example, would you and I enter into an agreement to proceed this week, or do you need to involve other people or follow a different timeline? If so, what do those steps look like?

Sales stars know that when a customer's curiosity is piqued and their guard is down, it's the best time to extract information about their decision process, budget, or levels of authority. It's also a good time to suggest your Mutual Project Plan and get dates into the diary.

However, if you've completed the P-R-E string and there's still a substantial amount of time left in the meeting block, you could go further. But what do top sellers talk about next? The temptation is to start selling your solution. Don't do it. You're still not ready.

Instead, high performers move to a deeper level of questioning in the second string that seeks to *expand* on the themes of three key areas: Consequences, Impact Points, and Scope (Figure 4.2).

Figure 4.2: The C-I-S String

STEP 4. CONSEQUENCES

You need this information to spot the serious buyers from the tire kickers. Prospects who tell you they see no real downside to keeping things as they are (or no upside to making a change) are lacking in hard motivation to take action. Unless there are definable consequences for "doing nothing," it's doubtful the customer will part with any money. So you must establish that consequences exist for doing nothing or that a payback awaits for making a change in the status quo.

These questions look like this:

> • "How quickly companies choose to deal with [insert the trigger] varies from case to case. To what extent is there a timeline in mind for your own company? Who set that? Why is this date important to meet? Is it realistic in your opinion?"
> • "What's likely to happen if you don't have a solution in place before the end of [insert date]?"

- "What are the risks that the complexity of choosing the right path could create a delay that causes you to miss your launch date?"
- "How will completing things on time and on budget create a 'win' for you in the short or long term? How important is this on your list of priorities?"
- "To what extent are the performance goals of you or your department tied to delivering a solution into the company?"

Additional questions to ask in this step might include these:

- "To what extent is doing things this way costing you money?"
- "How long do you have before people start raising red flags?"
- "Why is making a change a priority for you now?"
- "When do you need to make a decision by?"
- "Where are people feeling the most pressure today?"
- "Who is feeling most of the heat? Who felt it first?"
- "What would be the most damaging or embarrassing aspect of failure?"

We're looking to qualify the pressure people are under to make a change. If there is no pressure, why will they buy anything?

Is this prospect talking to you because they are simply looking for free education to keep up with their peers? Do they have an idle curiosity about "one day" improving a chronic problem the company has learned to live with, but there is no acute trigger or budget for taking action now? Do they have a "use it or lose it" budget, and do they need to empty their budget to qualify for the same draw next year? Is it because they're going to show too much profit and they figure they may as well spend it rather than pay taxes on it? Is it because they're flush with funds and want to go on a shopping spree for wants as well as needs?

These might be termed *soft consequences* because if they don't act, it's not going to cause their business to shred cogs or bleed red ink. They can live with the consequences. This means any investment with you is *discretionary*. They can take you or leave you. Knowing a customer is soft on taking action is an important thing to know when qualifying deals on your forecast. It's the lament of many sales directors that their teams' pipelines hold too many deals that are based on enthusiastic and speculative discussions that have no hard reasons for the customer to act.

Have you heard a customer guarantee you a sale, only to see it evaporate later? Do they ever tell you, "Actually, I never had the authority to spend money, and I was just wasting your time to feel important"? No, usually they'll roll their eyes in a way that mimics irritation, explain that there were "sudden budgetary or political reasons outside their control," and buy you a coffee for being a good sport.

The real cause for the sale stalling was that the consequences were never qualified properly. When people have no budget, no authority, or no trigger to act, they usually won't act.

Since they don't always volunteer this confession, the only way to know for sure is to ask consequence-focused questions and then to triangulate what one person tells you with what other people in that company tell you. They might confirm or refute the first person's claims, put them into a new perspective, or even share additional problems, risks, and consequences that expand what your solution needs to be.

Where you hear that consequences exist, always ask how they are measured. Is it a qualitative measure such as frustration, reputation, or embarrassment, or can it be expressed in quantitative terms such as time, quality, and money? If so, how much? How often? By when?

What does performance look like today, and what do they want it to be three months from now? Two years from now? How does this compare to industry standards or competitor performance?

Always collect *their* measurements because you'll need them when building value propositions later in the sale.

This is why learning who else is impacted—and to what extent—is what top sellers explore next.

STEP 5. IMPACT POINTS

Here you suggest other people, functions, or departments that might be impacted, based on your Trigger Map and knowledge gained elsewhere in similar sales. Because you want to manage this discussion in a way that implies deep expertise, this middle step of the C-I-S string might again be delegated to your techxperts:

> Your Problem is that public relations is at an all-time low. One Reason you cited is that at peak call times, customers have to wait nearly an hour in a telephone queue to talk to a real person. But you have no way to anticipate when these peaks will be because they come at random times.
>
> What we've learned with prospects facing similar challenges is that before customers ring your call center, they try to solve the problem themselves by hitting your website for answers. Then they Google your company name and a phrase that describes the problem they have.
>
> If you could spot this surge of keyword searches online and anticipate that customers will soon be calling, you'd have time to open up more call center seats to meet demand. This would alleviate the waiting time they experience and solve the public relations problem that happens when customers can't easily connect to you.

What we don't know yet is why your staff members aren't already solving this problem on their own. Maybe they have their own challenges. To what extent do you feel your call center supervisors, database managers, and web analysts should be part of our next discussion?

When you do a good job of explaining cause and effect, and you open their eyes to how problems in one department can bump into other departments or functions (remember the Trigger Map here), it begins to paint you as a player with experience solving this problem. This is a key foundation to developing a trusted advisor relationship.

By mapping which functions or people are impacted along this chain of cause and effect, you might identify that the problem doesn't in fact originate in the department of the person you're talking to. This department might simply be drinking the water downstream from a poisoned well. That's important information if you're going to truly solve their problem. Getting credit for spotting unseen truths like this is worth its weight in gold. Doing so helps you build a map of the key players you need to connect with before you can truly present a "whole solution." Until you do this you're not ready to propose *anything*.

As a result of the Impact Points step in this questioning model, it's more difficult for prospects to put up roadblocks that stop you from meeting others because the *logic* of networking has been established, and the *emotion* of confidence and trust in you is building. People are more willing to introduce you to others. You're starting to become an insider.

Another benefit to you of exploring the Impact Points is that by confirming the ripple effect of the Trigger Map and meeting the other people who will be direct or indirect beneficiaries of the changes you will usher into their world, you can start to catalog individuals' descriptions of how their business works, as well as the names of actual people, the work they do, the challenges, delays, or inefficiencies they face, and their personal vision for improvement.

As stated earlier, eventually you're going to present a value proposition. The value of your solution can be made very personal to the stakeholders who have a voice in the final buying decision—if you take the time to drill into the Impact Points, learn all you can, and show how your solution covers the bases. You'll need to explain specifically how each person's job will be impacted. Do this, and people follow with their hearts, minds, and budgets—in that order.

STEP 6. SCOPE

We're back to a step with a padlock icon. The purpose of this step is to confirm that the people you're meeting with agree that the consequences for inaction are something they want to avoid, that your Trigger Map has pinpointed different people who should have a voice in the final solution, and that these people are now locked in to connect you to those stakeholders.

The S in PRECISION is where you summarize the Consequences and Impact just agreed, so you can confirm the full **Scope** of the solution they're going to need. You see this at the bottom of the F2F Meeting Planner in Figure 3.1.

The Consequence + Impact = Scope string goes like this:

- "It sounds like the [trigger] behind your project has ramifications across the company. You've given me a clear idea of how important it is to put the right solution in place and who needs to be consulted as part of that process."
- "Getting the scope right shapes the solution you eventually put in place. I'm sure you agree that it makes no sense fixing only half the problem, especially with [consequences] riding on this."

- "Facilitating this discovery is a logical first step when it comes to evaluating your options. I'd like to meet some of the people you mentioned, to scope this in a little more detail. Maybe you'd like to attend those interviews? For example, how would we go about setting up meetings with [list each name and role]?"

Getting this confirmation (with a closed-ended question that they have to answer with yes or no) is what you need to lock down here.

Do you see how these question strings follow a repeating pattern?

The first step is always about using open-ended questions to provoke a discussion and hear the customer's opinions.

The second step is always designed to establish your company's credentials as you drill into the issues using your unique insights and expertise.

The final step is always to lock down what's been agreed in this line of discussion and to make sure you're still aligned.

If you thumb back a few pages to the F2F Meeting Planner (Figure 3.1), you'll see that Step 5 is a column labeled "Expand" that contains headings for the C-I-S string. This is where you use it in a first meeting.

Top sellers use this string as the basis for scoping the prospects' true needs and as a justification to ask for introductions and referrals to the other people whose departments are impacted upstream or downstream.

When meeting each new contact, prepare a fresh F2F Meeting Planner, and repeat the P-R-E and C-I-S strings for every person you interview.

As you do this, you will hear some of *the same information* repeated by different people; this validates it from more than one source.

You will hear *new information* about Problems, Risks, and Consequences. This gives you added insights that will be helpful when changing or weighting the decision criteria so they play in your favor.

You may even hear the names of *different people and departments* who are affected by this situation, who you will attempt to get connected to. All of this builds relationships and social capital.

STEP 7. IDEAS

So let's roll forward in the sales cycle now. You've repeated the P-R-E and C-I-S strings for multiple people. Through this exercise you've heard new information about their problems, needs, and the effect they want a solution to have. You've explored the consequences if they don't act, the impact points to their people, role, and functions, which gives you the full scope you need to work across.

Along the way you've built belief and advocacy with key people. You've shown you're different to those sellers who are eager to push their product. You've kept your product in your pocket until now. You've taken your time to really understand the customer. This differentiates you right away.

And in asking these questions, you've triangulated information from the key people, until you're sure you've dug to the bottom of their needs. Only now, after restraining yourself for so long you thought you might burst, is it time to talk about you. Now the diagnosis is done, it's time to give the patient a prescription for their medicine. Now you've earned that right.

The Lead column (Step 6 of Figure 3.1) on the F2F Meeting Planner is a tool to use when trying to see what a solution looks like through your prospect's eyes. After doing so, you need to make your own capabilities so compelling that the prospect can't see themselves going ahead without you. This is about learning their decision priorities, then embedding your solution inside those priorities.

This is the purpose of the I-O-N string. Now you're ready to use it. As you now know about the PRECISION model, there are three steps in this final string: Ideas, Options, and Needs (Figure 4.3).

Figure 4.3: The I-O-N String

This second I in PRECISION is where you pause before talking about your solution and learn their existing Ideas about what they think they need. The Ideas step is achieved with open-ended questions.

If they say they are a blank canvas for you to paint on, you might question how far along the thought process they really are and how much of a learning curve you're going to need to invest in them. As much as it sounds like a great opportunity to shape their thinking, the reality is that a lack of maturity and consensus in their ideation process can have repercussions on the close date, and on profitability.

If they give you a shopping list of preformed ideas, it's good that they're clearly on the road to investing in something, but you might question who's been informing them already, especially if the capabilities look like they were lifted from a competitor's brochure. Are you sure you're not being lined up to be one of several competitor quotes that an arcane buying policy requires they collect?

Perhaps the main value in asking about their ideas is that you learn their priorities for what they already value and believe to be an appropriate path. There's a saying that you have to make yourself equal before making yourself different because if you don't respect their current thinking, you risk their closing their mind to what you have to say. You certainly don't want to unwittingly present your solution and have it challenge their best thinking or embarrass any of their key players. You also want to avoid selling them features you think are wonderful but that they have a strong aversion to. You must learn what's in their mind before playing your hand:

- "What ideas have you already had for solving this?"
- "What good approaches have you seen other companies use?"
- "Do you know anyone who solved this problem else-where? What did they do that might work here?"
- "If you had unlimited resources to do this right, what capabilities would be on your shopping list? Why?"
- "Do you know of any companies that you respect that have dealt with this? How did they do it?"
- "Out of all the things you need, what are three must-haves that are a priority for you? Why?"

Before looking at the next step, pause to consider this next idea. Let's say you did a great job mapping the ripple effect in the Impact stage of PRECISION. In the Scope stage, your prospect will have agreed that the Problem may be broader, higher, and deeper than they first thought, with more moving parts than they accounted for when they developed their first ideas about what they need as a solution.

What will they be feeling now as a result of the rules having just changed? Uncertainty? Irritation? A sense of heightened risk? This can sink you, or it can give you an advantage, depending on how you play the next step.

Top sellers congratulate their prospect for holding any Ideas that favor the solution the seller can offer. Making yourself equal to their vision puts the prospect at ease that their original thinking remains sound, and it paints your offerings as meeting those needs. This is a double tap of relief for the buyer. But they may still have nagging doubts about how to deal with the *new* issues you've just opened their mind to. So your next task is to explain how your solution embraces their current thinking, improves on it, and covers all the bases.

STEP 8. OPTIONS

The O in PRECISION is where you show how their Ideas have a place within your solution, then how your solution includes additional options they haven't considered (or didn't know were possible) that yield a higher output than can be achieved without your company (or with another supplier). The goal here is to present **Options** on top of what was just outlined in their own Ideas, so that their vision begins to look a lot more like your products and services.

Think of it this way: their current ideas are a racing car pulling into the pits during a race, and your crew is about to tweak their engine, change the tires, and add new options that affect every aspect of their performance so they can get back in the race and win. This step begins with a statement like this:

> Your **Ideas** make a lot of sense for "some" of your needs. Given the full **Scope** you've shared, may I share how we could offer **Options** to this list that will help create a "whole" solution?

When they answer in the affirmative (they'll rarely say no), it's an opportunity to ask two follow-up questions to secure information they may not give as easily later in the call:

Follow-Up 1

> "Just so I'm clear on what to emphasize, where do you see/ feel/think your biggest risks are?"

If they didn't sense any risks or weaknesses, they wouldn't be talking to you. Be assured, risks are there to be mined. You want to get these on the table for two reasons. First, you genuinely need to know what part of your solution to emphasize. Second, they need to hear themselves admit they need you—this admission will focus their thinking. This question and answer should not be confused with their learning the Consequences of inaction, which you covered in a previous step. If they're a little slow in putting into words the risks they feel, you can draw them in using open-ended questions like these:

- "To what extent are you concerned that learning to use a new solution is going to take people away from other priorities and be a risk to 'business as usual'?"
- "To what extent do your internal team members have the right resources/talent/experience/funding/time/credibility for handling an initiative like this? Have they handled a project like this before?"
- "Which people/departments/roles most need to be involved soon, so that later they don't hassle you for being excluded?"
- "What was the last project your team members worked on that felt like 10 miles of rough road? Where were the points of failure you don't want to repeat?"
- "If anything could go wrong, what is it most likely to be?"

Follow-Up 2

Hot on the heels of those answers, you ask the following question and thus collect just one more piece of information:

What I'm about to share with you is based on my company's engineers/scientists/architects/designers spending an enormous amount of time and money reviewing the same problems you've told me about today. I'll be sharing some very special intellectual capital with you, and I'm pleased you want to know about it. [*Unspoken subtext: We know what we're talking about, and this information is high value—a dopamine hit.*]

Solving this has been important to us because it's important to our customers. And the good news is, we've cracked the problem. And even better: when our customers let us lead them through what can easily become a minefield of unexpected challenges, we've never failed to delight them. That's what I hope you'll allow us to do for you. [*Unspoken subtext: You could sink without us. We're a safe harbor.*]

So let's say that after I share these ideas today, you see/feel/think our solution satisfies your needs. What then will be your next steps for moving forward? [*Unspoken subtext: An expectation is seeded that they will be required to take some action—your meeting isn't just an information-sharing exercise.*]

In their reply, you will gain the information you need about their internal decision-making process and whether they have the decision-making authority themselves to take action or they need to seek the approval of others. The reason you ask these two follow-ups *before* discussing your solution is that "muscle memory" from having been on the receiving end of sales pitches tells your customer that after you present, you'll try to close them.

They may be on guard at the end of a sales call because they fear being manipulated; hence they'll be less likely to impart information they think you might "use against them." Let's face it, no matter how good the rapport between you (or how much dopamine you've sent into their brain), customers grow cautious at the end of a sales call. It's natural.

But because you covered "risk and commitment" in these two follow-up questions before your presentation, you already have this information locked down so discomfort isn't felt at the end of a sales call—you prehandled it. Like the fitness infomercials on late night television, this achieves a state of "muscle confusion" that prevents your buyer from hitting a plateau. This is a small but potent technique applied by elite sellers.

STEP 9. NEEDS

Only after you have completed this level of professional due diligence can you credibly "pitch" your solution in terms of how their Ideas and your additional Options are a solution equal to their real Needs. Your presentation can now be put together like a jigsaw puzzle that includes references to the information they shared with you and leads them to understand how your services and products embrace and improve the options they are considering.

Top salespeople avoid presentation slides on a first meeting, seeing them as the default tool of lazy salespeople. Instead, they open a tablet, whiteboard, flipchart, or the back of a napkin, and they literally connect the dots while they have a real conversation.

Check out Figure 4.4, which demystifies the approach. Starting at the top left and working clockwise, you can present ideas that are based on the discussion you've shared. The conversation begins with your research into their *drivers*, and it is underpinned by PRECISION at every step.

I call this flowchart "The Chemistry of PRECISION" because it gives a dose of sanity to the overhyped word *solution*, which actually originated as a chemistry term. In scientific terms, it's impossible to have a solution unless you first have two other substances: a *solute* that is dissolved in a *solvent*.[1] Think of a packet of flavored drink crystals.

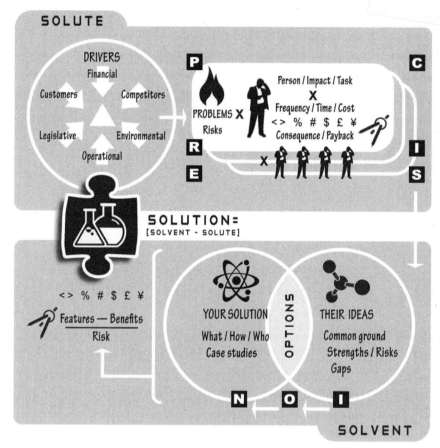

Figure 4.4: The Chemistry of PRECISION

Source: Concept and design copyright © 2012 by SalesLabs, Inc.

The crystals are the *solute*. You pour the crystals into a jug of water, the *solvent*. When they both mix, you have a *solution*.

You may hear some salespeople calling their products and services "solutions," but as you can see in Figure 4.4, this is not strictly an accurate label. Their products and services are actually a solvent. The solvent's purpose is to dilute a customer's problem, which is a solute. The act of applying solvent (your offerings) to a solute (the customer's world) is what creates the actual solution. Selling is an act of chemistry, a matter of science. It's impossible to offer solutions unless you first do your due diligence to understand the customer's situation.

What you find in the patterns of top sellers is they start at the top left of this diagram learning about the solute before they move down to explain the solvent. This allows them to connect both, forming a solution in the middle ground. The flow of this conversation inside a sales call might go something like this:

> You told me that as a result of [driver], the [problem] occurs when [person in role 1] is doing [task].
>
> This happens [frequency] because of [reason], and you measure its effect by [time/cost].
>
> You've thought about using [ideas] here, but you feel the [risk] could lead to [consequence].
>
> To deal with these issues, we developed a solution called [what] that takes the unique approach of [how]. We deployed this solution to help a very similar client need [case study]. This client achieved [measure] within [time]. Another customer achieved [measure] in [time]. The funny thing is, every time we help our clients, they see a measurable benefit.
>
> As you can see, our solution includes your [ideas], and it adds options [feature/benefit 1] that are unique to our approach. We also offer [feature/benefit 2] and [feature/benefit 3]. When you join your [ideas] to the options offered by our [solution], it serves to eliminate [risk] and remove the [problem]. Is that what you Need?

You repeat this flow for each key stakeholder uncovered by your Impact questions—after you know enough about them to discuss their needs. When it's too early to know much about these other people (that is, you may not even have met them yet), the following step in the conversation provides a bridge to start developing the person you first meet into an internal referrer:

> Clearly I don't yet know enough about the views of these other people to explain what our solution would mean to them. I recommend we go talk to them together so their needs are represented in your final solution design. Is that fair? Now based on what I've explained so far, what would you change to make this the perfect solution for you?

As a litmus test, this helps you gauge if they've started to emotionally and logically embrace your solution. It also starts the process of developing this person as an internal door opener. This is important because as you learned in the Impact stage of the PRECISION model, other people may be affected upstream or downstream from this person's department, role, or function. To secure a budget and win against rivals for that budget, you'll need to meet these other people and convert as many as possible into supporters for your solution.

If they are higher up in the company hierarchy, getting on their calendar is made easier when someone on the inside is vouching for you. My *Selling to the C-Suite* research revealed that in every company you find doors open and information is shared through tribal connections. If you try to cold-call people who don't know you, you'll rarely get lucky. When someone with credibility on the inside refers you to meet a senior manager, the door opens 84 percent of the time. Your bank account of social capital starts to be credited or debited from the very first call.

You might complete the whole PRECISION sequence in one meeting, but that's unlikely in a long sales cycle. You want to keep your powder dry and only reveal the I-O-N string after you've laid the appropriate groundwork. Pitching your solution before people feel a trust connection with you usually invites old preconceptions, past biases, and skepticism to torpedo your efforts. Never pitch your solution before laying the right foundation.

It's more likely you will want to complete P-R-E in the first meeting. When you come back for the next meeting, you can use E to recap your findings from the previous session, then progress to C-I-S. At that point, the very act of having uncovered additional people who are impacted may lead you to network to these other people and repeat the P-R-E to C-I-S steps as many times as it takes to see the full picture.

These iterations may take several weeks or months, but it's the preparation you need to be sure that when you eventually propose a "whole solution" in the I-O-N steps, it takes into account the entire scope of solvents (products and services) that are needed to dilute every solute (problem or need) your customer is facing.

Some salespeople confess to getting comfortable—they "settle" if they're meeting two or three contacts for each prospect company, especially if their early sales career exposed them to negative feelings about prospecting. However, the best consultative salespeople use the PRECISION questioning model as a method to prospect by gaining an introduction from one person to the next. Prospecting is easier when you're referred. As a result these reps typically call on three to four times as many meaningful contacts than transactional salespeople reach. They've learned that to engineer a customer's decision criteria, they first have to mine information from as many people as possible. In selling, knowledge really *is* power.

As a result of each meeting you have with different contacts, there's a chance you'll hear of different ripples, new people, extra pains. Then something happens. You get to a point where you stop hearing the names of new people, ripples, symptoms, or pains. It's here that you realize you've reached the bottom of the well. This is a defining moment in the sale. It means you won't be leaving any money on the table because finally you've mapped the full extent of your customer's Needs for this single sales opportunity.

So let's recap. In a first meeting (or series of meetings), you've discussed your contacts' business drivers and asked open-ended questions to uncover **Problems**. You've used your techxperts (or your own experience) to discuss how jumping at what looks like an obvious solution is one of the reasons why projects of this nature can fail, and that your mastery of such issues can remove the customer's **Risks**. Then you've used closed-ended questions to gain agreement on the **Effect** they really need a supplier to have in their business. This is to be sure you're both on the same page.

Next you asked open-ended questions to uncover the negative **Consequences** if they don't take action (or the payback consequences if they do). You or your techxperts have gained additional credibility by drilling into how this situation usually ripples out to **Impact** people, roles, and functions in other departments, higher up the food chain, lower down, and sideways. Then you've used closed-ended questions to lock down a summary of the full **Scope** of this initiative so the prospect understands you're all on the same page.

Finally, once ready, you asked open-ended questions to uncover their current **Ideas** or shopping list. You've explored how the added capabilities of your products, services, partners, or other differentiators serve as desirable **Options** on top of the prospect's current thought process, which will deliver to them a stronger solution. Then you've used closed-ended questions to lock down a summary of the **Needs** they need a supplier to fill, so be sure you're both on the same page about what that now looks like. You would expect their list of requirements to now morph around the unique elements of your solution, thus placing your competitors at a major disadvantage.

It's taken a few pages to spell this out, but I believe it's important to do so as a way of highlighting the quality of questioning that customers now expect from trusted advisor salespeople. Sure, you might be able to "wing it" and get to the end result without writing this approach on a F2F Meeting Planner. But if you want to send the message that the customer is so important that you would professionally prepare to meet them, and if you want your customer to see you respecting their ideas enough to write them down, managing your meetings using a tool like the F2F Meeting Planner (or any similar version you choose to employ) really is a minimum standard today.

THE PRECISION QUESTIONING FRAMEWORK

Before adding it to this book, this PRECISION Questioning Framework, Figure 4.5, was tested in the market for five years by 2,000 salespeople in small, medium, and large companies on five continents.

It works for them, and it will work for you.

Do you see how much more information you can extract from a sales call with these types of questions, using this logic flow?

But there's a danger to this. Because you get so much new information flooding out of the customers, it's unlikely that any slide deck created *before* the call is going to hit all the right points anymore. How can it?

So be careful. Whipping out a canned presentation now will undermine the value of the PRECISION discussion you've been having. You risk making the customers feel that you've only been biding your time to give a presentation that was always going to be the same no matter what they shared. You don't want to come across as insincere and manipulative, but salespeople rushing to pitch their wares too early is why some prospects can be excused for thinking the job title "rep" is an abbreviation of *reptile* instead of *representative*.

A final observation. Does your company use a sales methodology to help plan complex solution sales? You know what I mean—a set of pages, screens, or templates you fill in to show your managers that you're in control and have a game plan. So often, a big assumption made when these are rolled out is that everybody comes preinstalled with the basic sales questioning skills needed to feed good information into these sales plans. This assumption stems from the fact that when most of these "top-tas-tic, fox-storming, strategic-pain-sheets" were first released, it

Figure 4.5: The PRECISION Questioning Framework

was in an era when companies gave new salespeople months of training to master the skills of selling, and their basic training may have included SPIN or MANDACT or AIDA questions. Time marched on, and it was taken as "a given" that salespeople came with these skills long after companies stopped investing in such long induction programs.

So if you use a sales methodology and see that plans are being filled in with weak information and limited insight, if salespeople aren't close enough to their customers to have a clue what's really going on in the sale, and if deals slip off the forecast and don't close as planned, a primary cause can be traced to a dearth of curiosity and questioning skill. Better questions leads to better planning, execution, and control. It's not rocket science.

Chapter 5

Qualify Their Interest

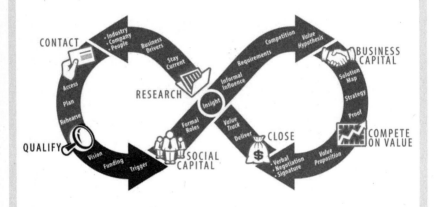

Sales Expansion Loop: Qualify

A smile always crosses my face when I'm facilitating workshops on how to sell inside a target opportunity and I ask my audience: "How do you qualify whether to pursue a deal or walk away?" I smile because the answers are always thoughtful and based on shared experience that has allowed the topic of sales qualification to enter the common vernacular, whereas 15 years ago a repeatable framework for doing this was something most road warriors were learning for the first time. I get a genuine kick out of seeing the profession achieve milestones like this. Their answers, sometimes in the language of whatever sales process they've been trained in, typically include qualifiers like these:

- "Does the customer have budget for this?"
- "Who's the 'economic buyer' that can spend the money?"
- "What's the 'compelling event,' 'pain,' or 'burning platform'?"
- "When will they make a commitment?"
- "Who are the evaluators, decision makers, and influencers?"
- "What issues, agendas, or rivals am I competing against?"
- "Do I really have a solution for them, and do I have a fair shot at winning?"
- "Why do this? Why now? And why with us?"

Qualification helps you identify vulnerability and strength in a sales opportunity, both yours and, depending on the quality of your information, that of your competitors. Near the start of a sales cycle you qualify in order to decide if there's a real opportunity that's worth investing your time on. It may take several meetings with a prospect for you to have enough information to make this judgment. Where you (and your solution partners) are noncompliant to the buyer's criteria, . . . or where it appears the purchasing manager is shopping around to drive the price down but has already decided who they're buying from, . . . or where a competitor has clearly written the evaluation requirements (so what you regard as the start of your sales cycle is actually near the end of theirs), . . . or where the customer and the project looks like a dog with fleas that will be costly to support and a pain to work with—where such situations exist, you need to assess the landscape objectively and decide that instead of racking up a $100,000 cost of sale for half a year of effort that won't be rewarded, it may be more prudent to disengage early.

But because your company may have a never-say-die attitude, . . . or when deals are thin on the ground and your managers want you to chase down every opportunity in case you get lucky, . . . or out of the hubris of wanting to be visible in every large tender, . . . and of course, if sales *profitability* is not a metric you're rewarded on—the act of walking away from a sales opportunity may be something you would never entertain or even be allowed to do by your line manager.

I submit that this is old thinking. There *are* companies today that take a hard line on sales qualification, and most important they profit from it. They've figured out what their hit rate is, and they challenge their reps to identify which deals *not* to go after. So if I average a 40 percent win rate from my proposals, my boss might choose to reward me not just on the 4 sales I win out of every 10 but also on the 6 sales I make a case for walking away from if I can show a validated business reason for qualifying out of them. If, as a salesperson, I could then fill the time those 6 deals would have otherwise sucked up with another 4 wins, I would have doubled my revenue performance for the year and actually expended less effort overall. Do you want 100 percent growth this year? Try working smarter, not harder. Others are doing it. You can too. The starting point is to have a standardized, repeatable rigor built around how you qualify each deal. If you don't already consistently apply a qualification framework to all deals in your pipeline today, this chapter will give you clear direction on how to do so.

Is qualification something you do only once at the start of a sale when making a go/no-go decision? By no means. As the sale progresses, we must continue to qualify to make sure we understand the customer's requirements and our competitor's position, and we need to be clear about whether we're in control of the field of battle, all the way through to the finish line. At each stage of the sale, we would want to be qualifying different things, and we should have this clearly understood throughout the sales and management teams. The rule of thumb is that anytime we start a sale, anytime we move from one stage of the sale to the next, or anytime there's a change in the landscape as a result of our actions or those of the customer or competitor, we should look through the lens of qualification and ask ourselves, "Am I winning or losing right now?" Then, depending on the answer, we should decide what the next best steps are to gain the advantage over the competition. Doing so informs our focus for strategy and tactics each week so we're doing things to advance the deal and not getting lost in unfocused tactics. We need to stand back a few paces to avoid getting lost in the detail. This is how you gain greater control over the outcomes.

THE *ART OF WAR*

The ability to see the landscape for "what it is" was a concept made popular by Sun-tzu's book the *Art of War*.[1] I know, I know: most enterprise salespeople today have heard all about direct and indirect strategies, flanking, niche selling, delay, and so forth. These are some of the "strategy labels" that come to mind when people hear the name of Sun-tzu invoked in a tome on selling. But for now, just park what you've learned from last century's sales classes for a moment. I'm talking about Sun-tzu as his teachings relate to *Qualification*. You haven't seen *this* before.

Sun-tzu was a Chinese nobleman born in the fourth century BC who saw his country ravaged by feuding warlords. This time is commonly known as the Warring States Period. He paid careful attention to how battles were fought, and he began to see patterns that gave foresight into who was most likely to win or lose based on the size of the army, the terrain they fought on, the tactics they used, and other factors. He realized the importance of positioning on the field of battle, and he saw that the decision to position an army must be based on an objective assessment of the conditions in that time and place.

He observed that military strategy was not about working through an established list of actions or a fixed plan, but rather, it required quick and appropriate responses to changing conditions. He knew that a plan that was drafted in a controlled environment would not necessarily work in the field. In a dynamic environment (like a strategic sale), army soldiers need to rely on their own powers of observation, not on a handbook of instructions. This means "constant qualification." Therefore, teaching warriors how to read situations in the moment, how to communicate those findings up the line, and how to respond to what they saw were of paramount importance to his methodology.

Master Sun wrote out this methodology in a journal of 13 chapters called *bing-fa*, which translates as the *Art of War*. This journal came to the attention of the provincial king of Wu, who asked Master Sun to demonstrate if *any* army could be led to victory by its teachings. After successfully proving that his disciplines held true under different circumstances, Sun-tzu was appointed general over the king's armies. According to legend, he conquered all the neighboring provinces in flawless victories, and he restored peace to the land.

The *Art of War* was used by the feudal Japanese daimyo Takeda Shingen, whose *Furinkazan* approach to warfare granted his forces near invincibility without the use of guns. General Vo Nguyen Giap taught his guerilla fighters the *Art of War* in 1954 for the epic Battle of Dien Bien Phu, which led to the ouster of France from its Indochina colonies and the partitioning of North and South Vietnam. Other military leaders from Napoléon to General Douglas MacArthur have claimed to draw instruction from Sun-tzu, and the book is now required reading in the CIA and the U.S. Army's Command and General Staff College, and it is featured in the Marine Corps' professional reading program. It is also being included in the playbooks of sporting coaches worldwide.

One key takeaway is that from the earliest moments of a battle, you can qualify who is most likely to win based on their positioning. You can make decisions based on this insight to change the balance of power; and for each specific condition, you can formulate definitive strategies and tactics that will propel you to victory. Much has been made of Sun-tzu's writings with respect to their applicability to sales strategy midway through a sales campaign. But my observation is that these ideas need to be used much earlier than that because only if you have accurate data upon which to make your calculations early in the sale can you set an accurate competitive strategy to guide the whole campaign later in the sale. That's where Qualification comes in. Constant qualification and requalification of the terrain are critical elements of Sun-tzu's philosophy. Constantly requalifying allows you to see several steps ahead of the competition and thereby stay in control of the sale.

I recommend a study of Sun-tzu and the *Art of War* to everyone, even those not in business. There are practical reasons for doing so that are likely to become very relevant in this century.

When I lived and worked in China for several years after that nation entered the World Trade Organization in December 2001, I took the opportunity to learn of Sun-tzu directly from old silk Mandarin texts and members of the country's 2.3-million-member military.[2] Much of Sun-tzu's spirit continues to animate the mindset of people in China today, and Westerners would be well advised to learn something of these teachings to understand the hearts of their Sino brethren better. Why? Because China has filled its war chest with billions of dollars from granting business licenses to allow Western companies to trade on the Mainland, it has learned best practices from them, and it has opened thousands of factories built to compete using low-cost labor. China flawlessly executed a public relations coup in using the 2008 Olympic Games in Beijing and the 2010 World Expo in Shanghai to show the world that "Made in China" was synonymous with a modern, progressive, and prosperous country. Visitors could see that gleaming towers of glass and steel had replaced poor shanty towns and magnetic levitating trains and a rising class of nouveau riche have established China as a land with one foot planted firmly in its heritage and the other stepping into the future.

In 2004, a card-carrying member of the Communist Party waxed prophetic for me over one glass too many of single malt while I soberly sipped a Sprite, listening intently to every word. He let slip what he called "the Grand Plan," the content of which I have no reason to believe he exaggerated. There in the musky oak-paneled room of a Shanghai country club, he opined that opening its doors wide to foreign trade, learning and copying the latest practices to make up for lost time, and collecting a massive fund surplus were the first three steps in a five-step plan the nation's leaders had hatched long ago.

Steps 3 and 4 were to play out through to 2020, he said, and see China and its allies using the savings accrued by being "the world's factory" to buy controlling stakes in marquee global companies, as well as underwriting the debts of whole nations. "Eventually," he said, "the dragon will roar, and China will swallow the world."

I could have put it down to the whiskey talking. But was it?

In 2004 China's Huawei Technologies started winning European work, and then it spread its business dealings around the globe. At the time this book was being written, Huawei was beating once top dogs Nokia Siemens Networks, Alcatel-Lucent, and Ericsson to integrate Orange UK's and T-Mobile's 2G networks.[3] In 2005 China's Lenovo acquired IBM's personal computer division for $1.75 billion, and by 2010 it was funding ventures in the coal-to-chemical industries, which are gateways into everything from pharmaceuticals to food cropping.

China's state-owned shipping giant Cosco spent $4.3 billion in 2010 to seize control of one of Greece's beleaguered shipping ports in Piraeus. Cosco's chief executive Wei Jiafu told Greece's Skai Television: "We have a saying in China, *Construct the eagle's nest, and the eagle will come.* We have constructed such a nest in your country to attract such Chinese eagles. This is our contribution to you."[4]

Chinese money has flexed its muscles in energy, oil, mining, and natural resources investments around the world, especially in Canada, Australia, and Africa.

In the article "China Buys Up the World" (November 11, 2010), the *Economist* stated:

> *Such concerns are likely to intensify over the next few years, for China's state-owned firms are on a shopping spree. Chinese buyers—mostly opaque, often run by the Communist Party, and sometimes driven by politics as well as profit—have accounted for a tenth of cross-border deals by value this year, bidding for everything from American gas and Brazilian electricity grids to a Swedish car company Volvo.*

It's worth noting that in 2011, foreigners owned $4.45 trillion of U.S. debt, or approximately 47 percent of the $9.49 trillion debt held by the public and 32 percent of the total national debt of $14.1 trillion. Of the stake owned by foreigners, China owns nearly one quarter. In March 2011 China surpassed the United States[5] as the world's top manufacturer, having previously vaulted over Japan.

In October 2011, headlines in European media reported how Klaus Regling, chief executive of the European Financial Stability Facility (EFSF), was cozying up to Chinese vice finance minister Zhu Guangyao about injecting funds to help bail out the eurozone.

Trevor Royle, diplomatic editor for Scotland's *Herald* newspaper, wrote:

> *China has entertained ambitions about investing heavily in Europe, and this would be facilitated by a major contribution to EFSF. A successful deal could also open the door for more subtle investment in banking, industry and property, which would give China a huge amount of leverage in Europe. In turn, that would increase the country's global reach and influence—from claiming more authority in bodies such as the IMF and resisting U.S. demands for raising the value of the yuan.[6]*

Max Hastings from London's *Daily Mail* added:

China has reserves of £2.1 trillion in foreign exchange, growing at more than £300 billion a year, with no place for most of the money to go. The dragon state already holds 10 percent of America's enormous overseas debt, a trillion's worth. But most of its money remains in its banks, to be used as munitions in the campaign to extend its global reach and influence.[7]

Make of this what you will. I'm joining the dots between my experience of immersing my family inside the Chinese economy and now reading the world's headlines to simply say there's a good chance you or your kids will be selling to, working for, or partnering with Chinese-controlled companies more often this century than has been experienced in the past. As a result of pure pragmatism, learning Mandarin is something I've long advocated to my own children even if their school doesn't offer it. Understanding Chinese philosophy and business rituals goes with the territory, hence the *Art of War* is right up there as required reading, along with the ancient *36 Stratagems* that have been quite well adapted by Krippindorf in his masterwork *Hide a Dagger Behind a Smile* (Platinum Press, 2008), plus Terri Morrison and Wayne Conway's indispensable *Kiss, Bow, or Shake Hands: Asia* (Adams Media, 2005).

I suggest that like Sun-tzu leading the emperor's armies, you also are the general leading your own forces across the landscape of your sale. Sun-tzu wrote:

Now the general who wins a battle makes many calculations in his temple ere the battle is fought. The general who loses a battle makes but few beforehand. Thus do many calculations lead to victory, and few calculations to defeat: how much more no calculation at all! It is by attention to this point that I can foresee who is likely to win or lose. (Art of War 1:26)

You win the sale by making many calculations, which means constant qualification. This is the foundation for all military and commercial enterprises. But to constantly qualify, you must cultivate a hunger to know about the customer and your competitors. You must be a curious salesperson. You must learn to research and to ask the types of questions that tell you what you need to know, unlike those salespeople who believe their job is to do all the talking. When you are talking, you're hearing only what you already know, not what you *need* to know. You get what you need to know by asking smart questions and *listening*, by keeping your eyes open, and by *discerning*. Yes, selling is as much a set of skills as it is a science.

So in a sales situation, is it possible to define the specific qualification criteria the top 20 percent of salespeople use *most of the time*? By doing so, can we arrive at a potent distilled formula? Will doing so grant us a repeatable approach for understanding the *landscape of the sale* and thereby direct our strategy and tactics so we too can achieve "near invincibility" in battle?

The answer is yes.

THE OPPORTUNITY SNAPSHOT

As mentioned earlier, adopting these qualification criteria may require us to unlearn some of the dogma we've been fed in the past. My researchers used the litmus test of "What do the top performers use *most often*?" instead of the many ideas on this topic that are interesting but rarely applicable. We culled our list accordingly. Some other criteria we encountered in the market were described by salespeople as "helpful to know, but you need telepathy to find out." There was a temptation to cut these as well in the interest of giving you an easier list to work with, but in actuality you don't need to read minds—you need a better questioning strategy. These criteria were retained where they added value, and we collected the best questions to help you get the answers. The remainder of qualification topics out there were duplicates that we merged.

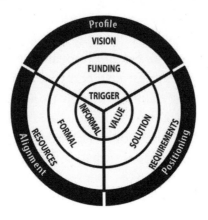

Figure 5.1: The Opportunity Snapshot

What remained from this sorting exercise across multiple companies, industries, and training methodologies was a filter of nine factors that shone through as essential to qualifying every dynamic, strategic sale. I call it the *Opportunity Snapshot* because its intent is to capture how the sale looks at a moment in time. As shown in Figure 5.1, it looks like a dartboard or an archery target.

THE THREE TRIMESTERS OF A DEAL: PROFILE, POSITIONING, AND ALIGNMENT

The nine criteria are grouped into three wedges that make up the circular diagram you see in Figure 5.1. Each wedge serves a specific purpose and is timed to what some top performers called the *Three Trimesters of a Deal*—where the first trimester is about understanding the customer, the second trimester is about defining what you need to sell, and the third trimester is about managing your perception in the deal. Let's explore these, starting at the center top position.

- **Profile: Qualify Their Interest.** The first wedge holds three criteria that relate to the customer's world. Together they answer the question: Is the customer ready to buy? This trimester of activity is about building a clear opportunity *Profile.* Sun-tzu tells us we need to understand the terrain of any engagement, and in a sales setting, this means understanding the client's world: their *vision* (criterion 1), their *funding* for the project (criterion 2), and their *trigger* or motivation for taking action now (criterion 3). The Profile speaks to the client's *readiness to buy.* If they're not in a position to buy, there will be no sale for anyone.

- **Positioning: Qualify Your Seat at the Table.** Coming around to the right, the second wedge holds three criteria that answer the question: Are you ready to sell? This trimester of activity is about *Positioning* yourself. Sun-tzu tells us our army needs to arrive at the battle ready to fight. Do you understand the customer's stated and unstated *requirements* (criterion 4)? Do you have a compliant *solution* to offer (criterion 5)? Does the customer see the *solution* as useful and differentiated and therefore to be of *value* (criterion 6)? Your Positioning speaks to your readiness to engage in the sale as a true contender, and it can be achieved only after building an accurate Profile (the first trimester).

- **Alignment: Qualify Your Ability to Win.** The third wedge holds three criteria that answer the question: Are you perceived as the winner? This trimester of activity is about *Alignment* between your resources and the customer's formal and informal buying criteria. Sun-tzu tells us that in any siege or battle, we can gain an advantage from local guides who provide intelligence on things we can't know on our own. Have you accumulated sufficient *resources* with which to win? Do you have people on the inside of the account helping you win? Are you using their insight for your people to be at the right meetings, locations, and conference calls for demos, presentations, and credibility-building discussions (criterion 7)? Do you have access to all the people with a *formal* role to play in the evaluation and decision-making process (criterion 8)? Are your personal efforts, support staff members, partners, or lobbyists bringing you closer to the people with *informal* influence inside the customer's office and closer to their idea of what the right supplier will look like (criterion 9)?

Top salespeople confirm that researching the *Profile* of the sale, improving your *Positioning* in the customer's eyes, and orchestrating *Alignment* of people and resources are three battles that exist in every complex sale, and usually one follows another, hence the nomenclature of calling them "the three trimesters." They report that when sellers concentrate on one of these wedges to the exclusion of the other two, they will seldom win the deal. But when they do a good job in all three as part of a coordinated campaign, victory can almost always be assured. Because it makes sense to review what each of these criteria means and how you can use it, I will explore each of the nine in sequence—the first three in this chapter (Figure 5.2), the second three in Chapter 6, and the last three in Chapter 7.

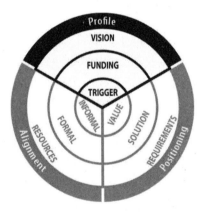

Figure 5.2: The Opportunity Snapshot for Trimester 1, Profile

CRITERION 1. VISION

For clients to be ready to buy, they must decide a *change* is needed. Lots of people talk about change, so for it to go anywhere, the people advocating it must have credibility in the organization, and they must have spent time socializing the idea to build support for it.

If you meet a prospect who tells you about their vision but they can't articulate it clearly and nobody else in their organization has heard of it, chances are it's a half-baked idea with no formal backing, and certainly it's doubtful the project is funded. Maybe you can help them develop the case for this idea if you arrive early enough in their thought process.

Whatever its origins, the vision needs to be sufficiently developed and far enough along in the planning process for it to be considered a formal project that people are authorized to spend time and money on.

You need to look for the extent to which they have a clear vision of what success will look like, how they'll get there, and what changes and benefits they expect. It's a question of "Why do this and how will it help?" Plus: "Can the owner of the vision carry it to completion?"

If the vision is fully formed when you first get involved, it is a good idea to find out who was first heard talking about this idea, where did they get their inspiration, how did they research to decide what direction to take, and what external influences shaped their ideas. You need to know if they're following one of your competitors, if they're following a leader in their market, if they're evolving along a safe trail someone else has already blazed, or if it is a revolutionary idea that may or may not be embraced by their company depending on its appetite for risk and innovation.

Experience suggests that if you didn't set the vision at the start of the sale, you're going to need to shape it and improve it if you want to be more than "column fodder" where the purchasing managers want your information only so they can show others they considered multiple options before deciding on a preordained supplier.

To get a positive score on the Snapshot in this field, you need to understand the customer's vision for the project and solution, and you must be able to explain it clearly to others. You should understand it so well that the client might ask if they can use your presentation material to brief their own staff members.

Questions to Ask About Vision

- Is the prospect troubled enough to seek an external solution? Is it because of a problem or inefficiency they want to eliminate (how much, how soon?), or is it because of a window of opportunity they want to exploit (how much, how soon?).
- Have credible stakeholders confirmed their vision of this business initiative? Have they shared it with others as a corporate vision, or is it only a personal curiosity?
- Which other people have heard about the vision? How are they each affected? How does this business initiative relate to the client's overall business strategy?
- What are their individual and collective expectations for what success looks like?
- Has this information been validated by a credible source in the client's business?

CRITERION 2. FUNDING

This is about the customer's ability to buy when the vision has formal approval. The funding should be adequate to pay not just for the ticket price of your solution but for *all* the resources required. If the client talks only about funding enough to buy your solution but not any of the other services, equipment, change management, third-party contracts, or other elements that typically accompany a large purchase, then you have to wonder if they've really thought it through or if they're simply comparing your price to the prices being offered by other vendors who have already talked to them. If they truly have a limited budget and are buying everything they need with *insufficient funding*—which may indicate they'll need to request steep discounts to get the whole job done—then they'll decide the project is unrealistic and push it back as a nice idea that never went anywhere.

You simply cannot afford to engage in a sale if clients can't pay you. You are not employed to give away free consulting or be their sounding board unless there is a certified paycheck on the horizon.

There are some salespeople in the world (such as those who sell exclusive superyachts, expensive cosmetic surgery, or prestige estate properties) who won't even speak with prospects until reference checks and lines of credit have been established. They don't want to waste their time with tire kickers. Don't waste yours.

However, if you are creating the opportunity by taking a speculative idea to the client, there may not yet be a budget assigned because a formal project is not yet approved. In such cases you use this criterion on the Snapshot as a reminder that you need to engineer the budget. You'll need to ask about their funding approval process. Do the people you're talking to already have surplus budget funds? If not, do they have access to discretionary funds? Do they have a track record of pulling money out of thin air, or will this be their first attempt? Can funding approval happen quickly, or is it burdened by red tape or competing projects that are already in the approval cycle? Is your project seen as strategic enough to bump any of the other projects and get fast-track approval? Do the business aspects of the project make it similar to any other projects about to receive funding, and if so, can it piggyback the same request to save time? How could you help your contacts paint the idea as a high priority?

If they want to do this project, they will appreciate your candor in exploring ways for them to build an internal business case. But if there really are no funds available or the people you're in contact with lack the credibility or commercial acumen to find the funding, you need a splash of cold water on your face—which is what this qualification criterion provides. If you see that the path you're on will lead to a dead end, the question shifts to what you can do to change it. You may need to find another point of entry and build other relationships.

Questions to Ask About Funding

- Does the client know what a solution will cost? How does your cost fit within the total budget they have for the project?
- Have they approved the funding required? Do the people you're selling to have the authority to approve this expenditure?
- Which executives will sponsor this project through the funding process?
- If there is no budget assigned, do the people you are selling to have access to discretionary funds? What is their funding approval process?
- Have they purchased solutions of a similar size and cost before, or is this a new experience for them?
- Does this prospect have a policy to negotiate vendors' proposals down by X percent? Will you need to price your solution with this in mind?

CRITERION 3. TRIGGER

Behind every investment is a problem the customers want to solve or a window of opportunity they want to exploit, and a consequence if action is not taken before that window closes. This is known as a *trigger*, and it is sometimes known by other labels like *motivation*, *compelling event*, *pain*, or *burning platform*.

- Businesses around the world spent $50 billion on the pending threat of the Y2K bug when ignoring it *might* have led to catastrophic failure of their computerized systems.
- Companies spend huge sums every year to be compliant with the Sarbanes-Oxley Act or the carbon emissions legislation when failure to do so *might* lead to heavy fines.
- Wars have even been fought, countries invaded, and civil laws changed when the rationale for doing so has been justified against what the consequences of inaction *might* be.

In all these cases, as with every investment decision your customers will ever make, there is a trigger that spurs people to act. Sometimes it comes in the form of the "fear, uncertainty, and doubt" of what the future might hold if they don't take action, as seen above. The flame is either already burning bright for you to throw kindling on (a *recognized need*), or it's no more than a small ember you'll need to coax to life (an *unrecognized need*). For your prospects to take action now and not put it off till next year, they need to feel some kind of heat.

This speaks to the axiom of "no pain, no change." Out of the three criteria in the Profile wedge, the trigger is regarded as the most important because if this isn't in place, your momentum can quickly shudder to a halt. Its importance is underscored by its being located at the pointy end of the wedge in the bull's-eye of the Snapshot.

So inside the prospect's business there will be a few people who first felt the heat. A few individuals shouted to get it on the company agenda. A few individuals have skin in the game and convinced others to follow them. These might be the contacts you are talking to, or they might be people you haven't met yet. When you understand who and what is triggering their interest in talking, you then understand where the sale will really be fought and won. This places you on the path to mapping how that trigger ripples out from these few people or this department and motivates others to take action. You need to look for the community of people who are joined by the same need, whose voices must unite around buying the solution from you.

But even when you connect to people who talk about wanting to buy a solution, you need to qualify hard to discern if they're talking soft triggers or hard triggers.

Soft triggers are the things that would be nice to do "one day," which a client toys around with as an idea, but only if they have nothing better to spend their time and money on. When a sales opportunity is based on a soft motivation, don't be surprised if nobody else in the client's organization has heard about it, or if the date keeps sliding back in your forecast. These are "pet projects" that are fun for the client to entertain, but they go nowhere unless (a) the client has surplus money to throw around, or (b) their situation changes and it suddenly becomes expedient to use the budget, such as a use-it-or-lose-it funding policy as they approach the end of their fiscal year.

Hard triggers are the things that must be done by a specific date or a specific consequence will occur. Some people call these *event horizons*, meaning that if the client doesn't change their current trajectory, they will fly into the heart of a black hole and be crushed. This type of motivation is a more reliable indicator of their willingness to take action. You know it's real when multiple people are talking about it and when they can tell you exactly what the consequence will be if they don't find the answers—and also what it means for their business if they do find the right solution.

When vice presidents have different managers and advisors under them suggesting a number of ideas for which they want approval or funding to explore, the VPs have to decide which of all these ideas are high priorities. When cash is tight or the economy is down, it's the hard triggers that get the green light over the soft triggers. So top salespeople suggest that just because a prospect is talking to you, it doesn't mean the discussion will go anywhere. You must qualify why they want to change, who first came up with the concept, when they need to act, and how they'll measure the change. It's no coincidence that what goes into a value proposition is often composed of the same ingredients. To sell value at the end of a sale, you must quantify the triggers at the start of the sale.

Questions to Ask About Triggers

- What is the trigger for taking action now (versus six months from now)? Why now? Is there a window of opportunity for taking action? Is there a date by which it is too late to act?
- What is the payback if this project is implemented on time or sooner than planned? What consequences will happen if the project is not implemented?

- Which other people or processes will benefit if action is taken? Which of these has the most to win or lose? Which of these is talking to us?

That's what the three criteria in the Profile wedge are about—understanding the landscape of the sales opportunity. If this wedge collectively shows good reasons why it's inevitable for the prospect to move forward and buy from someone (or if they're not at this point of readiness yet but there is reason to believe you can agitate that state of mind) then congratulations: the landscape is fertile, the prospect is serious about doing something, and they have the means to take action by a specific date. It answers the question: Why do this? But it doesn't yet answer the question: Why do this with *you*?

That's a battle that belongs in the second trimester: Positioning.

Chapter 6

Qualify Your Seat at the Table

The Opportunity Snapshot for Trimester 2, Positioning

The second trimester has a dedicated section in the Snapshot. This *Positioning* wedge focuses you on whether you're perceived by the prospects to be a supplier who should be given a seat at the table. For scoring to favor you, they must perceive that you fully understand their *requirements* and you can offer them a unique differentiated *solution* that represents *value* they find compelling enough to act on. Let's explore the Positioning wedge in more detail.

CRITERION 4. REQUIREMENTS

To score well in this criterion of the Snapshot, you need to know what changes the prospect needs to make in their world that your products and services can impact. Some of these may already be codified into a formal requirements list, a specification sheet, or set of decision criteria. It is common for these lists to be weighted, so when they evaluate different vendors, perceived compliance with the requirements of most importance will skew their formal evaluation. Sometimes these requirements lists will be split into different subject areas overseen by domain specialists in the account, such as those whose focus is to score all vendors on grounds of technical, service, legal, or relationship criteria.

If you are the first to talk to the client about an idea and they see merit in taking it forward, there's a chance you can impact how the requirements criteria are written to help your *solution* (criterion 5) be perceived as a natural fit, so your *resource* deployment (criterion 7) remains profitable, and your *value* (criterion 6) is perceived as strong. It's difficult for a latecomer to catch up when you've already spent months developing the relationships and requirements.

If you're not the first to talk with the prospect and you are responding to a tender or a request for proposal (RFP), either they genuinely want answers and are prepared to enter into a meaningful exploration or you've been invited only so that they can show their boss they pulled in several quotes to drive the price down (before they buy from a supplier they decided on long ago).

Either way, you need to understand the requirements they are using to evaluate you, how they're ranked, and what process they go through before somebody can sign off on a decision.

For example, let's say that after nine months of selling, you've succeeded in getting all the right people excited about moving forward with you. They started with a narrow set of requirements and decision criteria, and you reengineered these into a broader solution that will really help them achieve their goals—and they think you're a hero for helping them do that. Then they tell you that the size of the expenditure is now above their authority to approve locally and somebody from your organization will need to have meetings with an approval committee based in a city on the other side of the country. And let's say your company has just issued a travel freeze. How would this requirement impact your tactics?

If you have an office or a partner located near the approval committee, you're going to need to plan how to get someone else sufficiently briefed to represent you. Or you'll need to plan how to bypass the travel freeze and get approval to fly there yourself. You might want to check what coverage your competitors have at this location and see if you or they have the advantage. If it's you, one of your tactics might then be to emphasize geographical coverage and ease of service as a *requirement* they should weight, thus placing smaller or more remote competitors at a disadvantage. Once dealing at the head office, you might also decide to explore how this deal for one of the prospect's offices might enjoy an economy of scale if it were a national rollout, thus expanding the size of the deal.

Whether a deal goes to an approval committee far away or stays with the people you have already met, how does knowing the weighting of their requirements make a difference to *what* you talk about and *who* you talk to? Let's say you know that out of an evaluation committee of five people, two have the most say over the final decision, and that out of the 20 requirements they've listed, 3 are on their personal radar. Maybe you'll even uncover a requirement that isn't listed on the formal list but is still important to one of these decision influencers. Wrapping your arms around these requirements and making sure they are central to your solution is a smart way to sell.

When Dick Ebersol of NBC won the multiyear deal to broadcast the Olympic Games that shot him to the cover of *Sports Illustrated* magazine, behind all the many requirements and decision criteria that NBC had to satisfy was the personal agenda of then International Olympic Committee (IOC) president Juan Antonio Samaranch, and the legacy he wanted to leave, which was later dubbed the "Sunset Project." This was never going to be the type of requirement written into a public tender document. But being the only contender to understand its personal importance to a key decision influencer was paramount to Ebersol's closing the deal.[1]

Questions to Ask About Requirements

- Have formal criteria been published? Which are ranked as most important to the individual stakeholders?
- In your opinion is the list of requirements complete? Will the client get the solution they need by following this list, or can you add some thought leadership to modify the criteria in your favor?
- What are the key milestones for this specific decision? Have dates been set for passing certain tollgates for evaluating this project and its suppliers?
- Under what circumstances would the decision date be accelerated? Under what circumstances would it be protracted? Is the decision date something you can influence?
- Can you rewrite or rerank the criteria to create an obstacle to your competitors?
- What length or quality of documentation do they require, and how quickly do they expect it? Do you have the time and resources to comply with their expectations? Do you want to?

CRITERION 5. SOLUTION

Your *solution* (including third-party or partner components) must do what the client needs it to do so that their *requirements* (criterion 4) are met or exceeded. But you don't have a solution unless they perceive that you do. I've chaired countless deal reviews where, after the sales reps have waxed lyrical about how awesome their solution is, one simple question leads to mute silence: "What meeting were you in when all the people on the decision committee verbally told you that they believed all this?" It doesn't matter how impressed you are with yourself. If the other party doesn't see it, it doesn't exist.

Are there sales where the customer's list of requirements is a perfect fit for what you're selling? In the transactional world, sure, you see this. They know the brand and the model number they want. And in the solution selling world, you see it when they're responding to a case study about a company like theirs that put your services in place, and they want to do the same thing. But these are the exceptions to the rule. Top sellers tell us that if they engage prospects early enough, they typically see the requirements start as a "directionally correct" list, but through the give-and-take of meetings and discussions, that list will morph into a final form with your input, and typically, the input of your competitors.

This give-and-take process is a great opportunity for every sales professional because it means you can take a contact's initial vision of a solution and extrapolate where your product matches it. Then you can take the unique selling points of your solution and look for ways to reverse engineer their inclusion into the customer's specifications to raise the barrier to competitive entry. Sometimes this requires that you adopt the position of a thought leader and move the goalposts of their original *vision* (criterion 1). This in turn shifts their *requirements* (criterion 4) so that they align closer to your *solution* (criterion 5).

So in contemplating the validity of your *solution*, the first goal is to ensure that you're selling what they need. The second is that you ensure that they believe they need what you're selling.

Questions to Ask About Solution

- Can you explain how your solution meets all or part of the prospect's needs? Have you done so with the key stakeholders and influencers?
- What is the prospect's risk in adopting your solution? How will you mitigate these?
- What additional resources (internal or external) will the prospect need to install, run, and own your solution?
- Where is your solution weak? How will you mitigate the risk of competitors' exploiting your weakness?
- What objections need to be resolved before the prospect will commit?
- Has the prospect confirmed their belief in your solution, across different stakeholders?

CRITERION 6. VALUE

This is the second of the three criteria that are positioned directly in the bull's-eye of the Snapshot. Like criterion 3, *trigger*, in the first wedge, criterion 6, *value*, is this wedge's most important factor.

Top sellers report that when they close a deal and ask the customer to help them conduct a *win review* (or let them see their rivals' proposals to understand the enemies better), the customer goes straight to the value proposition. There they find three types of statements.

The most easily defeated is what they call the *motherhood boiler-plate*. This usually looks like it was carefully handcrafted by a word-smith in the vendor's public relations department, and it speaks in general terms about the advantages and benefits of each component of the solution and the vendor's company overall. Typical elements are the vendor's commitment to quality and service, their expertise and innovation, the awards they've won, and infamous Buzzword Bingo words like "partner," "synergy," and "optimize." This sort of guff belongs in a marketing brochure or annual report. In a discrete sales opportunity, it comes across as insincere when the specific *vision* (criterion 1), *trigger* (criterion 3), *requirements* (criterion 4), and *solution* (criterion 5) are not mentioned. How does the customer feel when they've co-invested months to answer your questions and help you understand their needs, only to see your value proposition ignoring these specifics?

Our studies into buying behavior revealed a corroborating complaint from customers that they often only see *one* value pitch, aimed at the macro company as a whole. Buyers say they respond more strongly when each key department is listed in a proposal and a separate value is proposed for each one, describing how their working environment or production output will be changed as a result of this purchase. Drafting it like a story that follows a day in the life of someone who works there, contrasting the before-and-after experience for each key role or function, resonates far more deeply because you're focusing on their world and what they most care about. As shown in the Prospect Call Plan (Figure 3.1), value needs to be quantified at the *enterprise*, *department*, and *personal* levels.

It's also difficult to dismiss the value proposition that makes a business case using spreadsheets and value calculators based on numbers the prospect has shared with you or those available from their own industry's trade magazines or government bureaus of statistics and labor. For financial-savvy buyers, numbers give a more objective rationale for buying, especially when accompanied by graphs and tables that show investment breakeven, projected improvements, net present value, or return on investment. North American companies like Sant and Kadient (now merged as Qvidian) have long been in the business of providing automation tools for this type of "evidence-based selling," as has U.K.-based Shark Finesse whose highly graphical online interface allows salespeople to draw from a pool of over 1,000 compelling economic arguments for why the customer should spend money and why they should do so now rather than wait till later.

There is certainly a clear advantage in being able to quantify your value. However, where top sellers find they can outclass these kinds of

value calculators is when the competitors' pitches are
who simply aren't wired to appreciate financial sprea
a focus on selling-by-numbers drives the vendors to focus on mak
their case to procurement or financial managers (who may be gatekeepers) to the exclusion of building relationships of trust with people
elsewhere (who may be the actual decision makers and influencers).
In a contest between an appeal to cold logic and an appeal to trust
and rapport, two old adages still serve: "People buy on emotion, *then*
justify with logic" and "People buy from people."

Put another way, if the people with the most influence over the
buying decision trust you, like you, and really want to work with you,
and if the cost-value equation of each different supplier is in the same
relative ballpark, a few extra dollars either way isn't likely to swing
the deal elsewhere, no matter how strenuously the accountants argue
their case. Strategic deals are never won on cost alone, and they are
rarely won on value arguments if trust and rapport are absent from
the equation.

So if a value pitch is vulnerable using either of these approaches,
what are the top salespeople doing to differentiate and stand out?
They use *both* approaches at the same time: an amalgam of *social capital* (the relationships) and *business capital* (the financials). It's a tough
combination to beat.

The first step is to establish social capital with each and every
person in the decision-making chain, building your personal brand
and creating positive word of mouth—even working to establish a
kind of *viral buzz* so you're talked about positively around the watercooler and it seems like you're *everywhere*.

Although you need to give some coverage to everyone who has a
formal role in the evaluation and decision, your primary focus must
be on the people who have the most *influence*. In Chapter 8, "Social
Capital," I cover how to identify and create a strategy for forming
relationships with these people.

It's also important (to the extent you can find them) to know if there are other people who influence your buyer's thinking who are not on their organization chart. For example, these may be external third parties who are used for advice or as informal sounding boards:

- People on their board or advisory panel you may be able to reach through other relationships your company holds or by being seen where they congregate—for example, online at sites like LinkedIn or Spoke, industry blogs, or company or trade conferences, seminars, or other events where these people are either speaking or attending as delegates
- Consultants or project managers who are working in other parts of the prospect's business or an affiliated initiative—that is, people who may be asked what they've heard about the different vendors being assessed

Bad press here is a killer, but positive word of mouth—even if it's only "Oh yes, I talked to one of their people a few weeks ago, and they seemed okay"—is absolute gold. They don't need to be raving fans or even satisfied customers. Sometimes it's enough for them to be the equivalent of a Facebook Friend or a YouTube Like. The tribal referral culture we see manifest in online social networks has now transferred to how people share opinions across business networks. If the jungle drums beat in your favor, today's time-poor buyers will listen in the expectation that groupthink has done some of the vetting for them.

So you should ask if the project you're selling to is a subset of something bigger or a new phase of an ongoing initiative such as a quality improvement program or a plant refurbishing project. If it is, chances are that other people have already earned their spurs from those projects. If you only connect and establish some kind of rapport in asking what they did, what the results were, and what they'd advise you about this customer's culture or their way of doing business so you can make the best contribution, you will enable them to say truthfully that they have heard of you should your target customer ever ask them. If you are only a small tick-in-the-box, a good reputation can be to your advantage if nobody the customer knows is saying anything positive about your competitors. So make those calls and shell out on those cups of social coffee. You can claim them back from your sales commission later.

After establishing their social capital, top sellers focus on putting their business capital in the bank using testimonials and spreadsheet calculations. But they do so in such a way that value is quantified for *each key stakeholder or department* instead of being a single company-to-company statement of projected value. It's more work to develop a dozen or so value propositions, but it's the final knot you must tie after having spent weeks or months learning all about the needs of the different stakeholders. Why would you not capitalize on all that intelligence to send you coasting across the finish line?

People respond to stories. It's wired in our social fabric from the times of gathering around campfires. So when you build your presentations and subsequent proposal around a solution, take time to explain what you're solving. Mention key people, processes, or departments by name. Personalize your value. Tell the story of how they perform certain functions without your solution and how your solution will create a different experience or outcome after they buy it from you, and describe the financial benefits of making such a smart investment.

It's this double whammy of building the right relationships and creating an effective financial or change proposition for each of these key people that wins deals today. Ultimately, you don't have any *value* unless all the right people agree that you do.

Questions to Ask About Value

- Do you know what value looks like to each buyer? Is it expressed as time, cost, risk, performance, visibility, service, revenue, profit, or personal value?

- What specifically will you help the prospect achieve that they can't do on their own?
- Does the value proposition use the client's internal jargon and metrics?
- How does your solution's value compare to the client's alternatives? Is your solution supported by a compelling business case? Have you quantified a cost, breakeven, and profit schedule for your solution? Have you involved the prospect in calculating this?
- Will the client gain a sense of urgency to own your solution? If not, how does the value proposition need to be modified?
- Are influential people speaking up for your solution internally?

We have examined the three criteria for Positioning. We'll now turn our attention to the wedge that explains Alignment.

Chapter 7

Qualify Your Ability to Win

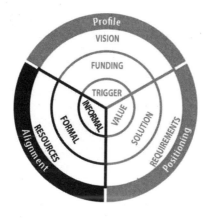

The Opportunity Snapshot for Trimester 3, Alignment

Alignment is the extent to which your resources of people, time, product, and expertise are understood by the key decision stakeholders, are seen as favorable, and impact the end result. It's also about everyone in your core and extended sales team being animated by the same spirit and strategy as they engage in the deal.

CRITERION 7. RESOURCES

Your people resources (including those from third parties or partners) must be available to sell, meet, demonstrate, and deliver your solution where and when the clients require. They must know what your value is and how you want it explained to different people. It is no good if you're presenting with a partner who tries to maneuver the deal to his benefit by talking about his own offerings to the detriment of yours. It is no good if you've sold expectations of product performance to the customers only to have a guileless technical specialist tell them where your solution isn't as good as a competitor's. It's critical that your sales resources are animated by the same spirit and guided by one plan.

This need for coordination also applies to the customer's resources: the people you're selling to. You need to know if they are all on the same page about what they want, why, and how soon. What are the steps they need to complete internally before a contract can be issued? What is their internal approval process, who gets involved, and how long does it take? Are their key people available for the important milestone meetings you need to have with them? Is someone inside the account coordinating all this so you're on the same page, moving forward in sync together?

This criterion is all about resources "being on the same page."

Many times I've seen a salesperson turn up at a customer's office to get the contract signed, only to learn that the customer left for vacation the day before. This simply cannot happen when your eye is on the ball to plan in advance how to coordinate your mutual resources.

For example, if you identified that their *motivation* (criterion 3) is to show that they have a solution in place before their shareholder meeting in four months but the decision process they have outlined to you suggests six months of meetings, you might point this out and suggest an evaluation schedule to accelerate the process so they can meet their deadline. But if you don't ask who's involved, what their top-ranked issues are, or the process they have to walk through inside their business before a check can be cut, all you can do is stumble through the sale until the client tells you the ride is over. That's a bit like being locked in the trunk of a car and trying to navigate, and it is as far away from being in the driver's seat as you can get.

Have you ever had a client who expected you, your presale team, and your partners to be available at times and places such that it placed a strain on those resources? Have you had clients that wanted free workshops, free education, and free evaluation periods? Have you ever had to fly in an expert witness or reference or use a third party with experience and then sensed a loss of control as the client spent more time with those people than with you? Have you ever taken presales resources or partners into a client call and cringed as they said all the wrong things?

Whenever we deploy resources in a sale, there is a cost and there is a risk. Resources need to be carefully managed so that you remain the leader of the band. We must identify the right people, make sure they are available when we need them, and ensure that they are properly briefed with more than a short chat in the taxi on the way to the meeting.

As leader of the band, the general of the sale, it is your responsibility to coordinate and rehearse with these resources to tell them exactly what you need them to do. You need to tell them what doubts to leave hanging in peoples' minds about their ability to do it themselves or with a competitor, and what strengths and differentiators you want them to seed so your offering is seen as superior.

You must also make sure your solution can be implemented properly after the client signs the order. It's no good setting an expectation of immediate results only to then find out the people needed to install the solution or train the customer's people are booked out for the next six months, which places at risk the client's meeting the window of opportunity that lies at the heart of their motivation to do the project.

To get a positive score on the Snapshot in this criterion, you must be sure that you have the resources needed, that they are available, and they can demonstrate why they are better, more plentiful, or more experienced than the resources being offered from the competition, even if that competition is the client's own team using a different approach to get the job done.

Questions to Ask About Resources

- Do you have access to all the resources needed to win, when you need them?
- Have your people all been briefed on how to articulate the value of your solution in front of the prospect?
- Are you following a budget to control the cost of sale? Will the value of this deal outweigh the cost of resources expended to pursue it?
- After winning, will you have the resources ready to deliver on time? Have you started scheduling these resources in anticipation of winning?
- Will diverting resources to this opportunity place other opportunities at risk?
- What countertactics can you apply or what traps can you set to defeat the competition?

CRITERION 8. FORMAL DYNAMIC

Some people will have the authority to evaluate you against prewritten *requirements* (criterion 4). Others will have authority to make the decision that contractually binds their company to a supplier. Others may reserve the right to approve or veto the deal after the decision is proposed. This formal chain of sign-off follows hierarchical lines. Your task as the general of the sale is to gain access to the highest relevant people, establish your relationship with them, and see to it that they pull rank to give formal direction to their subordinates that the sale can be awarded to you.

For example, if an evaluation committee decides to favor your competitor and they send their recommendation up to somebody who holds the budget as a decision maker, you're probably going to lose. But let's say you've already qualified that the decision maker is relatively new or is about to retire, and someone higher up in the food chain is appointed to oversee this person's decisions. You focus your efforts there, at the fulcrum. Instead of fighting the battle with the evaluators, you've already won the war with the approver.

So when the evaluators tick the boxes and pass their recommendation to the decision makers, who then internally announce their commitment to buy from your competitor, the up-line approver says something like this: "Bob, that's a good decision. But there are a few strategic reasons why we might want to go with Vendor B even though you're recommending Vendor A. I can't tell you how to do your job, but I wonder if you could take another look at Vendor B again and tell me if they're a million miles off the mark or if there is a way we could work with them?"

Rank hath its privileges.

To get a strong score in criterion 8, you must know who is evaluating you through the formal decision process, what they're evaluating you on, and how those criteria are weighted. Are there different subject specialists evaluating different aspects of the project? Who will they report their evaluations to? Is it a single person or a committee? Will it be tabled for discussion, and can you get copies of those minutes? How did they make similar decisions before? How long does it normally take? Are they following an evaluation checklist or project plan, and can you get a copy? Can you influence the evaluation check-list by suggesting steps they haven't considered that will save time or reduce risk? When the evaluation is done, who ultimately decides they will move ahead? Does this person also control the release of funds, or is there a separate process to be navigated? And even after the formal decision, is there yet a higher authority or panel who must bless the deal? Which way are they leaning?

Questions to Ask About the Formal Dynamic

- How high will this decision be made in the organization? Who is the highest-ranking executive likely to get involved?
- In whom does the authority reside to make a contractual commit-ment to a supplier?
- What other people reserve the right of veto or approval? Do you have access and credibility with these people? What evidence sup-ports this?
- Who is the competition meeting with? Whose relationship is stronger, and what evidence supports that opinion?
- Are your own executives talking to their peers in the prospect's company about this project? Have they been properly briefed on your value?

CRITERION 9. INFORMAL DYNAMIC

This is the third of the three criteria positioned in the bull's-eye around the Snapshot. Like criterion 3, *trigger*, in the first wedge and criterion 6, *value*, in the second wedge, criterion 9 is the third wedge's most important factor.

To score well in this criterion, you need to know who is going to most influence the decision, and you must have their support. Sometimes the people with influence *are* the same people as those with formal authority. But sometimes they're *not*, and because of this, you need to qualify hard if you're covering the people whose opinions and whims count the most.

It's like a *wagon wheel* of three concentric rings composed of the *hub*, *spokes*, and *rim*.

People in the *hub* are the ones who really decide what needs to happen; they have the insight to see what's coming, and they recognize the need for change. If they don't hold the functional job role needed to make that change happen, they connect to other people whose job it is (the *spokes*).

The *spokes* are the people who will ensure a project is legitimized and funded. They will speak on its behalf and shepherd it to become a formally mandated priority. If it's the *hub* that does the thinking, it's the *spokes* who do the speaking—literally they are the "spokespeople" for the project.

Outside the *hub* and *spokes* are the people on the *rim* who are involved because their job requires them to open doors, offer opinions, shuffle paper, or sign the checks. They don't exert much opinion or informal influence at all, even though they may be high-ranking officers in the company.

If people in the *hub* decide what should happen, it's the people who are the *spokes* who make those things happen. The closer people are to the hub of each project, the more influence they have on future decisions because they're part of "the club," the *sanctum sanctorum*, the power behind the throne. Look around your own company. Are there official department heads but then *other* people who *really* run things? You bet.

So we're looking to get inside with the advisors of those people with formal authority. The evaluation team might give you two thumbs up, but if the influencers don't, the decision makers will find excuses to rule against you. Have you ever had a sale ready to close, and a new player got involved or new decision criterion became overly important, and these late-breaking changes pulled the rug out from under your feet? If you thought you got blindsided because of politics, you were right!

To score positively on the Snapshot for this criterion, you need to have evidence of people exerting influence greater than their titles suggest they are capable of, and you need to make sure they know you and support you. Knowing *who they are* is not enough to rate on the Snapshot. They must know *who you are*, and they must be active in helping you win before you can score positively against criterion 9. You'll hear more about how influence works in Chapter 8, "Social Capital."

Questions to Ask About the Informal Dynamic

- Is there evidence of "power behind the throne" shaping the policies and ideas that the formal decision makers follow?
- Have you established rapport and credibility with these people? Can you count on these players to support your solution behind closed doors? What insight or information have they provided that has not been shared with rival suppliers?
- Which people have worked there the longest? What is their recent track record, and what level of credibility do they enjoy in the company? What is an example of their using their influence to get something done? How can you position your solution as a vehicle for them to use?
- Which people are candidates for retirement or transfer, or which people work in a department at risk of being sold or outsourced? How does this affect how other people regard their opinions?
- Which people have worked there a short amount of time? Were they recruited because of their past industry track record, and do they thereby have high credibility? Or did they join with no particular fame, and are they now in the process of building a track record and network? How will this project help them do so? How can you position your solution as a vehicle for them to use?
- Which people are known to have a tribal connection beyond the office? Did any of them work together in previous companies? Did any join this company in the same induction? Who spends time with each other socially? How can you join this network?

- How was the last decision for this type of investment made? Which people were involved in the decision-making process? How are the people in this project the same or different? Does this project show any different dynamics than seen in the past?
- Which other people (with no formal role in the decision process) are exerting some influence on the decision-making process (for example, users, advisors, consultants, or subject matter experts)? Where are they in the hub or spokes? Who is being influenced by their opinion? Are they supportive or nonsupportive of you?
- Which people are your mentors? Why do they see your success as desirable? How credible and influential are they? Where are they in the hub or spokes? How will they help you? What risks exist for falling out of favor with your mentors? What could cause this? How will your competitors try to weaken your relationship?
- Which people are or may become mentors for your competitors? Where are they in the hub or spokes? What would motivate them to favor a competitor or to become your enemy? How will you eliminate that risk?
- Is access blocked to any people you need to meet (for example, schedule conflicts, protective gatekeepers, or other people who don't see the relevance)? What is the risk of attempting to gain access to these people? What is the risk of not trying to gain access? What is your plan?

QUALIFICATION SCORING

That's an overview of how top sellers view their strategic deals as being composed of three separate time-based theaters of war, called *trimesters*. Winning in one trimester does not guarantee a win. Winning in all three trimesters does. So how do you score to see if you're winning or not? Is there a numerical calculation you can use?

There have been a number of scoring models used over the years for different qualification models. Some gave scores out of 10 or more points. Others allowed a positive, neutral, parity, or negative mark. In a team selling environment, there will always be debate about how to score the approach being taken, and people can spend too much time negotiating a number instead of agreeing what to do to advance the sale. The best practice is to discuss each criterion based on feedback from a reliable source in the customer's organization and then determine if you are *strong* or *weak* for each area. This polarizes the score and eliminates the anemic neutral mark.

The one exception to having polar scores is when you are early in the sales cycle and you have not had time to connect to all the right people yet. Given that these scores should be based on customer input and not your own subjective view, it's allowable early in a sale to include an *unknown* score.

Managers should encourage salespeople to state when something is unknown. This allows you to deal with what's real. When managers punish or ridicule their reps for not knowing everything, how do most salespeople fill in their deal plans? That's right—every field of their CRM or sales plan gets filled in, making it appear like no stone is left unturned. Most of the words are fiction, of course, but at least it keeps the managers off their back.

This is why I encourage managers to allow reps the freedom to state matters as they really are. Anything less only creates the syndrome of "The Emperor's New Clothes" where everyone says "how great the deal looks" while secretly knowing how naked and exposed they really are.

I see this type of "mitigated speech" regularly occur in deal reviews where local or corporate culture gets in the way of people telling each other the unfiltered truth. You might recognize it readily in Japan or China where "saving face" makes people overly polite and nonconfrontational in public settings. But people's mode of communication can also be diluted if their company has a push on for everyone to be "politically correct" or if it has roots in a genteel culture where what people really want to say is hidden behind so many layers of nuance and polite smiles that the important things never get said until it's too late.

In his runaway bestseller *Outliers: The Story of Success* (Little, Brown, 2008), popular intellectual Malcolm Gladwell explained the dramatic impact culture can have on business. In his book, he cited the August 1997 crash of Korean Air Flight 801 into Nimitz Hill in Guam. In a *Forbes* magazine interview about his book,[1] Gladwell said:

> *Korean Air had more plane crashes than almost any other airline in the world for a period at the end of the 1990s. When we think of airline crashes, we think, Oh, they must have had old planes. They must have had badly trained pilots. No. What they were struggling with was a cultural legacy, that Korean culture is hierarchical. You are obliged to be deferential toward your elders and superiors in a way that would be unimaginable in the U.S.*

In her review of Gladwell's book on *Asiance* magazine's website, columnist Sae Park noted:

> *The ability to retain your own decision making processes and exercise independence comes with the comfort of being able to challenge a superior without repercussion. This kind of impulse would not have been encouraged in the military settings where [the Korean pilots] learned how to behave in an aircraft.[2]*

To allow pilots to escape their cultural legacy, Korean Air mandated the use of English in the cockpit, which gave crew members the ability to use a different persona and be assertive with their superiors when their bosses were doing the wrong things. This allowed "plain speak," which reduced the number of Korean Air incidents dramatically—the airline's record became spotless.

How often does the hierarchical culture of a sales organization prevent salespeople and presales technical specialists from speaking up when a deal should be culled from the funnel? To what extent does the ego-soaked, command-and-control approach of top-down managers stamp out the ability of team members to have an open, honest, and strategic discussion about the state of each deal and the pipeline overall? How many deals that have ended up as "plane crashes" could have been saved with greater qualification and transparency?

Where this openness is absent it's an aberrant behavior brought on by tactical sales managers who mistakenly believe part of their job spec is to emasculate their salespeople for not having all the answers. A combative management culture makes deal reviews about as much fun as a tax audit or prostate exam. Not surprisingly, salespeople try to avoid these review meetings, or they fake the information they present in them to escape criticism. Before long everyone knows that it has become a massive game of charades, and the practice of running team analysis and planning sessions on your most critical sales opportunities falls into the category of "another idea that didn't stick."

It isn't that the business practice of opportunity reviews holds no value, and usually it's not that whatever sales methodology the company uses wasn't well designed. It's that without a clear executive mandate and regular inspection, the salespeople and sales managers become the ultimate arbiters of how much rigor, transparency, and accountability they're required to embrace, and so they let themselves off the hook. Those who allow opportunity reviews to fail do so because they're comfortable wading in the shallows of true professionalism while avoiding full immersion.

To combat this, top-performing managers who take over dispirited sales teams appreciate the value of having the team start to strategize the next steps to win each other's sales. They create a team culture, which may see them rename these types of review sessions as an "opportunity board," a "war room," a "deal dojo," or a "joint effort to success (JETS) session"—anything that removes the stigma associated with a particular salesperson facing a "review." In addition to the label change, they also run them in a way that creates wholly positive outcomes. I'll explain how they do this a little later.

To summarize:

- An *unknown* score on the Snapshot should alert you to the need to go out and execute a number of information gathering tactics where you ask lots of questions.
- A *weak* score should drive proactive tactics to defend or improve on the deficient area.
- A *strong* score should be a call to action to push the advantage and make your position unassailable.

So let's experiment with the Snapshot in action. Let's say the example in Figure 7.1 is for one of your colleague's target opportunities. They've been working this deal for two months, and they expect a decision two months from now: so it's a midcycle deal. Do any of the scores contradict each other? Do any of the scores look assumptive—

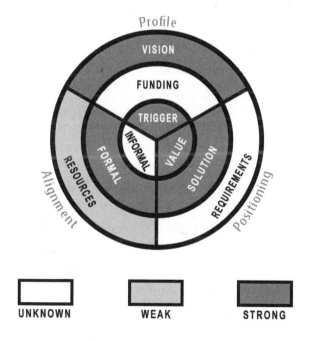

Figure 7.1: Example of an Opportunity Snapshot Showing Hypothetical Qualification Scores

that is, have any of the scores not been validated by the customer? What actions would you recommend as a priority?

One of the first things to jump off the chart is the unknown sources of *funding* (criterion 2) for the project. If the customer's *vision* (criterion 1) and *trigger* (criterion 3) for taking action are clear and compelling, we might question why the customer hasn't confirmed a budget to do something about it yet. If we are *creating the vision* through some evangelical selling, it may be that the customer has yet to create an internal business case to get funds assigned. This might explain why the *requirements* (criterion 4) also remain undefined. If so, with only two months left before the decision date, the *funding* really needs to be there to warrant further investment of time. Appropriate questions might be these:

- What is the customer doing to secure funding? *Who* is doing this?
- Does this person have a track record of securing unbudgeted funds?
- What are the steps in their internal approval process?
- How long does this usually take?
- How will this affect their decision date, and how firm is it? Why?

However, since this deal is midway through its sales cycle, it's reasonable to expect that the *requirements* (criterion 4) should already be in place, even if they're no more than a list of needs connected to the customer's *vision* (criterion 1). This is especially so given that the rep claims they are all over the *formal* (criterion 8) dynamic and so has scored their ability to provide the right *resources* (criterion 7) as weak. How can you make either of those claims unless you know the *requirements*? Either a positive score must be placed in criterion 4 (which is presently empty), or else the scores for criteria 7 and 8 need to be modified. Appropriate questions might be these:

- If you're competing against an incumbent, what are the existing features or relationship issues the customer likes and dislikes, and how can these form the basis for a *requirements* list (criterion 4)?

- If you're selling the customer on a new *vision* (criterion 1), what ideas have they bought into, and can these be considered as a shopping list?
- What are you doing to help the customer write their *requirements*, plus an evaluation timetable that doesn't open the door to competitors?
- You scored *resources* (criterion 7) as weak. What are you basing that on?
- How are you leveraging your strengths with people in the *formal* dynamic of the decision process (criterion 8) to clarify the *requirements* (criterion 4) and secure *funding* (criterion 2)?

You see from this simple example that each wedge is interdependent and uses the others as points of confluence. A shift in one criterion can create a domino effect around the disk, for better or worse. Your task is to look for those leverage points.

In the example given, a standout unknown is the *informal* dynamic (criterion 9) in this sales opportunity. If the rep were to learn that the person they've been spending most of their time with is relatively new to the company, has a limited track record, and is lacking the clout needed to get this project ratified and funded, then the salesperson driving this deal has a big problem.

If the person who most "owns" the *vision* (criterion 1) and *trigger* (criterion 3) is someone the salesperson has not yet called on, the rep needs to adjust his or her coverage of the account accordingly, along with floating the decision date until this new player's agenda and priorities are better known. But if the rep does get someone with informal influence engaged and this person starts helping them sell from the inside, this is a leverage point that could turn all the lights green.

This is how the Snapshot works around the three trimesters (or theaters of battle) in a complex, strategic solution sale.

The labels around the Snapshot are generic enough for you to figure out where specific terms from your industry's nomenclature belong. If you've been using one of the sales qualification models from last century's sales training, it should be easy to see where those phrases fit around the wheel.

The ability to take stock of your own current situation and then prescribe appropriate actions to advance the sale is made possible with an objective qualification model like the Snapshot. Indeed it provides a snapshot in time. If you like the picture you see, you create tactics to maintain it. If you see a picture emerge on the dial that has room for improvement, you take corrective action to line up the sale for a win.

By using the Snapshot, salespeople, sales managers, and everyone else involved in facing the customer can see what's real and understand that when you ask them to participate in customer meetings, demos, presentations, workshops, or lunches, the primary goal of all these sales activities is to know the unknowns, turn weak points into strong points, and then close the deal. Importantly, everyone sings to the same tune, which allows people to explain complex concepts using a form of "sales shorthand." This makes management and forecasting easier than talking about each deal in longhand.

So far I've talked about using the Snapshot to score your own vantage point in the sale. But that's only half of its utility. Sun-tzu tells us:

> *If you know the enemy and know yourself, you need not fear the result of a hundred battles. If you know yourself but not the enemy, for every victory gained you will also suffer a defeat. If you know neither the enemy nor yourself, you will succumb in every battle.* (Art of War *3:18*)

If your customer shares information with you about your rivals, or if certain things the prospect says and does imply to you that they're in discussion with your competitors, you can collate enough anecdotal or direct evidence to allow you to score the Snapshot to show where each competitor is positioned and aligned. When doing so, criteria 1 to 3 will usually be identical to your score for the same topic, since these describe the customer's situation.

However, if there are reasons to believe your competitors do not understand the *vision*, are at a disadvantage for *funding*, or aren't building their solution to address the customer's *trigger*, you may find it makes sense to score criteria 1 to 3 differently in the competitors' Profile trimester.

The two other trimesters have the same rules: *strong*, *weak*, or *unknown* scores for your competitors, based on what you hear about their positioning and alignment. When in doubt about their scores, default to the paranoia of giving them a strong score and plan actions to qualify accordingly. The purpose of scoring competitors on the Snapshot is to gauge where they stand relative to you and to come up with contingency tactics.

Some top sellers apply a weighted algorithm on these scores. Their aim is to calculate their opportunity's probability of being won against each of the nominated competitors.

Calculating this *win probability* is possible only when you have a normalized scoring method based on observation, validation, and competitive comparisons—like the Snapshot. To establish their win probability, top sellers establish simple rules for scoring the Snapshot:

- A *strong* score for each of the nine criteria rates a 10, except criteria 3, 6, and 9 in the bull's-eye, which each carry a score of 13.
- This means if all nine criteria are scored *strong*, the three bull's-eye criteria would score 39, and the other six would score 60, giving a total win probability of 99 percent.
- A *weak* score rates –10.
- An *unknown* score rates 0.
- If criteria 3, 6, and 9 score *weak*, each carries a penalty of –13.
- Opportunities are added to the forecast only when they have a better-than-average chance of being won. Typically this is at 70 percent.

With these simple rules in place, the calculations are possible, and they are shown in Figure 7.2.

		YOU		COMPETITOR	
		SNAPSHOT	SCORE	SNAPSHOT	SCORE
1.	VISION	+	10	-	-10
2.	FUNDING	+	10	+	10
3.	TRIGGER	+	13	+	13
4.	REQUIREMENTS	+	10	+	10
5.	SOLUTION	?	0	?	0
6.	VALUE	?	0	?	0
7.	RESOURCES	-	-10	?	0
8.	FORMAL	+	10	+	10
9.	INFORMAL	+	13	-	-13
	WIN PROBABILITY		56%		40%

Figure 7.2: Example of Win Probability Calculations

If this opportunity were near the end of its first trimester, criteria 1 to 3 are as good as can be hoped for. As the second trimester begins, it's clear where most effort needs to be applied. As the unknowns and weaknesses are improved upon, so the win probability will climb. It's also obvious that more needs to be learned about the competitors.

Top salespeople report how a competitor comparison is an invaluable lens to look through when qualifying their win probability:

- "I look at where our strengths are the same as a competitor's, and I ask if it's because the same people see us as identical (in which case we have parity and neither party is really strong), or if it's because we're selling to different contacts who value us for different reasons. This informs who we start to call on so we can cover all the bases at a relationship level."—VP Sales, Canada

- "On one deal my sales rep was in a pretty strong position against all the others. Then someone in my review team noted how two competitors each had half the sale covered, and we joked about what would happen if they partnered up. That was sobering because a week later that's exactly what they did. Fortunately with the Snapshot, being forewarned meant we were forearmed and already had a contingency plan in place." —National Sales Manager, New Zealand
- "It's like a game of chess. The Snapshot shows me what my competitors are likely to do next. If I can see five moves ahead, I can set traps and roadblocks with help from my supporters. That's not just strategic. It's kind of fun too." —Account Manager, Russia

Sales managers play an important role in helping salespeople qualify and "stress test" the qualification of a deal. Sales colleagues are also ideally placed to ask questions that cause you to question the validity of your knowledge and the approach being taken to move the sale forward.

Always remember:

- Qualify early in the sale, and do so again often as you move through it.
- Don't be afraid to walk if the deal doesn't look like it will pan out. The cost of pursuing dead deals and nonstarters is needlessly high.
- If you don't know it, don't fake it.
- Always create tactics to learn what you don't know.
- It never hurts to ask the customer what they're thinking.
- Any managers who put pressure on their teams to know all the qualification criteria early in the sales cycle only invite fiction into the Snapshot. Keep it real.
- The Profile of the sale may change if new players get involved or if the macro business environment shifts unexpectedly. Your Positioning and Alignment will ebb and flow; your win probability

can rise or fall. Remember these are *dynamic sales*, and by definition they are always in motion. Your Snapshot should reflect changes as they become known.

- Celebrate salespeople who gain a strength and never relinquish it, as long as their report is based on honesty, not hubris.
- Commend salespeople who report when a strength has become a weakness, as long as they have tactics to plug the gap.
- Caution salespeople who say they're doing well in a deal without applying any science to arrive at that opinion.

Chapter 8

Social Capital

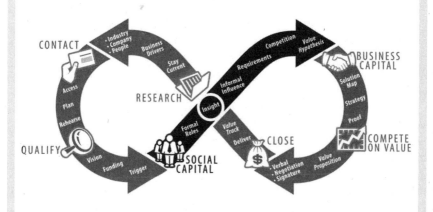

The Sales Expansion Loop: Social Capital

This step of the Sales Expansion Loop is of high importance, but it's often skipped. Looking at the diagram above, it's not uncommon to see salespeople go straight from confirming the budget (Qualify stage) to pitching their solution (Compete on Value stage) and miss the steps in between. For a simple sale in a linear sales funnel, this behavior may make sense, but it does not make sense in a large enterprise sale where personal agendas form aspects of the true decision-making process. If you don't navigate the currents of politics and whirlpools of influence, you will drown no matter how buoyant your value proposition is.

Think about selling to your customers: Are all the informal influences that shape their decision ever spelled out in a formal briefing paper, or is the reality a little more opaque than that? How do you get on the inside track and avoid the riptides that can otherwise wash you out to sea?

This very challenge is the intriguing premise behind Social Capital.

Developing social capital with your customers is an important stage in the sale between qualifying the landscape of the deal and building an offer to put on the table. Its position in this sequence is based on this logic: people decide with emotion (social capital) before they justify with logic (business capital), and if you wait until after you've developed your value proposition to begin recruiting mentors to help you close, you're missing the point of having mentors early to help shape your value proposition in the first place. The salespeople who exceed their targets every year make sure they're building supporters as early as possible. These are the reasons why we focus on Social Capital at this stage of the sale.

Robert D. Putnam is a Fulbright scholar, political scientist, and professor of public policy at Harvard University's John F. Kennedy School of Government. He devises *game theories* that distill human behavior and decision trees into a series of predictive mathematical constants—a branch of science used in politics, economics, and computing. One of his popular formulas that government trade officials base their strategies around can be adapted to our purposes. It shows how international agreements are successfully brokered only if they result in "domestic benefits" for the parties involved.[1]

In applying this game theory to selling, we might regard companies as "countries" and their key people as "provinces" or "states" within the country. A "domestic benefit" answers "What's in it for me?" to satisfy a stakeholder's personal agenda. Therefore, Putnam's logic is saying that no large strategic sale is won without the efforts of the people who gain a personal benefit pushing that sale over the investment line.

ACCESS

So how do you figure out who those people are, and then get close to them?

Reasons People Are Involved in the Buying Initiative

The primary motivations for people to become involved in the buying initiative are these: (1) they have some level of formal involvement in the investment decision, (2) they have vested interests in the final buying decision, or (3) they wish to advocate for the purchase because they believe it is truly in the best interests of the organization.

Formal Involvement

When their company evaluates suppliers, some people are assigned to the evaluation process because the investment requires their job title to be involved. They'll listen to your presentations, contribute opinions, offer an evaluation, and deal with the paperwork because doing so is part of their formal job. They may not particularly care which supplier is chosen, and they might not be entirely convinced their company needs to make this investment in the first place. But they turn up and go through the motions.

Think of your current biggest deal in the making. Which people you're in contact with are involved only because their job dictates that they be? Does it make any difference to them if the deal goes forward or dies on the vine? This information will direct you in how you pursue your target opportunity, what you say, and who you spend time with.

Vested Interests

Buyers are more likely to push a project forward when they see that doing so will help their personal agenda, as Putnam shows in his behavioral math. Perhaps they want greater knowledge, power, ease, comfort, or novelty. Or it might be to gain a first-mover advantage, prestige among their peers, the ability to push the envelope, right a wrong, climb the highest mountain, have the newest toys, or to leave a legacy. When they believe that making a deal with a supplier—any supplier—will advance these aims, they will support the change for its own sake.

Conversely, when buyers feel the proposed change will detract from any of their personal goals, when it creates a shift in the balance of power away from them, when it shines the spotlight on someone else, when it paints their past choices as outdated, when it allows another department to outpace them, when it mandates that they learn new tricks beyond their comfort level, when it erodes budget they earmarked for other purposes, when it in any other way creates a perceived personal risk, this is when people will work to downgrade the importance of the project and hope it will go away.

What you see here is that people can be supporters or resistors to a buying initiative, without this sentiment being about your competitors or you. To them, it's not about whom to buy from but whether they want this change at all. Think of your current biggest deal in the making again. Of the people you're in contact with, who are for the project (without yet caring who the supplier should be), and who are against it? To what extent does knowing this make a difference in whom you choose to spend most of your time with and what you discuss?

Often, the first battle you face is making sure everyone can answer the question: Why do this at all, and why do it now? This question must be answered to ensure that the deal has legs without the risk of its being sidelined, shelved, or culled from the list of approved expenditures.

You start by processing the PRECISION Questions on Consequence. You score your progress on Snapshot criterion 3, *trigger*. You keep stoking this until the parties agree that in general terms, it looks like you might have some capabilities of value. Through the rest of the sale, this *value hypothesis* will need to be tested and a business case will need to be added to give it substance, but before then you must mutually agree that it makes sense to explore the idea further. At this point you might seek to take control of their evaluation process by submitting a *Mutual Project Plan* (sometimes called a *Close Plan*), as detailed earlier (Chapter 3).

But even when they agree the project is worth doing, they're not actually supporting you yet. They can believe in the need for a solution yet not care where that solution comes from.

Advocacy

For them to nudge you over the line ahead of your competitors, to lobby and speak up for your solution when vendors are being debated in the canteen or the boardroom, they need a reason to choose sides. This is when they truly get off the fence and exhibit partisan behavior.

Partisans are fervent supporters of any party, cause, or idea—guerilla fighters who share local intelligence and attack or distract an enemy. Their help may be given overtly where they tell others what they think about you and your rivals, or their help may be given covertly as mentoring on what to say, how to act, who to reach.

As Sun-tzu said:

> *It is through the information brought by the spy that we are able to acquire local information.* (Art of War *13:22*)

To recruit people to believe that the project should happen and that you should be the vendor of choice, you're going to have to uncover their personal agenda. But you must also exercise caution in who you recruit. If you convince a number of people to be your internal advocates and everyone in their business has long thought of them as the village idiots, you may get a different result than you were hoping for. Therefore, it pays to assess which people have the most influence and to get close to these movers and shakers.

This makes political sense, but it's also practical from a bandwidth standpoint: developing social capital properly is resource intensive, and it requires consistency. You may not have time to do this with more than a handful of people. So make them the right people.

Let's look into the *how* and the *who* of social capital and influence.

How to Build Social Capital

Putnam found that social capital is accrued by two intertwined forms of social currency: bonding and bridging.

Bonding

Bonding occurs when people see you are like them: same age, same race, or shared interest or background. When people gather around the watercooler to chat about a new film or the weekend's football games, they're engaging in a bonding exercise that contributes to the social capital of that group. They are more inclined to repeat that gathering with the same members, becoming a clique.

If you've ever changed your dress code to mirror that of a customer (for example, leaving your jacket in the car and wearing an open-collar blue shirt when visiting a customer's factory, then putting on a tie and jacket when visiting the office), or if you've ever started a meeting with small talk about common interests, you've engineered a bonding ritual to break into other people's clique. It's relatively easy to adapt to other people and create bonding moments. It's not about being popular or liked as much as it's about showing them you belong in their circle as "one of them" and you deserve a seat at the table more than your competitors do.

Bridging

Bridging is what you do when you connect to people who are not like you. They may be from a different generation, industry background, culture, security clearance, technical proficiency, education level, job title, or something else. When a school jock befriends a school nerd, it's a bridging moment. Cold-calling is a bridging exercise. When a salesperson who typically feels intimidated calling on a chief financial officer takes time to learn the language of finance and then success-fully has a cogent discussion, this also is bridging at work. It's about moving outside your comfort plateau to connect with other people you normally wouldn't associate with.

Next time you're at a company social event, watch people divide into their natural cliques, seeking out people "just like them." Then watch closely for those others who move between cliques, like bees spreading pollen from one flower to the next. You'll see them. They're always there in small numbers.

You might first observe "the players" early in the evening dressed in their finery, pressing hands with the top brass, a champagne flute in hand, looking like a million dollars. Half an hour later you spy them casually pouring wine for a gaggle of neglected spouses, striking up a jargon-free conversation even nonemployees can enjoy. Later you see them crushing a beer can on their skull, their necktie gone, sleeves rolled up, trading fun with the beard-and-sandal brigade. None of these groups may be the players' natural habitats. But they under-stand the value of bridging, so they "play the room."

Where either bonding or bridging begin to break down, there comes a decline in overall social capital and—importantly for sellers—a rise in distrust and tension between the other parties and you. Think about when you've sold to prospects who didn't know you, had never used n before, and had nobody in their tribe vouching for you. Were they inclined to believe every claim you made, or did they demand to see other credentials, call your references, and read your testimonials?

Some salespeople believe this is a normal part of the sales process, something to endure. Yet why are there sellers who never get asked for referees? Because of their connections to key people? Because they're inside the circle of trust? Exactly. The difference is the level of bridging and bonding they apply.

The saying goes, "It's not what you know but who you know." But it's also "how well you connect on a personal level." People buy from people they trust, and the first echelon of trust is based on relating to the other party, having something in common. It may sound basic, but the more you learn about a person's background, history, and interests, the easier it is to strike up a conversation to achieve that bonding or bridging—and that's where social capital begins.

Look at their LinkedIn connections, groups they subscribe to, blogs they write, and Facebook photos and comments. Profile them using the approaches outlined in Chapter 2, "Research." It won't take long before you have a handle on how to walk and talk so they see you as someone worth bonding or bridging to.

Does doing so make you disingenuous, a fake, or a manipulator? The question of ethics is a topic some salespeople ponder when it comes to modifying behavior to make the most of customer interactions.

Yet as a society we hand out Oscars to actors who make us feel something from their performances, even though they're not really the character we see on the screen. Our television anchors and advertising voiceover artists don't talk at home the way they enunciate for the media. Judges and barristers don't wear their powdered wigs and capes when they clock off. The props and attitudes evinced on the job are all artifices of the "commercial masks" people wear.

It's the same with selling. It entails a little pantomime and draws the line at lying, cheating, and misinformation, the same as it would with any other respectable profession.

Once you're in the door through bonding or bridging, your goal is to demonstrate a mastery of their needs (from research and PRECISION Questions) to create opportunities that allow you to demonstrate your integrity by sticking to the timelines and outputs agreed to in the Mutual Project Plan. As people gain value from your interactions, word will spread about you through their personal networks. Your reputation and goodwill will precede you. Doors will open as people introduce you around to others. Almost like prospecting (only more effective) these referrals grant you mobility and credibility around the prospect's organization.

This currency is critical to establish early, before you begin to pitch your business value. If the prospects don't believe in you as a genuine person, they won't listen to anything you say about your company or solution.

Who to Build Social Capital With

One of Putnam's contemporaries in the field of research on social capital is Nan Lin, a Duke University professor who has taught at Johns Hopkins University and has served as vice president of the American Sociological Association. Lin observes that the society within companies is shaped in a hierarchical pyramid and that change within the pyramid is most likely to come from the middle.

He explains that at the top of the pyramid, there is not much scope to move up the ladder, so it's in the interest of people there to maintain stability and consolidate their power in the status quo with as little risk as possible.

At the bottom of the pyramid where agitation for change may be highest, there are so many people with so many scattered connections, approaching them all directly and attempting to herd them in one direction is nearly impossible in large organizations.

It's the *middle* of the pyramid where social capital gives you the best leverage. People there have ambition to scale the ladder or to shake things up to bring about change. They are few enough in numbers to make reaching them feasible, but they are well connected enough to wrangle the masses below.[2] They also have medium levels of authority, access to information, and the ability to schedule meetings others will attend—all helpful as you build formal and informal advocacy within the ranks. When you're looking for such points of leverage, Lin suggests the middle of an organization is the best place to focus.

This matches the research my team completed for the book and workshop on *Selling to the C-Suite*, where senior executives said they were 20 times more likely to meet people who had been referred to them by their "trusted lieutenants" compared to those who used cold-calling to reach them. By definition, the referrers who are in the executive's personal network already have social capital in the bank—so trade off their credibility until you earn your own.

But not everyone in the middle of the pyramid is of equal value to sell to. Within that population, you need to discern which people have low or high influence—and skew your relationship to the latter. It doesn't mean you abandon calling on the others; you just prioritize.

INSIGHT

If you are following our journey around the Sales Expansion Loop, you now curve back to the center, crossing the Insight junction for the second time. We are halfway through the sales process.

On this passage through the Insight step, you pause to ask yourself if you are extracting enough insight into the inner workings of your prospect's business, decision process, and key people. If it's like pulling teeth and few people are engaging with you, it might be worth asking yourself if you should make another go/no-go decision about the opportunity.

But before doing so, you must ask if you are giving enough insight to the customer so that you can build the right connections with them. If not, it might make sense to go back a few steps and double-check your facts and assumptions, and then make sure your customer and you are moving forward on the same journey at the same speed. You can always go back to the Research stage, find new triggers and stakeholders to approach, and see if another person will take you further forward.

Before deciding this, it's a good time to convene an opportunity review meeting with managers and peers and see what insights come from that. Top sellers run this as a formal meeting with the intent of turbocharging their approach to the sale.

Considered the most successful investor of the twentieth century and one of the world's three wealthiest people, Berkshire Hathaway chairman Warren Buffett once spoke about his strategy playing the game of bridge. He may as well have been talking about the virtues of running opportunity reviews at the key stages of a sale:

> *You gather all the information you can and then keep adding to that base of information as things develop. You do whatever the probabilities indicate based on the knowledge you have at that time, but you are always willing to modify your behavior or your approach as you get new information.*[3]

It pays to follow the advice of self-made billionaires.

How to Run an Opportunity Review

If you're a salesperson who understands the value of having extra eyes look into your sale to help you see the forest for the trees, an opportunity review can be incredibly motivating when properly facilitated by your sales manager. These meetings should be full of Aha! ideas that help you move the sale forward.

If you're a sales manager responsible for running an opportunity review, be careful that these meetings aren't confused with performance reviews or inspections of the troops. An opportunity review is not for testing the salesperson. It's for testing the sales situation. There should be no hint of criticizing or second-guessing the individual. If you allow any of that tone into a deal review, it will create a culture of fear and distrust, followed by falsification of information in an effort to avoid criticism. When this happens, you can kiss goodbye any semblance of value of the review for the salesperson or for anyone else who might have wanted to participate in such sessions in the future. Everyone will run for the hills and endure these meetings only under duress. That's not how you want these valuable sessions to be viewed.

Sales directors and other senior executives should be vigilant in patrolling the culture of these meetings. They should scour the calendar in search of these sessions and drop in on them regularly. Their purposes in attending should be to ensure that the meetings are happening on a regular basis in every team, for the right revenue opportunities, and that they're being facilitated professionally by the sales manager in charge.

It has been my sad experience to see many otherwise talented and personable sales managers come off as completely lacking in emotional intelligence when it comes to facilitating opportunity reviews. Like Dr. Jekyll transmogrifying into Mr. Hyde, they can take on a twisted persona intent on flexing their muscles to demean and beat up the poor reps who come to the table exercising faith and trust that the meeting will give them guidance and direction, not guilt and derision. Shame on any sales manager who perverts this sacred trust!

Here are guidelines gathered from elite teams that describe how top sellers are utilizing opportunity reviews for maximum effect.

Identify Target Opportunities

The sales manager should look at the forecast to identify deals most likely to benefit from deeper scrutiny. These deals may have stalled in their progression, or they may be approaching a critical juncture in each trimester, a key go/no-go decision point, or an important meeting or presentation. In short, something has either happened, failed to happen, or is about to happen that suggests it would be smart to look into the dynamics of the sale to identify the best ways to move the deal to the next level.

Schedule the Review

Invite relevant parties to a 45- to 60-minute meeting. The salesperson running the target opportunity review will attend as the presenter. The sales manager will attend as the meeting facilitator. Other people should be invited to attend as reviewers, even in small companies. These are people who bring a diversity of opinion and experience to the table, such as other salespeople, customer service staff who know the account being sold to, partners, or solution specialists. Ideally a minimum of three reviewers will be invited, not including the sales manager who must stay focused on being the facilitator.

Set Clear Expectations

When sending out the calendar invitation, it's always a good idea to explain the purpose of the review. Take care to explain why the specific opportunity was selected and what you hope will be achieved as a breakthrough from the session. This gives people a reason to attend and a context for why you hope their specific personal insight will add value. Letting people know this information will establish the review as something other than just another administrative meeting. It sets the expectation that the review will be a real business strategy session—for such it is.

Prepare with Purpose

When people are asked to look at the details of other people's sales opportunities, they are being asked to become conversant in a significant amount of new information in a short amount of time. One mistake too many managers make is waiting until they have people around the table to start sharing this information. Then they wonder why their review sessions take so long and why so few meaningful breakthroughs are achieved.

They're doing it the hard way.

Instead, ask the salesperson who owns the deal to print out or distribute a copy of his or her opportunity plan to the reviewers several days in advance. Send a five-minute calendar invitation for the salesperson to do this, to make sure it happens.

Give the reviewers time to look over the deal in advance, immerse themselves in the situation, and form questions and opinions. Send a 60-minute calendar invitation for the reviewers and sales manager to do this, to make sure that happens too.

In that calendar invitation or covering e-mail, suggest that as they read each page, they should write down questions on subject matter, historical background, or relationship dynamics they don't understand from the information provided. Time will be provided in the review meeting for these questions to be answered. Suggest that as they weigh how complete the information is or how well the sale is progressing, they should write down any risks or concerns that jump out at them. Time will be provided in the review to discuss these too.

With these preparations, when people get around a table to talk about the deal, they're ready to add value to a situation they already understand, rather than learning about it for the first time. As you prepare with purpose, the value of any opportunity review increases exponentially.

Run the Review

The date will arrive for the review to be run. The manager will place people around the same table, or people will dial in to a virtual meeting with screen sharing. The manager should thank everyone for attending and explain the breakthroughs being sought in the session. The manager should restate the amount of time reserved for the review and explain that the meeting will pass through three steps: (1) introductory comments, (2) brain trust, and (3) collaborative brainstorming.

Step 1: Introductory Comments. Step 1 is when the salesperson gives a 10-minute uninterrupted commentary on where she is now, where she wants to be, the challenges in her way, what she's doing about them, and where she needs help. The salesperson should avoid reading word for word each page of the opportunity plan—the reviewers have already read the outline, and now they need to hear the story behind the story.

Some background that is helpful for reviewers includes how the discussion started, who has attended sales meetings so far, how long the opportunity has been active, whether the evaluation criteria favor or disadvantage the salesperson's solution, how long the opportunity has been sitting at the current stage of the sales cycle, when a decision has to be made, each of the nine criteria on the Opportunity Snapshot, and the go-forward tactics that have already been planned. It's also helpful for the salesperson to share where she thinks things could go wrong.

Following this, the floor is open for 10 minutes for the reviewers to get answers to any questions they wrote in their preparation, if these questions were not already answered by the salesperson's commentary.

The purpose of this step is for an open exchange of information, pure and simple. Sometimes people will find fault or dwell on product-related topics instead of asking questions to understand the situation better. The best way to stay on topic is for participants to preface each question with: "Something I'd like to know more about is . . ."

It's the manager's job to ensure that each step of an opportunity review is run in an orderly and positive manner. Reviews should avoid any debate, conjecture, or interrogation. Being invited to these review sessions should be established as a coveted privilege, and the sessions should be considered collaborative forums in which salespeople are helped by a brain trust in a safe environment.

Step 2: Brain Trust. Step 2 is when the reviewers are put to work as that very brain trust for 10 minutes. Their task is to spot risks and gaps that could derail the sale. This part of the review might be introduced by the manager declaring: "Let's say we just received an e-mail from the future saying that we lost this deal, but it didn't say why. Based on how the opportunity looks right now, what might have gone wrong?"

To get a variety of responses, some managers will ask the reviewers to look at the sale through slightly different lenses:

> I want Jürgen to look at this deal through the perspective of the **customer**. Are we connecting to the right people? Do we really understand their needs? Are we guessing their decision criteria and weighting them? Is there evidence that real support is in place for us but not for our competitors? Who is really behind this decision, and how are we positioned with them? Will their business agenda or personal agenda really drive this decision? Look for anything in this sale that suggests we need to take action to get closer to this customer and exert more control over the buying agenda.

Another lens to explore may go like this:

> I want Maryann to look at this deal through the perspective of the **competitors**. Where are we underestimating them? Where are we overestimating them? What have we seen them do in similar deals in the past? What do we know about the strengths and weaknesses of the competitor sales teams? Have we had them in for recruitment interviews to test what type of people we're up against? In their relationships with key people, is there any evidence that they are stronger or weaker than we are? What strategy are they going to use to win, and what discussions do we need to have with the

customer now to make that strategy an untenable option for them? What if Competitors A and B joined forces in an alliance against us? Look for anything in this sale that suggests the competitors could outplay us, and write it down.

Managers might assign other lenses such as this one:

I want Donya to focus on the Snapshot scores and call out where they don't make sense or where we have a strength we're not leveraging enough.

Or this one:

I want Gavin to look specifically at the solution we plan to pitch here, and I want him to flag any risk that it might not meet the customer's expectations or that it will look like a me-too proposition.

The point is, you assign reviewers to get granular where needed, especially where they have subject matter expertise.

Reviewers use sticky notes, flipcharts, or pads of paper to write down obvious problems or nuanced risks. The resulting list reveals whether you are in a controlling or a reactive position, and it gives strategic insight into how the game could play out based on how the chess pieces are positioned on the board at present. This is the wisdom of crowds—and applying it to your sales opportunities gives greater clarity than individuals can see on their own.

After 10 minutes, have your reviewers read out loud their list of gaps and risks. Some may be duplicates (discard them). Others may touch on different aspects of the same problem (group these under a unifying heading). The aim is to distill their ideas into a short list. As these gaps and risks are read aloud to the salesperson, the best way to avoid tangents and debates is to ask the reviewers to preface their report with the words: "I see a risk that is . . ."

The salesperson in charge of the target opportunity doesn't need to respond to any of these gaps or risks. She doesn't need to debate. She just needs to listen and choose which risks to take onboard as the most critical, most timely, and most relevant.

This step confronts salespeople with a stark reality: if strangers to the deal are seeing certain things as critical risks, action is clearly required. When we hear a voice of doubt in our own head, we can rationalize it away. When it sounds in our ears through the warning voice of another, it's more difficult to ignore.

Step 3: Collaborative Brainstorming. Step 3 is for all parties to invest 10 minutes in collaboratively brainstorming as many ways as possible to fix the gaps that are shortlisted. If you are pressed for time, it helps to adopt a division of labor, but most companies using this approach prefer to move sequentially from one risk to the next and scoop up as many opinions as possible for each one. This is where teams are at their most creative. Managers need to channel this so the result is that the salesperson receives a clear playbook of the steps to take, in the correct sequence, who to talk to, what to say, and things to watch for. This level of detail should be written onto the tactics or actions page of whatever format of opportunity plan the team uses.

The first time you run an opportunity review following these three steps, it may feel a little formal, structured, and awkward—especially if your current way of reviewing deals is a casual chat over a coffee, or if in your company the word *review* has a negative connotation.

Just follow the process, and the result will speak for itself. Where sales managers create a transparent forum to review and improve the sales campaigns for target opportunities, people sell more. Is this just hype? By no means. Research proves it.

According to 422 companies interviewed by Aberdeen Group,[4] 81 percent of the businesses that showed the highest year-on-year gains in team quota attainment and revenue per rep used formal analytics to validate how their sales opportunities were tracking. In the middle performing companies of this sample group, only 55 percent of managers applied rigor to inspecting their team's deals. It was done only 34 percent of the time in the lowest performing companies. In this data the lesson is simple: what you observe, you change—and the more you observe and improve something, the higher your results will be. Ancillary benefits of running opportunity reviews and tracking the progress of sales are that the companies doing so typically outsell those that don't by a factor of 130 percent, their lead conversion is 150 percent better, and their forecasts are 146 percent more accurate.

If you're a salesperson who wants to close more business, insist that your sales manager should start running opportunity reviews on a regular and professional basis. It is your right to work for managers whose application of process and leadership is most likely to create an environment in which you can succeed.

If you're a sales manager who already runs deal reviews but in a casual ad hoc manner, tighten up your approach and watch the results climb.

If you're a company executive with patchy revenue in different sales teams, compare those teams for which managers run opportunity reviews and use sales analytics against those teams that don't. Which ones have the most reps on target and the most reliable forecasts? Catalog what they do on a regular basis and replicate their best practices across the other teams. A rising tide will lift all boats.

When you complete an opportunity review at the Insight junction and decide you're ready to move forward, the next step in the Social Capital phase will be to identify people you need to get closer to in order to win the informal comparison you and other vendors will be subject to. This is where a few tips to interpret and build influence come in handy, as you'll see in Chapter 9.

Find the Influencers

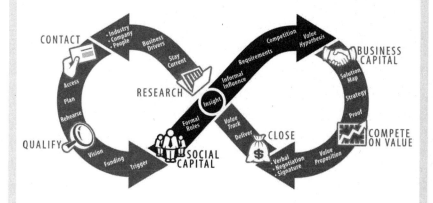

The Sales Expansion Loop: Social Capital—Influence

INFLUENCE: PERCEPTION AND REALITY

On the left side of Figure 9.1, we see three vice presidents who all carry the same business card, can probably sign off the same level of expenses, and by all appearances have the same authority. The Perception of Job Title paints them as peers who share an equal reporting line up to their CEO.

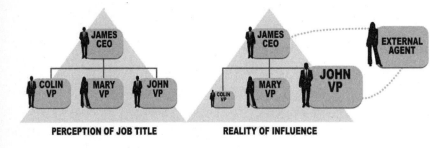

Figure 9.1: An Example of Formal Rank Versus Informal Influence

When the Reality of Influence is considered, however, you learn that one of them (John) has an enormously successful track record, and he is well liked and has his opinion sought on matters outside his area of the business. Another person (Colin) is "in the departure lounge" with limited currency after having fallen out of favor for missing his targets too many months in a row. Outside the organization chart is a former company executive (External Agent) who now works with an analyst firm and retains close contact with the current CEO (James), who she has been advising for more than five years.

UNCOVERING THE REALITY

Should this reality shape whose offices you spend the most time in? Of course it must!

But how do you uncover the reality of influence in your target sales opportunity?

Be a Detective

To identify these players, always look for the people who are linked to diverse projects and discussions. Look for the people who attend meetings and say very little, but whose few questions demonstrate insight beyond what they've heard directly from you (they're in the loop through other sources). Look for the people whose opinion others defer to regardless of their rank. Look for the people who seldom act surprised when they hear breaking news. Look for the people whose LinkedIn profiles place them in the alumni of companies whose staff now proliferate the account you're selling into. Do some digging. These connections all tell a story.

Make Them Dance

People may get close to you, telling you that they're your supporters, but when you need them to come through for you, they can vote for the other guy. Has that ever happened to you (if not you, then someone you know)? You must test people's loyalties early to midcycle in the sale to avoid surprises at the finish line. So even though you may have agreed to a Mutual Project Plan, it pays to set up some additional assignments for *them* to complete, and see if they come through for you. If they never quite get around to it time and time again, it tells you something about them. Talk is cheap.

For example, will they share with you the latest organization chart? Are they willing and able to brief you on the company strategy for the year ahead? Can they wrangle people you name into a business lunch, exploratory workshop, or reference site visit? Do they introduce you to others you want to meet? Are they willing to review your sales opportunity plan and validate your strengths and weaknesses? Do they volunteer good counsel? To the extent they are legally able, do they explain how you are perceived compared to your competitors, and do they offer suggestions that help you win?

If you're confident you have good rapport, try asking for any of these or similar displays of support. Then see if they're friends, foes, or fence-sitters.

Ignore Gravity

Influence doesn't always follow hierarchical reporting lines. Top salespeople learn to tell the difference between the formal authority that is granted by right of rank and the informal influence that is granted by other means (this dynamic was already covered when I discussed Snapshot criterion 9, the Informal dynamic, in Chapter 7). Influence can move sideways from peer to peer. It can reach across cubicle walls and oceans. It defies gravity when subordinates have more clout than their boss. It can flow into the company from outside agents who have history, relationship, and currency with key people.

MAPPING INFLUENCE

We all know this dynamic exists, and it's likely that you've been trained on a sales methodology that purports to help you map it. So a word of caution is appropriate here. I see some political maps in salespeople's account plans being drawn on top of the hierarchical organization chart they pull from annual reports or create using a widget in PowerPoint. Most salespeople get the formal line of reporting correct, and then over the top of this, they color, code, shade, or otherwise display the people they believe have the most influence in the deal. The theory is right. But the execution is frequently flawed—and I'll tell you why.

We conducted an experiment reviewing more than 500 deal plans where the traditional organization chart was the type of chart salespeople started with as a base when mapping contacts in the opportunity. Onto this the salespeople were asked to display the political influence of each person. One trend emerged in more than 76 percent of these maps: with the hierarchical reporting tree staring them in the face, it was nigh impossible for salespeople to see beyond each person's rank and instead draw how influence *really* worked inside the departments they were selling to.

This phenomenon was revealed when we transferred every name on those deals to a two-axis chart, as shown in Figure 9.2. We assigned the Y axis to denote Influence (low, medium, high) and the X axis to capture what level of Rank each person's job title gave him or her (top, middle, lower tiers). What did we find?

We saw an almost straight diagonal line from low rank/low influence on the bottom left to high rank/high influence on the upper right. What's wrong with that?

Everything.

It reveals that despite having attended one or more training sessions that taught these principles, three-quarters of those salespeople were still unable to tell the difference between rank and influence, so they wrote their sales plans by defaulting to traditional logic instead of demonstrating *situational awareness.*

This means they were selling under the premise that someone at the operations level (low rank) only had low influence on the decision-

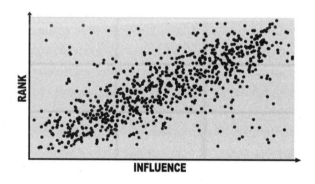

Figure 9.2: The Misreading of Rank as Influence

making process and that the higher up the ladder they climbed, the more powerful people became. And that's the problem when the sales planning tool you're using shows a hierarchical map: it's at cross-purposes with the task of focusing on the dynamic of influence, which is the sole purpose of such an exercise in the first place. Mapping it to a hierarchical chart defeats the purpose of the exercise more often than not.

Wondering what else these organization charts reveal, we note most opportunity plans show few enemies or naysayers, despite competitors being present. The people so many sales reps are spending the most time with are those they had already bonded to, and they are seldom spending a lot of time with people they need to bridge to. We checked, and the close conversion rate of these salespeople was in the 33 to 58 percent range. They weren't winning 100 percent, though their organization charts implied that they were covering all the right people and that all of those people were their friends. There's a term that describes salespeople who approach major competitive bids with such naïveté: "road kill."

When we inspected the other 24 percent of salespeople (who were closing 46 to 81 percent of their deals), the correlation of rank to influence was scattered across the chart—as is more realistic. They focused on selling to the *outliers*—those "movers and shakers" whose rank or title alone doesn't determine how they function, who they know, or what power they wield.

These top sellers showed some people with low rank having extremely high influence, and they could explain why their track records and connections granted this.

They were clued in to the fact that some people with the highest rank were no more than rubber-stamping figureheads.

They had mapped out the pools of support they could count on, and they knew each business and personal agenda that needed to be satisfied in return for buying their solution.

They had also plotted the cadres of nonsupporters who despised change of any kind and accordingly were making life difficult for *all* the vendors. And they had identified those who wanted change but were lobbying for a competitor's solution instead.

They gained this information by keeping their eyes and ears open, by being *curious* about the political dynamic in each sale, and by asking good questions to uncover it.

If you don't ask, you don't get.

For each of the people on their chart, they had a set of actions written down on their sales plan to neutralize the arguments of those who were against any change being made, to educate and win over those who were supporting the competition, and to leverage their own supporters to nudge the buying decision their way.

So how *do* these winners map the people they're selling to?

First, they *avoid* using those hierarchical organization charts that other salespeople borrow from the customer's annual report or account plan. Even if a hierarchical model is the only option provided by their CRM or sales planning tool, they go to the effort of creating their own chart format in PowerPoint, Visio, or some other graphic tool whenever they're planning a discrete sales opportunity.

Why? First, they do it to be accurate. Second, because influence is situational—even if a few company officers are *always* in the mix, deal by deal *different people* get involved to shape the outcome.

These sellers understand that no professional can afford to have their thinking on this topic skewed by the semipermanent structure of the company that you see at the account planning level. Instead, they use a different visual that focuses on the situational dynamic of the opportunity at hand.

By definition, such a chart does not include many "actors" or "personas" (as they are sometimes called in marketing-speak) because *only a few people matter most*, around which are others who *shape their thinking* (from inside and outside of the company tree). These are the people who have the most to gain or the most to lose by this project going ahead or being shelved. They have a vested interest in what's going to happen, they care more about it than anyone else, and they are active participants in the internal lobbying for and against the idea. These *must* be identified and categorized.

You may choose to include additional actors on your chart: the active channels through which you are seeding ideas or through whom you are gaining access. You achieve a diminishing return by mapping other people because it dilutes your focus. When salespeople mistakenly believe their job is to impress their peers by how many people's names they can cite in the account, they're missing the point of planning an opportunity-specific strategy to build their social capital. When it comes to drafting an Influence Map for a discrete target sales opportunity, less is always more.

Your choice of who to include boils down to this:

- Who has most skin in the game?
- Who most shapes these people's opinions when they have a choice to make?
- Who else must be involved because the decision-making process requires their thumbprint?

In sales to small businesses, our research shows the list of *meaningful* contacts averages in the range of 1 to 3 decision makers and influencers (though there may be more people involved at different steps of the buying process). In sales to medium-sized companies, it is typically 3 to 9 people. In large enterprise deals, the key stakeholders typically range from 5 to 15 people per community.

A *community* is defined as any group of stakeholders who must be on board with the decision to buy from you before the company can go ahead, whether they exert high influence or not. The community's size will depend on the scope of your deal. For example, a sale to a single branch office is likely to involve fewer people than a national, regional, or global deal. The size of community also depends on whether the company you are selling to is *consensus led* (where you have to get many people on board) or if it uses *top-down mandates* to bind the masses (where you sell to fewer people).

But whatever the size of the community, if the people in it don't match the descriptions provided here, you must ask yourself if they really belong on your sales plan at all. You must delineate between whether you're drawing an Account Plan (which can have a cast of hundreds) or an Opportunity Plan (where the cast is more compact). Let's face it, you won't have the time to cover *everyone* in the organization, so target with laser accuracy and *go deep with the right people* instead of going shallow across too many. Consider the individuals, and ask the following questions:

	Yes	No
If they went on vacation tomorrow, would this deal stall until they returned?		
If they voiced a lack of support, would the key players be disinclined or unable to proceed?		
Do they have a formal assignment to evaluate your proposal against a list of predetermined criteria?		
Are they responsible for getting their stakeholders "on the same page" and delivering a final recommendation on who to buy from?		
Are they the people whose jobs are to commit to the decision and/or sign your contract?		

Where you answer no to any of these five questions, it's likely you can deemphasize your coverage of those people with low risk to your campaign.

Accounts are full of people who believe they have a right to collect lunches and junkets at your expense, who will tell you how important they are to you for winning a specific deal or for your longer-term standing in the account. Don't take any of that at face value. Instead, be a detective, make them dance, and ignore gravity. Test their claims. Use the questions above to validate each person's importance in the scheme of things, no matter what level of the hierarchy they are at. You might be surprised how a list of 25 to 40 people who all seem important one day can be whittled down to a more manageable number of 5 to 15 people when they are viewed through a more critical lens.

If your sales managers criticize you for not having enough people listed on your opportunity coverage plan, they might have a valid point, or they might not. Their opinion is valid if you're stuck in the comfort zone of calling only on familiar people you already bonded with, if you're not active in all the impacted departments, if you are calling at only one level of the business, or if you're spending time on the outskirts of influence at the expense of bridging to the people at the heart of the sale. In such cases, listen to your managers, and take a fresh look at who you're contacting—the PRECISION Questions will help you find the right people to meet.

But when managers give you a hard time for no other reason than they like to see their reps calling on *as many people as possible*, chances are you have one of those transactional-minded managers described earlier who believe a higher activity level brings greater returns. With these, you may want to back yourself up by sharing a list of all the names you *could* have targeted in your buyer's ecosystem and explaining why you've trimmed that list down to a few points of leverage and influence. Help your managers and other team members understand your thought process so they see that you already weighed your options and made a deliberate, strategic decision on where to focus.

As mentioned earlier, top sellers avoid the trap of overlaying their analysis of the people in a sales opportunity onto a hierarchical organization map because it can so easily blind them into confusing the levels of authority with true influence. Instead, they simply draw a set of concentric circles. Some options are shown in Figure 9.3.

Figure 9.3: The Influence Map

In the center they draw a **hub** of the most influential people for a specific buying decision. These are surrounded by a network of people (the **spokes)** who feed information and opinions into them and out from them, like radio transmitters that run across departmental lines and even beyond the organization. Outside of this, on the **rim** of influence, are people who have a formal responsibility to be involved when purchasing decisions are weighed and made, who have opinions and biases, may be vocal, and cannot be ignored.

For the purpose of this illustration, let's divide the whole circle into wedges that represent the different departments you sell to in your deal. Department titles are shown around the outside of the wedges. Inside each wedge you place the people who report to that department, positioned in one of the three circles depending on whether they have high influence (hub) or low influence (rim) or they are the people who shape opinion and make things happen for the people in the hub (spokes).

This chart is easy for most salespeople to draw. While I've shown it with images of people, it's a popular practice to simply write people's names on the map where their level of influence intersects the department they report to. If you draw this "Influence Map" on PowerPoint or Visio, it's easy to draw the people's names and titles in boxes you can overlay. If you draw the circles on a flipchart, try posting sticky notes for the people.

Where you know one person influences the thought process of another, and especially when specific people are part of your access strategy to open doors to the hub or spokes, you might want to draw arrows to show which way influence flows between people or which paths of introduction are available to you.

These arrows become very helpful when you're reviewing an opportunity plan with your manager, partners, channels, or presales support people. They might know some of these people, allowing you to assign the best people on your virtual sales team to manage each relationship. They might have seen how a similar decision played out in the past inside the company you're targeting, and they may be able to draw additional arrow vectors or add people for you to consider in your plan of attack.

Spatially mapping the connections between people and talking about it to others on your team has the effect of activating the kind of right-brain creative thinking where what-if scenarios, gaps, and risks can more easily be seen, discussed, and mitigated. These never reveal themselves in the left-brain columns and rows of a spreadsheet or contact list of a customer relationship management screen.

You'll notice the illustration shows six department wedges. It's a neat way to divide the circle. You may not need to use all six wedges, but it's unlikely you'll need to use more than six. If the people with most influence reside in two or three departments, only show those and leave the others blank. The whole point of an Influence Map is that it's not intended to be a permanent chart of every person and every department in the company. You should have an *account plan* for that. As discussed earlier, the mapping of people in sales opportunities is dynamic and situational—the people with the most influence over a deal today may not be the same for a different opportunity six months from now, even when selling to the same department. So the rule of thumb is to avoid complexity, and distill your focus to as few departments and people as possible, even when you feel there's a need to list every department and subdivision. Focus.

Compared to the world's top 20 percent of sellers, the middle 60 percent of average sales performers (and sometimes their managers) demonstrate a peculiar penchant for trying to hoard more wedges, more departments, more people. Some opt to draw sprawling organization charts instead of a simple Influence Map. They spend their time making shotgun phone calls and hit-and-miss coffee dates to achieve the illusion of industry.

But being a "busyness person" is not the same as being a "business person."

Maybe you know salespeople like this. I used to see a salesperson like that every day in the mirror early in my career. We've all been there. You can get away with it if all you're doing is flogging a box, pushing tin, or selling a product in a numbers game. Hit enough random golf balls and eventually you'll get a hole in one.

But that's not how *you* like to play, is it? Your deals hinge on selling the right solution to the right people with the right message, and not spreading yourself thin. You can't be everywhere, and with the Influence Map you don't need to be. Just be with those who matter *most*. That's the utility of this approach to visualizing the organization chart as a circle instead of a tree.

If you or those around you find it too challenging to jump so far away from a hierarchical map, what some bright salespeople do is apply the Influence Map to each level of the company. This is what you see in the middle of Figure 9.3. There, the people on the first Influence Map are still shown in the department wedges they belong to, but their rank has been split to show if they're at the *executive*, *middle management*, or *operations* level of those departments.

While this is a little more complex to draw, the approach has the virtue of revealing reporting lines in the hierarchy, without losing focus on influence. When you review this with your manager or sales team for the first time, it's helpful to discuss what you know of each department. You might come up with the name of someone previously overlooked. When you review where you've been spending most of your time, this type of chart can flag if you've been calling too low, too narrowly, and who reports to whom.

It's easy to see if the people you've been spending time with strengthen your sale or create risks for it. For example, you might be calling at only the middle management level at the expense of having established ties higher up or lower down. Or you might be calling on people high up, but who are on the rim with low influence. Only this rigor of examination can reveal if your call pattern has been uneven to date. Perhaps you've been very *active* making sales calls, but have you been truly *effective*?

If you can show that a middle management contact is in the spokes of the business . . . connected to a person at the operations level in the very influential hub of the deal . . . who in turn has the ear of an executive who may be out on the rim but whose job it is to make a commitment to a supplier based on recommendations from these people—suddenly it becomes clear that you're following a deliberate relationship strategy. Sales managers are much more likely to support salespeople who show insight into who they need to close.

Conversely, if the people you're calling on in middle management are shown to all be on the rim, you can use the hierarchical version of the Influence Map to spot another route into the hub. You may need to go down to the operations level or up to the executive level to find the path you need.

Remember though, "calling high" is not the sole aim of the game. The most influential people at the hub of your deal can be at *any* level. Your job is to identify them, then broadcast your value through one of the spokes connected to them. Piggybacking the credibility of these people is always a better strategy than trying to build your own when you're establishing new relationships. You have to bridge before you can bond. If they believe in you and see how your solution advances their business or personal agenda, those in the hub will hear of it soon enough.

A manager interviewed during the research for this book said it this way: "Surely a salesperson's job description is simple: identify and sell to the spokes. The rest will follow."

In Chapter 4 of *Selling to the C-Suite* (McGraw-Hill, 2009), you'll find additional detail on how to identify the people with most influence in a sale. I won't recycle the pointers I gave in that book because they're set out well enough there. But let me simply draw from page 76 of the hardcover edition of *C-Suite* and invite you to view people's influence through four lenses:

- What they did in the past: Is their credibility in credit or debit?
- What they do now: Are they perceived as building new currency?
- Who they know: Are they connected to the ruling regime?
- Their ability to drive change: Are they opinion leaders?

You'll find some people belong in the hub or spoke because they have a vested interest in making a change, and they had enough credibility to pull a project together to the point where people are evaluating suppliers and a budget is attached. But just because they had the ability to get it this far, will they be able to retain the budget if the CFO mandates austerity measures? Will they be able to keep the project on a dais as a high priority? Can they defend it when naysayers lobby to preserve the status quo?

You see, membership in the hub isn't restricted only to people who want to see the project go ahead. When funds are budgeted and approved, there can be others who begin to circle the project whose goal is to divert the funds or repurpose the project so the investment morphs to serve their own goals. They may represent internal competition to those who originally initiated the project—people who lacked the resourcefulness to get something off the ground but who are more than happy to hijack it now that it's in flight. These people may be voices others listen to—opinion leaders. They might speak with the silky voice of reason and enjoy high popularity, or they may be prickly individuals who make life a living hell for everyone if they're not consulted and involved. You may know people like this in your own organization.

If they reside in the organizational hub of influence, they can elbow their way into the hub of your opportunity. Watch for people like this: they will have their own spokes extending through the organization, sending their own messages out through the jungle drums in the battle for mindshare. Sometimes these drums will be beating for your competition to win the deal, or their message may be to keep an incumbent product or service in place as a low-risk alternative to swapping for a new brand.

Can you afford to ignore these people? Of course not. Keep your friends close and your enemies closer. So double-check each player's influence using the four criteria above, as an exercise in risk mitigation. Make sure you know what players are on the board, and why.

THE DIMENSIONS OF INDIVIDUALS' INVOLVEMENT: FORMAL ROLE, ALLEGIANCE, AND SIGNAL STRENGTH

Because people will display different loyalties to you as a supplier or to the evaluation process itself, there is one final addition to the Influence Map that high performers always add. Rather than write notes on their opportunity plan about each person in longhand, they standardize on a form of shorthand notation using symbols to denote three different dimensions of the individuals' involvement:

- **Formal role.** Each person's formal decision-making assignment
- **Allegiance.** The level of support they display to you
- **Signal strength.** How well you're covering the relationship

We'll examine the formal role in the rest of this chapter and cover allegiance and signal strength in the next chapter.

FORMAL ROLE

Not everyone plays a formal role. Some circle the decision without any official responsibility, some are involved out of curiosity, and some attend your presentations so they can offer an opinion about you behind closed doors. You will meet numerous people in the various meetings and lunches where you're invited to bridge, bond, and present your credentials. Only a few of these people will be part of the official committee whose responsibility it is to spend their company's money. Within this group there are three main roles people fill: evaluators, decision makers, and approvers.

Evaluators

Evaluators review you against technical fit, legal compliance, customer and analyst opinions, service capability, business footprint, company reputation, or other aspects on their company's shopping list. Because some aspects require an experienced eye to make a comparison, there can be many evaluators each focusing on their area of expertise. They may compare each supplier against a list of criteria with weighted scores to come up with a manageable shortlist of frontrunners that all parties can agree are in the race on the basis of merit. Companies that need to prove impartiality, abide by antitrust laws, or show an audit trail of how they choose to release funds without corruption or laundering tend to favor such delineation when making a formal evaluation.

Those tasked with making this happen are clear about their responsibilities and the criteria they are scoring you against. If they're a public company or government organization, they may be legally bound to share with you what they're assessing—if you ask to be told.

The reason you want to know people's roles in the evaluation process is so that you can deliver a focused message instead of giving generic information to everyone. When you know what it is they're looking for in a supplier, you tailor what you talk about so these aspects are accented. There may be other accomplishments and features your company is proud about. But if they're not a priority on these people's evaluation list, there's little point in talking about them. Learn what's on their shopping list, know which items are must-haves, and show how well you fit these. Manage your choice of customer testimonials, case studies, demonstrations, and site visits based on this information, and remember to adapt to each evaluator's unique list.

Gone are the days when one pitch is good enough. To win consistently, you must flavor your message using what you know of each evaluators' focal areas. Your goal is for the evaluators to say you look like a perfect fit for the criteria they are assessing (to the extent you can do so factually).

If you sell as part of a team where presales technical or industry experts get involved to convince the prospect's equivalent contingent of propeller-heads, it's even more important to know who the evaluators are and what their fields of evaluation are to be for this sale. Smart people on your presales team who hold a lot of specialist information in their heads can be the fastest points of failure when you let them run wild. Have you ever had one of these resources go down a rabbit hole you wished they'd avoided or been too transparent in telling a prospect what your company *doesn't* do very well? Who's responsible when they go off-message? We are, when we fail to brief them properly. If you're not scripting them on what to say and what to avoid on a customer call, these resources can easily go feral.

A way to keep them on the leash is to arrange to share roles in each sales call. You accomplish this by handing your evaluators over to your experts, and the experts drill into the individual evaluators' areas of focus:

- Your techxperts ask about the **reasons** the evaluation criteria have been formed and share stories of why these and other evaluation criteria have proven important to other customers you've served. This is a credible way of implanting ideas in the customer's mind about how they should weight their criteria—and you aim to focus them on those areas where you have a competitive advantage.

- Your techxperts discuss the ways in which these evaluation criteria typically **impact** other systems, processes, and people across the business, which can help you identify other evaluators or open up the customer's thought process if they've been approaching the project with a silo mentality when it really needs to be seen as an enterprisewide initiative.
- Your techxperts serve as gurus who share insights on what ideas other customers have taken on board and which **options** from your product or service portfolio work best. This establishes your credibility as a solution provider with an established track record plus additional value to add beyond the customer's original thinking. This is where reengineering their evaluation criteria can pull out the rug from under your competitors.

You might recognize these three topics from the center column in the PRECISION questioning model you read about in Chapter 4. In addition to its utility as a consultative questioning tool for solo sales calls, the PRECISION model has the added virtue of helping you manage double-headed meetings when you bring along your expert witnesses, product specialists, or subject matter experts (as you know, I call these *techxperts*). Give them the center square in each PRECISION row where they can use their deeper knowledge to impress the customer. You should open and close each PRECISION row and allow yourself time to watch your customer's body language and reactions as your techxperts handle their parts of the call. Evaluators aren't the ones who make the final decision to buy or not to buy, but they *are* the ones who decide if you're going to be on the starter's block and stay in the race after the marathon starts. So it pays to ask the people you meet what role they play in their company's decision process and how they plan to evaluate you against other options. If you don't ask, you won't know.

Decision Makers

Decision makers listen to the recommendations of the evaluators and so form an opinion about each vendor's strengths and weaknesses. The questions they ask and the capabilities they choose to grill you on may be informed by what the evaluators have dug up on you. Decision makers are usually senior in rank to the extent that the task of committing their company's funds to a vendor is something they own the budget and authority for.

Sometimes salespeople report being confused about who the final decision maker actually is because it looks like there are multiple players who serve in this capacity. This occurs when the evaluation committees are led by one or more project managers whose role is to coordinate everyone's efforts and facilitate consensus. These people may be from outside the prospect's organization chart: hired guns from industry bodies or independent third parties such as consultants, project management firms, or other prime contractors who are involved when your sale is a smaller part of a larger overarching initiative.

So how do you identify the ultimate decision maker? Ask. It shouldn't be a state secret. There is usually *one person* with the responsibility of saying that the decision to appoint you—and all the success or failure that follows this decision—was their call. That person is the one staking their reputation on this decision. Even in the most egalitarian of work cultures, it eventually comes down to one person who asks for everyone's recommendation and assurance before committing to buy from you. Follow the money to find whose budget is being spent, or look for the person in charge of the department that will be involved the most with your company after the contract is signed and the installation or implementation begins.

Evaluators are legion, and their interests are diverse. Decision makers are singular, and their interest usually boils down to the equation of risk versus capability. If they don't believe in you—if your social capital and business credentials don't add up in their book—even if the evaluators recommend you, the decision makers may go another way, especially if your competitors have bridged and bonded to them in your absence. You must know who casts the final vote and if they decide on logic or emotion!

Let me share an example from my own experience that echoes what top executives and sellers confirm about this. My team was working on a million-dollar deal to provide consulting and change management services into a prospect's national sales and marketing function. What we were recommending was visionary, and because it required the type of change best implemented from the inside, we were going to embed our staff into an on-site project office for half a year to keep everyone on track during the setup phase and remove the customer's risk of their people getting distracted and running out of steam.

When it came to evaluating the project feasibility and planning how to make it work, there were about 20 competing voices at the local, regional, and global levels. Some wanted the project to go ahead, some were against this office blazing a new trail, and others felt the staff they hired should "figure it out" on their own without help from us. Amid the din of voices, we identified four people in the hub at different levels of the business, and we won their vote. The evaluation process had been completed, a Mutual Project Plan (close plan) had been followed, and start dates were penciled in.

The final decision was referred to the chief executive officer, a person who was not in the hub. She had founded the company and rated respect, but over the years, she had estranged her managers with a mercurial nature that saw her micromanage some projects while acting vaguely on others. But where she chose to focus, she was a control nut, borne out of being extremely risk averse. Managers had learned to keep projects off her radar as much as possible lest she get involved. Still, due to the size of spending, on this occasion her formal role afforded her the right to release or deny the budget.

I'd met her only occasionally, so it came as a surprise when her office issued a memo that the contract signing would be a meeting she and I would hold in private with none of my supporters present.

Behind closed doors, she confirmed that her company was inclined to move ahead with my company, but only if we cut our price by 20 percent. Yet based on what I knew of her, I realized she wasn't really asking for a discount. Remember, she was a control nut, and on this occasion she wasn't close enough to the evaluation process, so she felt there was a degree of risk that she wanted to cushion. Apparently in her mind a discount of $200,000 would offset this risk.

This was one of those moments where your mind has to weigh alternatives in a matter of seconds. I regarded my project plan and pricing as lean but effective. Based on what I knew of how cautious this decision maker was, if I granted a discount, it could call into question the whole integrity of my proposal, give rise to claims of overcharging, which might erode all the trust built over many months selling to this company. Based on what I knew of how little patience she had for detail, if I tried to explain how every cog in the machine was necessary in my price, I could easily lose her interest. I realized her request was based on emotion and not logic, so it needed to be answered by emotion, simply and without fanfare.

I repositioned in my seat to adopt an open pose (leaning forward, palms up, constant eye contact, nothing to hide), and I told her that there was no fat in our proposal, that the project was indeed very risky, but that every dollar was accounted for to reduce that risk and bring the results in on target and on time. I said I was confident our joint teams could deliver the outcomes. I then caught her gaze squarely and offered my personal guarantee. That was all she needed to hear, and she signed for our full price using the pen I pushed across the table with a reassuring nod. The meeting lasted a total of 10 minutes. If I had panicked and dropped my price, the deal would have gone nowhere.

What do we learn from this story? If I hadn't known in advance who the decision maker was going to be, and if I hadn't asked people how she typically made decisions, it would have been impossible to know with certainty how to respond in the moment of truth. Sales can turn in your favor or veer away from you in an instant as a result of such discussions. So identify where the buck stops, what they're most looking for, and be equal to it.

Approvers

Approvers may be a final step in the decision process, but not always. If the decision maker owns the budget and is trusted to make this commitment, there may be no approver required. If the decision is politically charged, if the budget is higher than the decision maker's clearance level and needs to go to a higher authority (for example, the board of directors), or if the decision maker is a new hire, under scrutiny, or about to leave the company, then an approver may be appointed who reserves the right to review, approve, or veto the decisions made by the decision maker.

Usually approvers offer a simple blessing and rubber-stamp what the decision maker wants to do. But sometimes they can change the entire outcome. For example, a multitude of salespeople cite cases in which they entered a deal where it became clear that their competitors had been present for months already, had gained the support of many, and were dominating everyone's calendars to leave little space for other contenders to have a real shot at winning the business. So these enterprising late entrants don't play on that turf. Instead, they map where the final approval resides, and they concentrate their efforts connecting their executives to these people (peer-to-peer selling) to discuss "future business" as part of a long-term account strategy. By so doing, they build their credentials and social capital under the radar where it doesn't look like an attempt to disrupt any current decisions. When their discussions rub up against enough of the approvers' current needs and future agendas, the approvers may wistfully say they wished a project existed that would allow them to move this budding relationship forward. To which the sellers reply: "Well, actually it's funny you should say that . . ."

Using this approach, their competitors might confidently win the evaluation and formal decision process, only to be vetoed at the final mile by an approver who invites the decision maker to take "a closer look" at a different provider—for "strategic reasons." It's a fine line for approvers to walk because if they don't handle it well, it can come across as though the project leaders got it wrong or as though they don't appreciate the weeks and months of effort the evaluation team already expended. It can quickly become political, and this is why it's a return volley best delivered as high up the tree as you can get.

Rank hath its privileges.

However people feel about the goalposts being moved, they're sent a clear message all the same about what outcome they need to engineer. Accordingly, you see the decision date shift, and new evaluation criteria get injected into the mix, weighted to favor certain criteria so the decision is legitimized. In this way, approvers can be powerful allies to cultivate when you know who they are, opportunity by opportunity.

Now that you understand the three roles people play in the decision process, you might want to add a level of greater detail to your Influence Map by writing the role each person plays under their name and title on the map. This can be abbreviated shorthand as shown in Figure 9.4.

Evaluator   Decision   Approver
Maker

Figure 9.4: Descriptive Role Labels for Individuals on the Influence Map

In Chapter 10, we'll discuss how to assess each person's *allegiance* to you and your *signal strength* with them, as we continue our examination of the Social Capital stage of the Sales Expansion Loop.

Align to Key Stakeholders

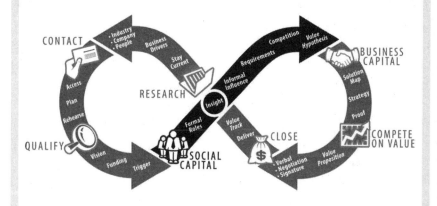

The Sales Expansion Loop: Social Capital—Competition and Value

COMPETITION AND INFLUENCE

In every project, the people in your target opportunity will either stay on the fence and let others choose who to buy from or they will take sides and shape the outcome. Some will want change; others will want things to stay as they are. Some will want an external supplier; others will want to build an internal solution. Some will want you to win; others will want your competitor to win.

Allegiance

When you're selling, you need to know which way people are leaning so you can direct them in your favor. You must question where their allegiance lies and decide what you can do to bring the key decision influencers to your side when votes are cast. To help communicate, plan, and track their progress in building this aspect of social capital, top sellers grade the level of allegiance exhibited by each person they are selling to in a target opportunity. The labels they use are descriptive of each person's proclivity to help them win in the specific opportunity they are pursuing at the time.

Let's look at the most common descriptions, and as we do so think about the largest sale you have in your pipeline right now and decide how you might describe each of the people you're selling to. After you decide which labels best describe these people, I'll delve into the relationship strategies you can apply with each type.

We're going to look at people who you might choose to label as resistors, enemies, neutral people, supporters, and mentors.

Resistors

Some people are **resistors** to change. They aren't so much against you and your solution as much as they are against *any change* being made to the status quo. Maybe they've seen their company undergo so much change that they feel fatigued and just want a season of calm. Maybe they're laggards who are the last ones to adopt any new trend. Maybe they're risk averse and like to wait for new products and services to become mainstream (and less expensive) before they jump on the bandwagon. Maybe they were raised to be frugal and prefer to repair existing investments, happy to put up with inconvenience if it saves them a dollar. Maybe they played a role in a previous decision, and they believe any change might be interpreted as a reversal of their past choices. Maybe they've been so busy working with their head down that they have never looked up from their bunker to see that there are now better ways to get the job done. Maybe they fear what your solution might mean to people's jobs if it includes the possibility of outsourcing or automation.

To deal with resistors from the outside of the company they belong in is a tall order. You're going to need help from the inside to understand the cultural appetite for change and have someone help build a case to change the resistors' minds. For this reason, top sellers who identify individuals as resistors resist the urge of selling to them directly until they've first built an adequate support base with other people from the customer's organization who the resistors respect, who can help nudge them along the road to acceptance. This is really an exercise in change management, and it is necessary only if you realize that if a specific resistor doesn't get on the bus, your whole project might jackknife.

Dr. A. J. Schuler, PsyD, is an expert in leadership and organizational change.[1] A graduate of the Wharton School of Business, Dr. Schuler served as the operations director for the global human resources consulting firm Talent Plus, and he has coached change across different cultures in businesses as varied as Sony, Ritz-Carlton, Pepperidge Farm, Godiva Chocolates, and Bovis Construction. Germaine to our discussion here, his insights offer eight reasons why resistors dig in their heels, and what to do about it:

1. **The risk of change is seen as greater than the risk of standing still.**
Making a change requires a kind of leap of faith: you decide to move

in the direction of the unknown on the promise that things will be better. But you have no proof. Taking that leap of faith is risky, and people will take active steps toward the unknown only if they genuinely believe—and perhaps more important, feel—that the risks of standing still are greater than those of moving in a new direction. Making a change is all about managing risk. If you're making the case for change, be sure to set out in stark, truthful terms why you believe the situation favors change. Use numbers whenever you can so the rational mind is engaged as much as the emotional mind.

2. **Resistors identify with the old ways.** As a social species, we like to remain connected to those who taught us. If you ask people in an organization to do things in a new way, you set yourself at odds with all the hardwired, emotional connections they retain for those who taught them the old ways and the successes they achieved using those ways—and that's no trivial obstacle to overcome. At the very least, as you craft your change message, you should make statements that honor the work and contributions of those who brought such success to the organization in the past because on a very human but seldom articulated level, your audience will feel asked to betray their former mentors (whether those people remain in the organization or not). A little diplomacy at the outset can stave off a lot of resistance.

3. **Resistors have no role models for the new activity.** It's great to be a visionary, but most people don't operate that way, and merely communicating the new solution is not enough. For most people, seeing is believing. Even customer site visits and case studies may fail to impress resistors because these examples were "not invented here." The closer you can offer these from inside their own industry or other parts of their own company, the better. Some resistors may not convert until you complete pilot programs that work out the kinks with people they know and trust, citing their achievements and candid opinions. The goal is to move the resistors from "There's no need!" to "How can we get it done?"

4. **Resistors fear they lack the competence to change.** This is a fear people will seldom admit. But sometimes, change in organizations necessitates changes in skills, and some people will feel that they won't be able to make the transition. In most cases, their fears will be unfounded, easily solved with effective communication and training. Town hall information events are popular for presenting the rationale for change and showing how people will learn the specifics of what will be required of them, from whom, and when. In this way, you can minimize fear by showing how people are not expected to change overnight and that provision has been made for them to gain competence throughout the change process. Then you have to deliver.

5. **Resistors feel overloaded and overwhelmed.** When you're introducing change, be aware of fatigue as a factor in keeping people from moving forward, even if they are telling you they believe in the wisdom of your idea. If an organization has been through a lot of upheaval, people may resist change just because they are tired and overwhelmed, perhaps at precisely the time when more radical change is most needed! That's when you need to do two things: reemphasize the risk scenario that forms the rationale for change and be very generous with praise when the resistors start to migrate their thinking. When you reemphasize the risk scenario, you're activating people's fears, the basic fight-or-flight response we all possess. But that's not enough, and fear can produce its own fatigue. You've got to "catch people doing things right" and praise that progress.

6. **Resistors have a healthy skepticism.** It's important to remember that few worthwhile changes are conceived in their final, best form at the outset. Healthy skeptics perform an important social function: to vet the change idea or process so that it can be improved upon along the road to becoming reality. So listen to your resistors, and pay attention because some percentage of what they have to say will prompt genuine improvements to your approach (even if

some of the criticism you will hear will be based more on fear and anger than substance).

7. **Resistors fear hidden agendas.** If you seek to sell change into an organization, not only can you expect to encounter resentment for upsetting the established order (and for thinking you know better than everyone else) but you may also find the motives of those who support you come into question by resistors. What's the solution? Showing that your solution is being considered for the right reasons and not for factional advantage. Being open with information and communication. Not overreacting to accusations and provocations. Exhibiting good faith and genuine interest in the greater good of the organization. If your solution implies a reduction in the workforce, then be transparent about that, and show an orderly process for outplacement and in-house retraining. Avoid the drip-drip-drip of bad news coming out in stages, or through indirect communication or rumor.

8. **Resistors feel the change threatens their sense of identity.** Sometimes change on the job gets right to a person's sense of identity. When factory workers begin to do less with their hands as automation sees them watching a monitor, they can lose their sense of being craftspeople—the very thing that attracted them to the job in the first place. When medics see decisions about prescriptions and treatments shift to the insurance companies and managed care organizations, these professionals may feel they've lost the ability to do what they thought best for patients. It's surprisingly easy for people to feel the intrinsic rewards that brought them to a particular line of work will be lost with the change. And in some cases, they may be absolutely right. The only answer is to help them understand the new rewards that come with a new work process or how their own underlying sense of mission and values can still be realized under the new way of operating.

Enemies

Some people are **enemies** to you and your solution. Beyond the resistors who don't want to see *anyone's* new solution put in place, the enemies have decided *you* should lose the deal. Sometimes they take this stance because they are your competitors' mentors, and they are working behind the scenes to help them win by making you look bad because something they perceive in a rival's offering advances their agenda better than you do. Sometimes they are simply bigots for your competitors' solutions due to past positive experiences with them or due to negative experiences with your brand. The roots of these opinions may have grown because your competitors were the first to bridge and bond to them, perhaps beating you by mere days. At other times their opinions may be deep seated, decades old, and out of date—part of an emotional embalming process that has left them rigid in their views.

When enemies are operating *overtly*, they're the ones who torpedo your presentation by asking questions about customer sites where your company has experienced a troubled implementation or customer satisfaction problems. They make mountains out of molehills. They throw the curveballs and sling the mud. They speak of your competitors as though they're the gold standard, and they demand that you justify yourself in comparison. They set meetings that are canceled at late notice, publish the wrong meeting times, or delegate what should be important interviews with you to their minions without adequate briefing. They ensure that your final presentation is cut short or that it is scheduled to coincide with everyone's after-lunch sugar low on a long day of vendor reviews that bleed everyone into anonymity, while ensuring that your rivals are allowed special dispensation to be the sole presentation the following morning when everyone is fresh and attentive (and you can be sure the competition will be coached based on people's reactions to you and others the previous day).

When enemies function *covertly*, they might present themselves as your biggest allies. "Show me your presentation before taking it to others, so I can help you fine-tune it . . ." say some. "I'll send you to the people who matter most. Trust me . . ." say others. These are common tactics that allow your rivals to steal your thunder or that see your resources depleted in meaningless and costly tangents while your competitors seem to get all the shortcuts and lucky breaks. This isn't coincidence, and you should follow your nose if you think something smells fishy. As a rule, you can flush out covert enemies by asking them to do things for you that supporters or mentors would readily provide. If you get a lot of verbal commitment but they never quite get around to delivering the goods, it's a safe bet their heart just isn't in it. Actions speak louder than words.

Once identified, if you want to play the game of counterespionage, enemies are a good way to lull your competitors into a false sense of security by feeding them misleading information about what you're planning to present and propose and who else you're talking with. As Sun-tzu wrote:

> *All warfare is based on deception. Hence, when able to attack, we must seem unable; when mobilizing our forces, we must seem inactive; when we are near, we must make the enemy believe we are far away; when far away, we must make him believe we are near. Hold out baits to entice the enemy. Feign disorder, and crush him.* (Art of War *1:18–20*)

You have to make a conscious decision to put a fence around the enemy (and your chance of success improves when guided by a mentor you trust), and you have to manage the information that goes in and out of the gate in this fence. Meanwhile, you proceed with other people who offer more fertile ground to plant seeds, and keep this activity (and the content of those conversations) off the enemy's radar.

Neutral People

Neutral people haven't made up their mind if they support you or not, or they don't really care what solution is selected. They may be content to follow the decisions made by others, or they may subscribe to the idea that all suppliers are the same. If being dispassionate is their default position—the typical approach they apply to any purchasing project—they're unlikely to pose a risk by staying neutral, and you're unlikely to gain much benefit by expending time and resources trying to nudge them off the fence. Such battles don't need to be won.

But if there's a risk they won't remain neutral forever (as a result of being educated or wooed by other parties), you have to weigh how helpful they will be in your camp as supporters or how damaging they could be as enemies to you if they start to favor your competitors. If they are in the hub or spokes of influence, it's desirable to see them become a voice for your solution, and this is treated below when discussing supporters and mentors. If they are on the rim of influence, it won't matter how they feel about you.

Supporters

Supporters *prefer* your solution to other options, but they have less of a vested interest in pushing an outcome than the mentors do. When asked for their opinion, they will vote in your favor, especially when they see others doing the same. The advantage of having supporters prefer your solution is that many voices can influence what the collective does. A good bridging and bonding meeting, a stellar presentation that leaves people buzzing, and/or a spirited discussion over lunch that hits all the right points can all turn people from having no opinion to giving you every indication that they're on your side.

This can be a benefit to you as a seller, but it can also lead you to think you have more people in your corner than you can actually count on when the chips are down. Your competitors (and their mentors) will be actively bridging and bonding just the same as you are, and their first target in the war for votes may be to turn neutral people into their own supporters, and then to convert those who support you. If the tide of popular opinion should shift, supporters may swing their vote. It's nothing personal. But when this happens the support you *think* you have can evaporate, leaving you grossly overestimating your chances of winning the deal.

Have you ever committed a sale to your forecast only to see your competitor eating your lunch? We all have. What reason do we most often give our manager when they ask, "What happened?" Rarely do we commit career suicide and admit "I was outsold." More often we ascribe our failure to "something political" going on. The truth is a combination of both reasons: "I was outsold because my competitor was more politically agile than I was."

The danger of supporters swinging their vote underscores the need to avoid complacency. I've seen salespeople fill their Influence Map with lots of people who "like" them, will have coffee with them, or will always answer a phone call from them. But the reality is that these people do no less for the competitors. It's *their job* to meet vendors and get the best from them. When I see reps rate people as supporters, I want to know what it is that demonstrates real support for their solution as opposed to these people just being friendly? It's frightening how many times good salespeople can't tell the difference (or don't want to). So ask yourself these questions:

- Do I know *why* they support me?
- Do they see me as the *sole source* of this differentiation?
- Do they announce to *others* in their company how they feel about my solution?
- Have they turned other people from neutral to supporter?
- Is their opinion firm or fickle?

To consolidate their support and immunize them from sliding to a competitor's camp, try sitting down with each of your supporters and cataloging the answers to the questions above. Ask them to do things for you. You might consider putting all supporters in a webinar or workshop with your company where other people in their business or industry vouch for your solution, thus reinforcing that the support they give you is a safe bet. The success of the old marketing slogan "Nobody ever got fired for buying IBM" is a potent example of how that company tapped people's need to identify with the herd and so won their hearts and minds. Herd mentality is the principle upon which most supporters operate.

Building Supporters: A Social Capital Experiment

To test the ideas in this chapter, I ran a controlled experiment on Facebook. There's a strong correlation to what you see on Internet sites like Facebook and LinkedIn and the way popular opinion is forged in a corporate community. This is because the choices people make on social sites to "Like," "un-Like," or "Talk About" a topic are based entirely on influence from others and the personal preferences that the sharing of news and opinions can create. There is no hierarchical rank or authority to force any top-down compliance, so it's a perfect microcosm to illustrate how influential opinion moves the masses.

For this experiment I set out to bring a newly written science fiction novel to market over the 2011 to 2012 holiday period (deemed the most difficult time of year to get noticed). At the time, publishers like Titan Books in London and Random House Worlds in New York told me the market was experimenting with cross-platform properties that told aspects of the same tale in book, videogame, television, film, or "augmented reality" formats (something we're likely to see more of as devices like Google Glass start placing images in front of our view of the real world). The television drama *Defiance* is one example of this kind of multimedia play, where viewers could experience the characters' expanded world by playing a videogame to explore their backstory and side adventures between the airing dates of episodes.

The idea appealed to me. I understood the power of multichannel marketing from my days consulting to Siebel, a pioneer in the concept that the more places a customer can experience your brand, the stronger it resonates, the stickier it gets, and the more likely they are to buy.

To launch the book quickly, I hired "speed author" Alan Dean Foster as my coauthor in producing a manuscript for a book I called *Endworlds: Echoes of Worlds Past* (ReadBooks, 2011). I was always impressed with the work Alan did novelizing the first *Star Wars* movie for George Lucas, along with his work with Gene Roddenberry on the original *Star Trek* screenplay and dozens of novels since for the *Alien, Transformers,* and *Riddick* franchises, among others. After a year of writing and editing, *Endworlds* was given a synchronous release on Facebook, Amazon.com, iTunes, Barnes & Noble, and other outlets worldwide.

I didn't have the budget to add a multimedia television show or videogame, so instead I created a way for readers of the book to immerse themselves into the world Alan and I had written by treating the book as if the characters' adventure was unfolding in the real world, in real time. An example is a Qantas flight between Japan and Sydney in which part of the fuselage blew out in midair, forcing an emergency landing in Manila. In the real world, the cause remained somewhat unexplained, but in my book it was two of the characters who were behind that accident during a skirmish with bad guys in the hold of the plane. Dozens of similar headlines and Google links were added to the footnotes in an attempt to suspend disbelief that a purely fictional tale might actually be true.

Knowing my competition would be all forms of cross-platform entertainment, I applied a process I named "reality literature" to include a substory of puzzles and ciphers the book's main characters were trying to solve and invited readers to visit a website I had built where readers could collaborate to solve these puzzles. The website and Facebook page leaked the idea that the puzzles pointed to actual GPS locations where objects of alien technology were buried. The characters in the book needed these found to advance their cause.

Before people actually went to dig at these locations around the world, I had to send a team of people out to actually plant brass and crystal artifacts at these sites in America, England, India, and Australia. Fortunately I've lived and worked in a lot of places over the years, and I was able to call in a few favors to achieve this feat. The book's sequel will include each of these readers' real world adventures to find these objects, thus fiction drives reality, and reality gets written into the next work of fiction.

On top of the book, the puzzle site, and the "game layer" in the real world, I added a soundtrack for the book which was composed in England and recorded in the Czech Republic by a 70-piece symphony orchestra. While this was being mastered at Abbey Road Studios in London, we embedded "Easter eggs" of Morse code that revealed the GPS coordinates of the buried artifacts, or which showed photos of Babylonian numerals for the latitude and longitude points when the music track was played through a spectrograph like iTunes Visualizer. These tracks were embedded into the chapters of the e-book and also released as a stand-alone album.

All of this was achieved on a modest budget and without any publisher or film studio support. My goal was to prove that an unheralded, no-name, self-published e-book with associated multimedia assets could achieve mindshare against more established film, television, and literary franchises, such as *Harry Potter*, *Twilight*, and *The Hunger Games*, that were already riding high from millions of dollars being pumped into their marketing. I wanted to show that a David could beat a Goliath.

As sellers, is it any different when we dig into our bag of products, case studies, customer testimonials, media coverage, and other "cross platform" tools to make our proposition sticky and memorable enough to combat a much larger rival that expects to use its dominance to wipe the floor with us?

Did my experiment work?

I set a lofty goal to collect 10,000 Facebook fans within two months of launching the e-book, solely by applying the principles of bridging and bonding that you've read about in this chapter as well as Chapters 8 and 9. What was learned can be summarized as follows.

At first it was slow going and disheartening. People didn't respond. But this was to be expected. When you're selling a new idea, people avoid being the first to support it if there's no prebuilt following,

, herd, or community to join. As salespeople, we understand this. After all, showing new prospects that there's already a party going on is the very reason why we use testimonials from past customers.

To show this was indeed a party worth joining, I needed to engineer a sense of community so like-minded people would relate to the book and start to talk about it. Inexpensive Facebook ads targeted specific demographics with customized messages designed to appeal. I tested the water with sidebar ads in different choices of content, color, messaging, and headline. You can do the same sort of thing with targeted LinkedIn and e-mail marketing campaigns to new prospects.

I monitored which ads hit their mark with the largest communities, then dropped anything that didn't create buzz. This was tested every few days. I quickly learned there's no point flogging a dead horse.

The corollary to selling is that it's important to know what issues, drivers, triggers, and headlines are topical and how these can ebb and flow over time. Keep your ears open, and then paint yourself as the enabler of the most popular goals so crowd momentum lifts you up as the standard to flock to.

It remains unclear who the first people were to start the landslide. One night I went to bed with six followers (thinking the experiment was going to be a failure). The next morning I awoke to more than 3,000 fans of which a massive 72 percent were actively talking about the product to their friends. Where conversion rates of 4 percent are deemed good for this medium, 72 percent is almost unheard of.

I kept fueling this by keeping the Facebook page updated with new headlines, comments, anecdotes, and invitations designed to keep the product fresh and newsworthy. With so much competing for their attention, my message had to repeat regularly enough for it to cut through and be heard. It's the same when you're managing any sale. You must choose the right message and hammer it home again and again until you're seen as embodying something unique and special that people in the customer's organization will relate to and share with each other.

Using this approach, by the end of 14 intensive days of constant course corrections and avid blogging, this e-book had gained my target of 10,000 fans. I was amazed how quickly this was achieved. Then seasonal competition destroyed this mindshare: Hanukkah arrived, followed by Christmas and other year-end activities that dominated the business and social landscape. The number of people talking about the product plummeted 70 percent over the December 2011 holidays. As a sales corollary, it was like thinking you had 10 people inside a customer organization whose support you could count on, only to see 7 of them turn their backs on you. All that progress blown away in one week!

But the 30 percent who remained did so because they were truly hooked. Facebook told me that far from being transients who hit the fan page once or twice, these individuals had visited the e-book's Facebook site more than 20 times each as it was updated with fresh content. They were solving puzzles on the *Endworlds* website and commenting on the soundtrack. I could see which people had many friends on Facebook, so I created a discussion forum for each area of interest to tap their referral network even deeper. The corollary for selling is obvious.

At the end of Week 8, the e-book had 170,000 fans and 50 percent of these were telling their friends about it. This was a higher fan reaction than most novels on the *New York Times* top 10 bestseller list,[2] and it blew away the Facebook fandom of many other book, television, and film franchises that were popular at the time.[3] Such was the buzz around *Endworlds* that mainstream media, print, and online editorials started to review it, and it hit the number 3 spot on Barnes & Noble's top 20 enhanced e-books, just behind Stephen King's *11/22/63* and JRR Tolkien's *The Hobbit*. It was a meteoric rise for a book nobody saw coming, peaking and holding steady at 250,000 fans.

I don't know how long the Facebook site will stay at those levels, but at the time of submitting the manuscript for *Target Opportunity*

Selling, these followers are holding steady at www.facebook.com/longcoats, and Hollywood has asked to know more.

The experiment proves that when you need to build a support base in an environment where nobody knows or values either you or your product and your message, *anyone* can build a following in as little as two months of part-time effort, even against tough competition. This is incredibly good news if you've ever felt your competitors had all the mindshare in a deal. Forget what came before you arrived on the scene. Ask instead what imprint you want to leave on that landscape, and set out to make it so. You *can* change your stars.

Whether you're selling to people face-to-face or going viral on the Internet, at the heart of the action is your ability to generate social capital that creates its own buzz and branding around you. To create this, you need to know the right topics and craft the right messages to the right people (it's difficult to do this if you don't put in the effort to do the right *research* at the start of the Sales Expansion Loop). Once you have buzz building, then you map which communities of people are connected by a common interest, and then you say or do something topical to get the people in these groups talking about you. Make sure the few people who first champion you gain a platform to speak up and share something positive with others.

Give something away for free (it might be a webinar presentation, video, brochure, trial demo, or something else this community values). Give them a reason to like you, and let the weight of popular opinion build into a landslide.

As you do so, neutral parties will become supporters, and some of these may turn into mentors. This is how social capital is built from scratch. Whether you're connecting to people via LinkedIn, a blogsite, face-to-face, or some other way that motivates people in your target community, you can use these principles to your benefit in every sale, even when nobody in the customer organization has ever heard of you before.

That explains the principles for how supporters can be built. Let's now look at mentors.

Mentors

Mentors believe in you, your brand, your company, your reputation, and your product. They want you to win, and they will share information and open doors for you.

Their reasons for mentoring you might be transparent to everyone in their company: they simply believe your solution or team is the better choice. They have worked with you before and trust the quality of your work. They've worked with your competitor before and don't want to repeat or continue that experience.

At other times their reasons for supporting you may be less public. They feel it's time for a regime change of suppliers to "keep people honest." By shepherding a different solution across the finish line, they change where the project will be managed from, which helps certain people in their business to consolidate their power or gain new career experience. The inclusion of certain capabilities in the final requirements list means their department might benefit downstream without having to contribute their own budget. Or they enjoy a business, social, or personal relationship with someone on your team.

Whatever their motivation, they see you as the vehicle for it. Beyond mere words of support, they are prepared to act in your favor, to steer people's preferences, to point out the competitor flaws behind closed doors, around the watercooler, and in the hallway discussions that are the petri dishes where opinions spread like a virus.

If they don't mind others knowing what side of the fence they sit on, they'll sell your solutions in your absence. If they're prickly people that others try to stay on the right side of, they might even make it clear what an unpopular decision it will be to choose anyone but you.

Yet sometimes they play their cards close to their chest so they don't appear to be taking sides. They might listen to your presentations and then go into detail about where you're deficient, why they couldn't support you unless you fixed certain things, and where they want to see more emphasis. At first blush this might come across as extremely negative. But when you step back from the emotion and

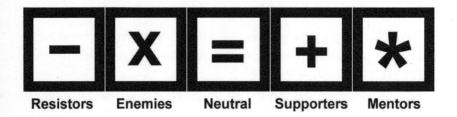

Figure 10.1: Descriptive Allegiance Labels for Individuals on the Influence Map

look at what they're really telling you, it might become apparent that they're drawing you a treasure map of how to win. True mentors will always point you in the right direction no matter how friendly or gruff they seem.

Search for mentor candidates. Cultivate them. Leverage them.

Now that you understand what the labels mean for each person's allegiance, you might add this information to their names on a chart, using the simple symbols shown in Figure 10.1.

Signal Strength

When drawing your Influence Map, it's helpful to show who you've been spending your time with. Salespeople in our research revealed a variety of ways for doing so.

Some simply had a box that gave a numerical score for the number of meetings held with each customer contact—and they were quick to point out that they counted only those meetings where the sales opportunity was discussed. Numbering only the opportunity-specific conversations prevented overconfidence that could have easily occurred if they had known these people for a long time while working the account. They might have had 50 meetings with a person over time, but if none of these were recent or helped their current sale advance to the next step, why count them?

Other salespeople say the number of meetings is wholly unimportant to track at the opportunity level. What matters the most, they suggest, is the content and quality of those meetings. Rather than track time spent with each contact, they track how the level of contact is boosting their *signal strength* in the deal. Questions they ask to determine this include these:

- Are these meetings superficial or going deeper? How deep?
- Does the customer say my value comes across "loud and clear"?
- Are they "broadcasting" my signal to others?
- Are they opening up on issues, concerns, logic, and feelings?
- Are they asking for copies of my material to share with others?
- Are my meetings yielding new insights to them or to me?

The measure of signal strength might be likened to the bars on a mobile phone. When your battery is charged and when the place in which you are standing is unobstructed and free from interference, you get a better quality of conversation. As a measure of social capital, top sellers like to track how clear their signal is with each person. They use this indicator to examine who they've been spending most time with and to assess if key people are being covered appropriately. Five criteria are used.

1. If they have never met the person, they leave a blank box signifying **no contact**. If a person with no contact resides in the hub or spokes of influence, it reveals a significant risk in the coverage plan for that opportunity.
2. If they have only talked superficially by **phone** (or only by e-mail exchanges), the person rates one bar on the signal chart.
3. If they've had at least one face-to-face **meeting** with the person, the person rates two bars.

It helps to see where you've only contacted people by phone and where you've been in person. Some salespeople report having brilliant first meetings in which they solved all the world's problems and the customer loved them. These still only rate two bars—if the meeting was so good, the person will invite you back. *Then* you rate that person with a better score.

4. When you gain that repeat audience and can say you've met **multiple** times, it's a good indicator of interest, so you can claim three bars of signal strength. Yet even after meeting someone three, six, or nine times, you can still find yourself having hollow conversations where it seems that no matter what you try, the person won't open up and let you inside the kimono.

5. That's the difference in scoring the full four bars on the signal strength icon. When you find yourself having **in-depth** conversations with your contact; when that person truly meets you halfway; when the person gives full disclosure on his or her needs, fears, and vision; when the person treats you like a consultant—these are signs that your signal strength with this person is high. You're getting through.

To avoid a common misnomer, note that you don't need to have multiple meetings to achieve an in-depth conversation. It's not uncommon to see people on an Influence Map jump from having one meeting to an in-depth relationship, bypassing the multiple label altogether because the conversation is immediately rich and meaningful, and it will help you win.

Now that you understand what each label means in terms of your signal strength with each person, you might attach one of the labels to each person's name on your Influence Map, using symbols as shown in Figure 10.2.

When you put formal role, allegiance, and signal strength together on an Influence Map, it creates a summary profile of the individuals. This paints a picture about your relationship with them and the

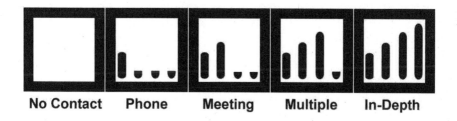

No Contact   **Phone**   **Meeting**   **Multiple**   **In-Depth**

Figure 10.2: Descriptive Signal Strength Labels for Individuals on the Influence Map

people around them. Salespeople who chart the organization this way try to keep it simple. They know that all the detailed information on each person's likes, dislikes, birthdays, spouses, past purchases, and so forth will be held in a customer database (if they ever need to look it up), so there are no prizes to be had from cluttering an opportunity plan with that type of data. They try to keep things as uncluttered as possible, hence boiling down the information about people to the essential basics.

One sales manager created a PowerPoint image like the one shown in Figure 10.3 and sent it to a self-inking stamp supplier. Next day she gave all her reps an inexpensive stamping device that left an outline of boxes with blank spaces inside for writing (a) the person's name and job title above (b) boxes for the symbols that explain the contact's formal role, allegiance, and signal strength. This made it easy for her salespeople to run a deal review. They would stand in front of a flipchart, then draw an Influence Map of concentric circles to show the hub, spokes, and rim. After dissecting this wheel into wedges and labeling these for each main department, they stamped the boxes directly onto the page (or onto yellow sticky notes they could easily reposition) at coordinates where people intersected the department and each level of influence. Then they filled in each person's profile information as shown in Figure 10.3.

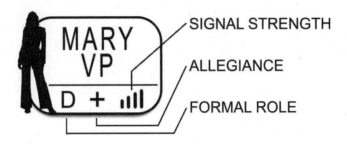

Figure 10.3: A Personal Profile on the Influence Map

Whether you stamp it, hand-draw it, or use PowerPoint, Visio, or some other sales software to chart it, an Influence Map gives a helpful overview of your social capital, where its iconography and shorthand can abbreviate how you share your plan with peers and partners. A picture paints a thousand words, and having a common language brings better understanding of where you stand in the deal. You can then spend less time trying to agree where you are and invest more time planning how to get where you need to be.

VALUE HYPOTHESIS

After they've developed adequate social capital and credibility with those who wield the greatest influence, sellers who sit in the top 20 percent of the performance curve report a step where they pause to "throw around some ideas" with the prospect. They describe this as a **Value Hypothesis** step. Note that unlike the better-known "value proposition," this has nothing to do with the provision of calculations, formulas, or business cases.

The word *hypothesis* comes from a Greek word that means "to suppose." It is used by scientists when they put forward an "educated guess," then prescribe a method to confirm or disprove it.

This step is where you look at the customer's problems and ideas, and you have a discussion in general terms about how your company might add value based on your capabilities and the work you've completed for other customers in the past. In essence you're saying this:

> Based on past work with other customers, we can certainly help you. We've done this before at ABC [examples]. My guess is that in your business [based on industry, size, need], the results we can get for you would look like XYZ [case study or impact measure]. I'd like to talk with your people and test these ideas. From there we can put firm numbers into our proposition. Can we agree on a way to do that?

You probably wouldn't say all of that in one breath, but by the end of an exploratory meeting, this is the message you want to deliver. The utility of a Value Hypothesis is threefold:

1. It builds the customer's confidence that you have answers worth exploring together.
2. It further rationalizes why it's a good idea to network you to other stakeholders.
3. It reinforces the value of following the Mutual Project Plan you authored—through which you gain a greater measure of control over the decision process.

As you move around the Sales Expansion Loop, the Value Hypothesis may expand based on who you meet, what they tell you, and what issues matter to the most influential people. Always keep a record of what individuals share about their vision and the problems they need solved.

Gathering these insights in a discussion about your Value Hypothesis is relatively easy because if you handle it correctly the conversation is nonthreatening. You aren't trying to convince them about anything—you're not deemed to be *selling* yet. At this stage, all you're doing is drawing flowcharts, circles, and arrows on sheets of paper and whiteboards as you explore and test some ideas together. Through this you aim to help people open up and share important information, especially in response to your application of the PRECISION Questions.

You'll need this information later when you actually *do* present a full *value proposition* and business case, linking back to everything in the hypothesis they revealed about their needs and how they measure it. This paints your ultimate solution as something you proved together—an idea they already have co-ownership of. This can make all the difference as you get closer to the finish line.

Chapter 11

Sell Your Solution

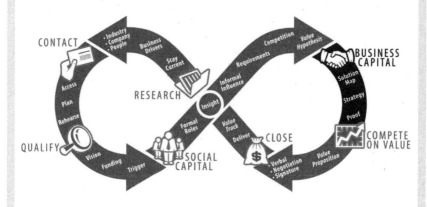

The Sales Expansion Loop: Business Capital

Having completed the previous steps in the Sales Expansion Loop, you now hold an abundance of insight into the people, issues, and competitors that make up the topography of your sale. You know most people's opinions, biases, and allegiances, and they should regard you as a credible player they could see themselves being in business with.

Perhaps most important, if you've completed the previous stages correctly, the customer and you will be in sync; you won't be trying to close the deal before they're ready and able to commit. This means your forecast will be more bankable with less slippage.

If the preceding phase of the Sales Expansion Loop was about selling yourself by building your social capital, networking, and connecting to the people with highest influence, this next phase is where you pull together all the information you've collected and finally put an offer on the table by ticking three interconnected boxes: Sell Your Solution (this chapter), Form a Competitive Strategy (Chapter 12), and Establish Your Proof (Chapter 13).

The Solution phase we'll discuss in *this* chapter is when you list the customer's evaluation criteria, decide if you can win the sale if the battle is fought on that landscape, and define exactly what product or service in your portfolio best fits their needs.

MAPPING THE CUSTOMER'S CRITERIA AND YOUR SOLUTION

If you believe the criteria were written to favor another supplier, you have three decisions to make:

1. You can stay in the game, do nothing about changing the criteria, and hope your value, brand, product, people, or price will land the deal.
2. You can try to modify the evaluation criteria to favor your strengths and shift the advantage to your company.

3. You might withdraw from a rigged race and save the cost of what would otherwise be spent in the weeks or months ahead.

If you continue to engage, you'll decide if the best solution to put on the table is one of the preconfigured products your company offers. Pricing will be straightforward based on the scale of the customer's usage and the fees your finance manager, marketing team, or product managers have predetermined.

If the customer's need is unique, you may need to talk with others in your company to decide what you should be offering. Most large companies employ specialists who have an encyclopedic knowledge of their products and different ways customers are using them to solve specific problems. They will need to be properly briefed by you on what *Problems* and *Risks* the customer is facing; what *Consequences* they seek to avoid if delays occur; how different departments or business functions are *Impact points*; and what *Ideas* and *Options* the customer is contemplating. You see PRECISION at play in the italicized words. See how useful those questions become as the sale advances?

It's always helpful to review any Trigger Map you created when deciding which products, services, or accessories are going to be relevant to the customer. The techxperts in your company should be able to help you decide what your solution should be, and they can give advice about where third-party products or services might be applied to complete or boost the offer. Their thinking can be diagrammed in what is called a *Solution Map*, an example of which is shown in Figure 11.1. Pricing will be unique in these cases and therefore difficult for a procurement manager to commoditize and compare.

It's relatively easy to extrapolate your Trigger Map onto a Solution Map you can share with the customer—and you *should* share it with them. You do this by summarizing the **Key Issues** that appear from your analysis, listing them by department or by the name of the person most affected. These issues can then be summarized into a list of real **Needs** that should be in line with what each person you've

SOLUTION MAP

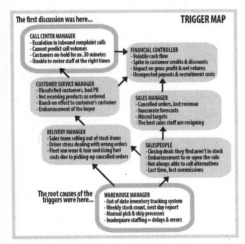

TRIGGER MAP

The first discussion was here...

CALL CENTER MANAGER
- Escalation in inbound complaint calls
- Cannot predict call volumes
- Customers on-hold for av. 30 minutes
- Unable to roster staff at the right times

FINANCIAL CONTROLLER
- Volatile cash flow
- Spike in customer credits & discounts
- Impact on gross profit & net returns
- Unexpected payouts & recruitment costs

CUSTOMER SERVICE MANAGER
- Dissatisfied customers, bad PR
- Not receiving products as ordered
- Knock-on effect to customer's customer
- Embarrassment of the buyer

SALES MANAGER
- Cancelled orders, lost revenue
- Inaccurate forecasts
- Missed targets
- The best sales staff are resigning

DELIVERY MANAGER
- Sales team selling out of stock items
- Driver stress dealing with wrong orders
- Fleet van wear & tear and rising fuel costs due to picking-up cancelled orders

SALESPEOPLE
- Closing deals they find aren't in stock
- Embarrassment to re-open the sale
- Not always able to sell alternatives
- Lost time, lost commissions

The root causes of the triggers were here...

WAREHOUSE MANAGER
- Out of date inventory tracking system
- Weekly stock count, next day report
- Manual pick & ship processes
- Inadequate staffing = delays & errors

Key Issues

- The Call Center is actually a victim of bad communication between the Warehouse and Sales.

- Other departments face collateral damage, such as Delivery and Customer Service.

- The financial and cultural impact is high. Staff are resigning, including their top salespeople.

- $6Mn in orders has been lost to competitors.

- Credits and discounts = $1.5Mn per month.

Needs

- Real-time inventory control, not weekly.
- Automated restock from suppliers.
- Current information to sales team, with data on restock dates and alternative offers.
- Interactive voice response for calls on hold.
- Auto queuing & routing of service calls.

Our Solution

WAREHOUSE:
RFID inventory control system (laser barcode scanning as a lower-price option) with order entry automation to key suppliers over an extranet ecommerce portal. Hardware, software and monthly service fee.

DELIVERY:
GPS-directed delivery management to route vans to the most efficient route. Tablet-based proof of delivery with signature capture and e-mail of dockets & cross-sell offers.

SALES:
Tablet-based presentation playbook with real-time order entry screens and signature capture. Provision of real-time stock lists with click-to-order (and back order) functionality. Auto prompt for alternatives when preferred products are out-of-stock. Sync to adaptive pricing database with inbuilt discount codes.

CALL CENTER:
IVR2000 call queuing, routing and filtering with voice-to-text capture and manager's dashboard. Predictive module CTF8XA to provide website, SEO and blog spike monitoring to anticipate and book staffing needs.

Figure 11.1: An Example of a Solution Map

talked to agreed to when you processed them through the N square of the PRECISION dialogue. You complete your Solution Map by describing which products or services best serve the needs (**Our Solution** on the illustration provided). Sometimes you might suggest alternatives and options the customer can weigh and choose from.

This step-by-step approach to solution development makes it easy for the customer to follow your logic and reasoning. There can be no doubt that you're *not* trying to force products your company is having a promotion on but that instead, you've tailor-made a solution to real needs, sufficient to satisfy the triggers in their business. Having a map like this on file also comes in handy later in the sale if someone in the customer's business tries to cherry-pick, dismantle, or discount your offer. You can visually show how each part of your solution plays an essential role in the bigger picture and why removing any of those links increases their risk. Being able to see the names of departments, people, and how the jobs they perform are affected makes the discussion much more personal—any attempt to discount *you* can more easily be seen for what it is: something that impacts *them.*

Of course, it makes sense to be certain the items you list as issues and needs reflect what the customer is using on *their* list of decision criteria or what you want them to change their list to, if doing so is in their interest. If you do stellar work developing a Trigger Map and a Solution Map, the ultimate compliment is to see the customer draft their internal documents using your ideas.

But beware: those tasked with protecting expenditures (such as procurement, purchasing, and contracts managers) will always try to boil your solution down to its basic elements, free of the marketing gloss they've learned to distrust. They don't care about your cup-half-full claims of value added, synergy, or partnership. They prefer to focus on why the cup is half empty and why they should pay less for that.

To gain a small insight into the thought process of buyers, I share one of billionaire investor Warren Buffett's gems:

The most common cause of low prices is pessimism. We want to do business in such an environment, not because we like pessimism but because we like the prices it produces. It's optimism that is the enemy of the rational buyer.[1]

They have a shopping list of evaluation criteria, and it's common practice for them to draw tables in which each requirement on that

EVALUATION CRITERIA	WHO IS MOST VOCAL FOR THIS?	RANK	YOUR POSITIONING L M H
1. Reduce out of stocks in w'house	Bob Coates	1	X
2. Give real-time inventory	John Horne	2	X
3. Route nearest van to next job	Sally Jepson	3	X
4. Reduce reload time at dock	Bob Coates	4	X
5. Reduce manual calculations	Steve Hansen	5	X

Figure 11.2: An Example of Weighted Decision Criteria

list is weighted in terms of importance (see the example in Figure 11.2). This helps buyers decide which items might be excused for commanding a premium and which might be targets for culling if the price ends up too high.

If their thought process has been influenced by an incumbent supplier, consultant, or a convincing white paper they downloaded as a touchstone, they may already lean toward a favorite supplier or product, or the list may be an amalgam of features from different sources they hope someone can cobble together for them. Whatever its source, let's call this the "Column A list." Your solution will need to appear as a logical fit for Column A if you are to stay in the running as a contender in this stage of the sale.

Though it sounds obvious, sales stars take care to understand what those evaluation criteria are, how they came to be, and how flexible the prospect is in fulfilling them. Questions top sellers ask include these:

- Is there a formal list of evaluation criteria you will be using? Who was in charge of the team that compiled the list?
- What sources did they use to inform their thinking?
- What information from other departments, external companies, or thought leaders helped shape these criteria? Whose ideas were used?
- Have you used products or services like this before? How is this list the same as or different from what was used in the past? Why?

- Which people's needs are best represented in this list? Are those people on the evaluation committee? Will I have the opportunity to discuss their needs personally with each of them?
- Is this list set in stone, or can it change if better ideas come along?
- Walk me through how the evaluation criteria might be modified if there were a good business case for doing so. Who would get involved? What meetings would they attend? Would you see yourself inviting vendors to add ideas at these meetings?
- How are these criteria weighted in terms of importance to you?
- How was this weighting agreed on?
- Was it unanimous, or do differences of opinion exist? Who is the most vocal for other criteria that are not at the top of the list? What are those criteria?
- Which people have needs that are not addressed here? Why were these needs not included? Who decided that? How do people feel about that?
- If you had budget for only half the items, would the rankings change?
- Do you see it as important that all these criteria be delivered by a single supplier? Why?
- Is there a reason you need all these criteria in a single purchase compared to progressive purchases that build on each other?

Because different people see reality through different eyes, the rank order may be different depending on who you talk to and how each item serves their department or function in the business. For this reason there can be a degree of internal conflict on these weightings.

Sales stars seek to minimize conflicts in the evaluation team by building consensus. They focus stakeholders on different lists of decision criteria: one list that best serves the whole business and other lists that best serve each stakeholder's department or personal agenda. Emphasis is given to talking about evaluation criteria that appear near the top of all lists. This approach helps you explain your solution in terms that resonate with all parties.

Personalizing the discussion about the solution can be its own form of differentiation, as they begin to see your intent is not just to sell *your* solution but to sell the *right* solution for each party.

DECIDING WHETHER YOU CAN WIN THE SALE BASED ON THE EVALUATION CRITERIA

I mentioned earlier that walking away from the sale is a viable alternative when the criteria are stacked against you and all the customer wants you to do is play a Master of Ceremonies role in a beauty pageant for which a winner has already been decided. There's no shame in bowing out of an unwinnable sale that's just a facade. If more salespeople were remunerated on profit instead of the top line, I'm convinced there would be more attention given to this.

Just remember as Buffett said, when buyers get their training, they're taught to be pessimists who strip away all points of differentiation to drive the discussion to the only variable remaining: *financial concessions.* To win in such an environment, you'll have to add resources or cut your margin more than the next guy is willing to. And even then it's no guarantee you'll win because these exercises are often a pretense to negotiate incumbents and preferred suppliers down to a lower price by showing how keen their competitors are to take their place.

Just as you have sales targets, professional purchasing managers have performance metrics of their own. Often these require them to prove to their bosses that they shaved 10 to 20 percent off every first offer they receive. As a result of knowing that a game will be played around price, few sellers think it prudent to make their first offer their best offer if they want to avoid being taken to the cleaners. In fact, most stars don't lower their price at all until they're on the shortlist for final negotiations (and even then some prefer to dig in to maintain their price rather than drop it and look like they don't believe in the value they're offering). They know if they lower the price too soon, it can only go one way from there: down further. So they focus on selling value to get the customer into the final stage of the sale. We'll explore value propositions and negotiating in Chapter 14.

Sales stars know a secret that allows them to hold firm on price as long as they have a viable solution the customer could use. They know the customer *needs* their quote in the mix. It's policy to get more than one quote. This gives you more power than you might think you have.

In the poker game of bluffing that buyers engage in, they act aloof, as if you're fortunate they would deign to talk with you. Some sales rookies believe this falsehood, and it can stay with them their whole career. They cling to excuses for staying under the buyer's thumb, such as: "They'll disqualify me if I ask for something nonstandard." "Their corporate governance rules won't allow them to share extra information. I have to work blindly." "I can't call over their head. I should count myself lucky just to be in this race!"

This is learned behavior, taught by the procurement people who throw this kind of fear, uncertainty, and doubt around all the time.

Don't believe them. They need you there.

Another tactic buyers often try is inviting sellers to the party late in the game and giving us tight deadlines to reply to their requests. It's like sprinting to an airport departure gate just as the flight crew is locking the doors and preparing to push back to the runway. It's stressful! Make no mistake, they're trying to condition you to be subservient and jump through their hoops.

Stars train themselves to step out of the sales situation and ask if what the buyer is doing at any moment in time would be reasonable in different circumstances. For example, is it reasonable to tell a real estate agent that you're in a hurry, don't want to inspect a property, but prefer to buy it based on the pictures on their website if they'll reduce the price by 20 percent and send the contract within the hour? Who would do that in the real world? The same can be said for buying a car, shoes, computers, and most things where it's important to get the right fit. The examples I've given are for personal purchases, and we see that this type of buyer behavior would be preposterous. It's only more so for corporate purchases.

When you see this sort of thing happening, don't kowtow. You're within your rights to say something like this:

> You've made the right choice asking me to respond to your buying project, but your request has come out of the blue. I can't do what you want me to do in the time frame and terms you've provided because I'm busy serving other clients who got in line months ago. Looking at my diary, I can help you jump the queue a little, but you're going to have to give me something in return. Are you willing to do that?

They'll ask what you want. Top sellers don't answer right away. First they say something like this:

> Based on your asking that, am I correct in thinking you have authority to agree to a new response date so my company can accommodate your request?

Few buyers say they have no power. They'll agree they have authority. As soon as they say it, they'll want to prove it. This is where you give them the opportunity to show just how powerful they are (and to show some of your own mettle at the same time):

I can work my schedule to respond to your request, but I need three things from you. First, I need time. My company delivers only quality, and this includes our approach to putting together proposals for projects like yours. If your deadline had been given to us two months ago, the timing would have been about right. But asking us to respond at the last minute? . . . Not so much. So I need you to push things out by several weeks in order for me to give you a quality response. That's fair, right?

Second, I need a meeting with you to get answers to questions we always ask, which are best discussed with a whiteboard, face-to-face. Your company might have tried to anticipate what we need to know in your briefing documents. But frankly, you probably don't buy solutions like ours every day, whereas we sell them every day, and we know what it takes for customers to be successful with them. Let me do what I know works best for our customers. I need only 30 minutes, and you can come to my office, or I can come to yours.

Third, I need you to confirm the process you'll be following to evaluate us, with a disclosure that this isn't just some price comparison exercise to keep an existing supplier honest. If I'm about to invest several weeks and several thousand [insert your own currency] into doing this for you, these are the things I require from you. Since you said you have this authority, I'm sure someone in your position can easily do these things.

In return for agreeing on a meeting this week or next, I'll open a file today and make a business case to my boss that this proposal is something we should definitely invest time and money in, and I'll expedite it so you get your information quickly. So when would you like to meet and get the ball rolling?

You'll put this into your own words, of course. But the intent is clear. You're showing yourself to be a busy professional who is willing to do them a favor, but since their request comes unexpectedly, there needs to be a quid pro quo—they need to meet you halfway.

If they do, go for it. If they don't, have the steel to walk away and see if they come after you.

There was a company in our study that sold solutions into federal, state, and local government agencies. These agencies often buy through tenders so there can be no hint of their giving any vendor a monopoly or favoritism. During one large project, they realized they were *always* involved in overlapping tenders in different departments, so they *never* got to have in-depth discussions with anyone. Their sales director saw this was costing them the ability to get close to any of the key people, and it was reducing them to little more than a proposal mill. So she instructed all her salespeople to withdraw, decline, or walk away from every sale that wasn't part of existing supply agreements. They all did this in the same quarter of the year so it would be noticed.

This was risky. Buyers wanted to know why the company wasn't bidding for business all of a sudden. Competitors seized the opportunity to spread rumors about insolvency. It caused quite a stir.

But it achieved its purpose. The government agencies that were famous for keeping vendors at a distance were now chasing the supplier for meetings. Now that the supplier wasn't bidding for any active deals, they were free from the "no contact moratorium" all their competitors were still bound by. None of the executive contacts in those agencies could then confuse a lunch, dinner, site visit, or ideation workshop as being a conflict of interest or breach of probity. Knowledge was exchanged. Visions and long-term strategies were shared. Understanding was developed. Relationships were formed.

The next three quarters drove business on an epic scale. Then each year, this team would step away from deal making for a couple of months in the interest of repeating this kind of unfettered access and dialogue. They had to let go of some things to take hold of better things. It all started with challenging the buying constraints placed upon them and flexing the muscles that come from knowing the customers *need* you. It pays to remind them of that now and then if they're not giving you a fair chance to develop the right level of relationship.

Top sellers tell us that buyers actually *expect* you to take charge and not simply go in asking for a briefing about what they'd like to buy. This sentiment escalates the higher up the chain of command you go. At the top of the tree, executives don't respect salespeople who fail to be assertive, opinionated, and provocative. They want meetings with you to be short but memorable, where you push their buttons and help them see something they didn't already know. You need to go in with *ideas* if you're going to win over Ideas Buyers. Have no fear: it's your job as a solution salesperson to sell this way. Go do your research, and stir things up!

Customers at all levels report being disappointed when salespeople don't do anything to challenge their thinking or commit them to action. Think about it: if you give no advice and don't show you already have future steps mapped out that you want them to commit to, how can you ever aspire to sell like a Trusted Advisor? You can't. You get relegated to the scrap heap of mediocrity.

Don't walk that path. It's too crowded. Aspire to something higher. Instead, build your solution *with* the customer.

DETERMINING EXACTLY WHICH OF YOUR PRODUCTS OR SERVICES BEST FIT THE CUSTOMER'S NEEDS

By using PRECISION Questions earlier in the sale, you demonstrated your ability to listen and place their interests first. You applied situational awareness of their industry and company in conversations about their problems, risks, opportunities, triggers, and needs. This earlier investment of time and effort pays off here in the Business Capital stage because the collaboration you've fostered puts wind in your sails, and the consensus you've gained gives you a compass heading.

Remember the final row in the PRECISION framework: you and your techxpert talk about the customer's existing Ideas and the Options you recommend they add, and then you confirm that this is what they Need. Here in the Business Capital stage of the sale, you rekindle those discussions with each stakeholder.

If you drew flipchart pages in past meetings, now is the time to take hold of those rolls of paper and post them on the walls again so the customers can see *their* handwriting all over *your* solution.

If you agreed on a Mutual Project Plan (your close plan), now is the time to go into detail about what product you recommend, how services should be added to remove any risk or to improve results, and what you need the customer to do on their side to create an environment in which your solution has the best chance of succeeding.

Always justify every recommendation you make by referring to the customer's own words. You should find these on the notes you wrote down on your F2F Meeting Planners or notes from other meetings over time.

The fact that you need this evidence in the closing stages of the sale is the reason why it's essential to write notes at every meeting *all through the sales cycle* and e-mail a summary of these immediately so that they become a matter of record in the customer's inbox.

When you bring these up again in this latter stage of the sale, the logic of your argument is irrefutable because it's based on what they already agreed to.

Salespeople who don't believe in going into their sales calls with a written plan rarely write notes or e-mail a summary afterward. Such dereliction of duty makes their life much harder than it needs to be when it comes to closing the deal.

The point is this: you don't wait till the end of a sale to design your solution and ask for commitment. You should be doing it all along. By creating many small incidents of "Yes" early and often, you condition the customer to say the big "Yes!" at the end of the sale—a Pavlovian response.[2]

So run regular meetings with individuals. Summarize by letter or e-mail what you agreed to. Then repeat the exercise with different people to learn who is on the same page, and who is friend or foe. Eventually, invite small groups of people with sympathetic views to come together and attend meetings where they can exchange similar ideas and workshop their needs with you as their moderator.

When inviting people to these sessions, include people who reside in the hub and spokes of the Influence Map and others who play the formal roles in the decision process. Use such get-togethers to turn people who remain neutral into supporters of your solution. They may get off the fence simply by seeing how the tide of popular opinion is flowing toward you.

Ask everyone to contribute their ideas to improve the final shape of your solution, and confirm that it is something they can *see*, *hear*, or *feel* themselves using.

The words in italics in the paragraph above are carefully chosen because there's a sales tip here you might profit from. The communications studies of *neurolinguist programming* (NLP) tell us that people receive and process information using three mental modalities, in which one will be most dominant: the *visual filter* (seeing), the *auditory filter* (hearing), and the *kinesthetic filter* (feeling).

According to NLP pioneer Richard Bandler,[3] you can determine which filters your buyers default to by watching their eyes as you talk to them, and especially *as they talk to you*. Test this out. Find people nearby, and strike up a conversation. Ask them to describe something to you, and watch where their eyes go as they access the information.

If their eyes *look straight up or to an upward corner* of their field of vision when they are trying to retain or recall information, it is a cue that they process information in the **visual** modality. Double-check if they talk using phrases like "in *light* of," "*see* eye to eye," "as you can plainly *see*," "it's not *clear cut*," "it was *under* my nose," "my *perspective* on this," "crystal *clear*," or "*appears* to be."

To fully engage the visual buyer, use gestures and facial expressions, brochures, charts, storyboards, photos, animations, or videos to get your story across, with sentences like these:

- "Imagine how your production line would *look* if you just . . ."
- "*Picture* this new equipment on your job sites."
- "*Imagine* the smile on your boss's face when . . ."
- "Wouldn't this report *look* much more professional if . . ."

If their eyes *move sideways from ear to ear* when trying to recall or process information, it is a cue that they may process things in the **auditory** modality. Double-check if they talk using phrases like "I hear *whispers* about," "it *sounds* to me like," "I hear what you're saying," "the *word* on the street is," "what I think I *heard* you say is," "didn't you *say?*" or "people are making a lot of *noise* about."

To fully engage the auditory buyer, don't open any slide decks, but instead talk in a quiet place where they will be able to hear every nuance and tone in a discussion that flows like a conversation instead of a presentation, with sentences that include this language:

- "Your colleagues will all *talk* about . . ."
- "You'll have *peace and quiet* once you . . ."
- "We've been *listening* to . . ."
- "Have you *heard* . . ."
- "If you have your *ear* to the ground . . ."
- "Let me *tell* you about . . ."

If their eyes move *down or to a lower corner* in their field of vision when trying to recall or retain information, it is a cue that they process information in the **kinesthetic** (touch and feel) modality. Double-check if they talk using phrases like "it *slipped* my mind," "starting from *scratch*," "*pain* in the neck," "gives me a *headache*," "tried to get *hold* of you," "goes *hand-in-hand* with," "*fits* like a glove," or "this *boils* down to."

To fully engage the kinesthetic buyer, put a pen in their hands, ask them to join you drawing diagrams on a flipchart or whiteboard, and encourage them to hold, touch, or use your product. Use language like this:

- "You can *take hold* of the situation by . . ."
- "Here are some available *courses of action.*"
- "It will *feel* good when . . ."
- "Let's *roll up* our sleeves and . . ."
- "Would you like to get *hands on* with this?"
- "Let's *take a deep dive.*"

When presenting to a mixed group, use all these communication styles by utilizing visual props, allowing hands-on interaction, or carefully scripting what you will say out loud. This way you have something for everyone to connect with. If you schedule a group meeting where those who process information using one style attend, tailor your approach accordingly.

The goal is to provide information in a format that will lodge in their brain and leave the deepest impression. Doing this helps boost your signal strength and build support for your solution, as discussed in Chapters 8 through 10 on Social Capital.

It's important that these kinds of discussions are held *before* you formally present your final solution to the evaluation team. You want your *final pitch* to be a no-surprises summation of the ideas that people have already endorsed, not information they're hearing for the first time.

How often have you (or someone you know) walked into the customer's office for that all-important day of vendor presentations with absolutely no idea how the individuals in that meeting were going to respond to what you were about to show them? We've all faced this when we've skipped the preliminary steps, and it can be very uncomfortable.

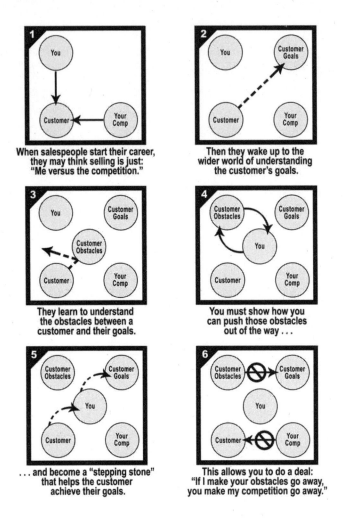

Figure 11.3: Positioning Your Solution

Try to ensure that each person sees your offering as a stepping-stone that helps them reach their individual or department goals. Imagine if most of the people in a deal you're trying to win right now believed that you had co-created a solution *just for them*. When they're talking in the lunchroom and hear your solution mentioned as *other people's favorite*, could this repetitive reinforcement cement your position as the front-runner in their mind? Of course it can.

Win over the people, and you'll win over the company.

Figure 11.3, "Positioning Your Solution," shows how this works.

The more you can get the customer talking about the emotion of how achieving their goals will make them feel, and the more you can show yourself as the mechanism through which that change will be achieved with higher certainty than the other options they could choose from, the less signal strength your rivals will have and the more yours will be heard.

Chapter 12

Form a Competitive Strategy

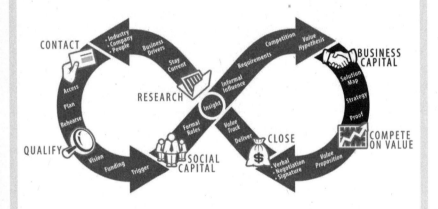

The Sales Expansion Loop: Business Capital—Strategy

Before his consulting career, William E. Rothschild was a 30-year insider at General Electric and the company's senior corporate strategist for three of those years. In his book *The Secret of GE's Success* (McGraw-Hill, 2007), Rothschild observed the relationship between objectives, strategy, and tactics:

> *What do you want to achieve? The answer to this question is the* objective. *How will you go about achieving your desired results? The answer to this you can call* strategy.

I would add: "What specific actions will you take? These you can call *tactics*."

Objective. Strategy. Tactics. These three elements of opportunity planning follow each other in sequence and in consequence to each other.

The first element, objective, is easy to see. When you want to close a sale to a specific company, for a specific product or service, by a specific date for a specific price—that's a measurable sales objective for your forecast.

The last element, tactics, is also easy to see. Tactics are the steps you (and others on your sales pursuit team) take to fill the days, weeks, and months of the sales cycle: research, meetings, questions, presentations, and so forth. Tactics are made easier when they're directed in sequence by a Mutual Project Plan the customer has agreed to follow. Often they become a balancing act between acting and reacting as some events go according to plan and others hit you from left field. But always they are focused on advancing the sale toward the prize: to achieve your objective of X revenue for Y solution by Z date.

Strategy is the element that *should* serve as a bridge between objectives and tactics. But of the three elements, strategy can be the most difficult to relate to because it's often taught as a quasi-intellectual exercise in divination that leaves people struggling to see how to give it practical expression—so they decide to just "make things happen" instead of directing their tactics as a subset of their strategy.

That works okay if you believe that the law of averages pays your commission checks. But if you want to *win* business more often, learn to understand and apply a sales strategy. As an unknown writer once observed (often attributed to Sun-tzu though it appears in none of his writings):

> *Strategy without tactics is the slowest route to victory. But tactics without strategy is the noise before defeat.*

So how do you set and then execute an opportunity-specific sales strategy? Top sellers suggest three steps: polling, positioning, and propaganda.

POLLING

First, you take a poll on how well you and your competitors fit the customer's view of the ideal solution, and then you seek to identify each other's weaknesses as they relate to this specific deal. For example, who are the people you and they have or don't have positive signal strength with, or have failed to cover adequately? Which of these have influence to other stakeholders? And is it in your power to win them over? What are the gaps in each other's armor? Which of these causes your customer the most doubt and concern? And is it in your power to ramp up their anxiety, then prove you offer something better (without directly bad-mouthing the competition)? In answering such questions of comparison, you'll find that you're either stronger than your competitors, weaker, or in exactly the same ballpark. You gain this comparison by applying the Opportunity Snapshot, as explained in Chapters 5 through 7.

Before two boxers face each other in the ring, they watch videotapes of each other's past fights to find their opponent's weak spots. They check if the judges of the coming match typically score one type of fighting move higher than others, and then the boxers will practice showcasing that move. They watch and learn. Top sellers do the same.

POSITIONING

Second, you search the Snapshot to look beyond "what is" to "what might be." From your current foundation of strength, weakness, or parity, is it in your power to reposition any of the criteria on the Snapshot dial so you increase in favor and your competitors fade into the background? With the Snapshot as your compass, come up with a list of things you must do so this will happen (tactics). Then anticipate what your competitors are likely to do in response (based on past encounters with them or their known default behavior), and work to block that path (countertactics). Then take stock of where you end up by rescoring the Snapshot for your competitors and yourself. After this effort, decide if you are now positioned stronger or weaker or if things have stayed pretty much the same. Then take additional actions as appropriate.

Clever boxers use what their polling revealed about their opponents and those doing the scoring. If the other fighter has a knockout left hook, they position themselves to keep their guard up on that flank. If their opponent took damage in a previous fight, they position their blows to reopen those old wounds until their enemy is disabled. If their polling revealed what a judge most likes to see in a boxer's routine, they position the fight right in front of that judge and flawlessly perform that routine to achieve a higher technical score.

In selling you need to use the information you gain from polling to decide how you want to be positioned in the customer's eyes. Achieving your desired positioning is a deliberate act, a choreographed dance.

PROPAGANDA

Third, if you applied your best efforts to the previous step, you now know what can and can't be physically changed about your position. Let's say your competitor just released their latest product with *better* technology and a *lower* price than you can come close to—and it fits *exactly* what the customer's evaluators say they're looking for. They will be better positioned than you are. This is where impressions come into play—and propaganda is the means by which you create or change the impressions by which others see you. This is the heart of strategy.

One famous boxer from the twentieth century was an upbeat fast-talker who charmed audiences and judges with his jubilant cries of "I am the greatest!" and "I float like a butterfly and sting like a bee." He had the brawn to back up his boasts, but the very fact that he proclaimed himself this way created a sense of expectation on the part of his audience. Sure, it began as clever rhetoric, but his next win made people wonder if it were true. Several wins later, even his opponents might well have wondered if they were indeed facing "the greatest"—exactly the intended fear, uncertainty, and doubt of any propaganda campaign.

Politicians do the same thing when they find a cause in need of a champion. Whether it's a theme of morality, security, or prosperity, if a gap exists in the other candidate's platform, the smart politician fills that gap, knowing that votes will follow.

Polling. Positioning. Propaganda.

When you view "strategy" this way, its function as a link between the sales objective and the tactics you use becomes much clearer. Once you calculate what your propaganda should be to give you the advantage, it follows that every conversation, presentation, e-mail, and document must be consistent with that theme, or there's no point having the strategy in the first place. All your tactics must be animated with the same spirit, to the same end.

You'll need to explain your strategy to others on your extended team (your manager, techxperts, partners, telesales team, service reps—whoever else will play a customer-facing role in helping win the deal) to ensure that their discussions are consistent with the impression you want to drive. It's the constant drip-drip-drip of consistent propaganda that builds mindshare and helps the customer know what you stand for and how you stand out from the pack.

You're competing to make an impression not just against your revenue rival in this opportunity but against all the other banner ads, blogs, tweets, headlines, and jingles your customer is exposed to daily—which some marketing analysts suggest total in the thousands every day. Think about it. Does your breakfast cereal have its own advertising slogan? How many ads did you hear on the TV or radio as you were preparing to leave your home this morning? How about since then—have you been exposed to billboards, posters, newspapers, magazines, movie trailers, e-mail spam, or SMS texts today? Of course you have; advertising is everywhere. It barrages your clients too.

If your connection to them is once a week, your message is being diluted by tens of thousands of distracting voices. If it's once a month, they've contemplated hundreds of thousands of consumer and commercial propositions since last seeing you. Even if your sales calls are the epitome of perfection and make the angels sing, it doesn't mean the customer is thinking about you in between calls. Most buyers see you on their calendar, they know you're coming, and you might even send them an agenda to ponder in advance of each meeting. But the reality is that in today's go-go pace of business, customers use the first moments of a meeting to reboot their brain and recall what you mean to them ("Oh right, it's *those* guys again"), and based on what emotion or logic you tap during the meeting, they use the last few moments of the call deciding if they like you, trust you, and are willing to do the things you ask to advance the sale.

So why not make it easy for them? Start and end every meeting with a headline that explains how you want to be positioned against your competitors in the deal. Make it catchy. Put this same phrase at the end of all your e-mails. Ask your presales techxperts and alliance partners to do the same. Unite your voice across the extended team with a single, memorable message that helps the customer instantly identify what you're selling them. Ideally they will use the propaganda you've seeded at internal meetings when different stakeholders are comparing notes on each vendor.

Some salespeople add their company slogan to their e-mail signature to leverage their marketplace brand. That's a good start. But what I'm describing here is opportunity specific. It's your theme and positioning—your banner on the battlefield. It's what you place in every presentation, letter, proposal cover, summary page, demonstration, and conversation.

So what does it look like? Let's look at the Strategy Map in Figure 12.1.

You begin by learning the decision criteria against which the customer views you and your competitors through a lens of perception. This lens can be shaped by personal **bias** or by how the **media** paint you (this includes Google searches that reveal how many times your company's name appears in articles about the solution you claim you're an expert in, and analyst opinions, press releases, and so on).

Perception may be built by what the **grapevine** says about you—by people who have worked with you before, past customers, by how many connections and referees you personally have on LinkedIn (people form judgments about you based on your perceived popularity and activity), or the opinion blogs that follow news stories about your company.

Most important, a customer's perception is built by **what you do and say**—the extent to which they see you walking the talk—from which they form their opinion about how dependable or knowledgeable you are, and a range of other tangible and intangible perceptions.

Knowing how they perceive you is where your sales strategy begins. Knowing how your competitors are positioned in the customer's perception also shapes your choice of strategy. Then your choice of strategy informs the headlines you use to give voice and substance to your strategy in every presentation, conversation, and document, as discussed earlier.

Polling, positioning, and propaganda are the three steps that inform your choice of strategy. And out of a multitude of variables

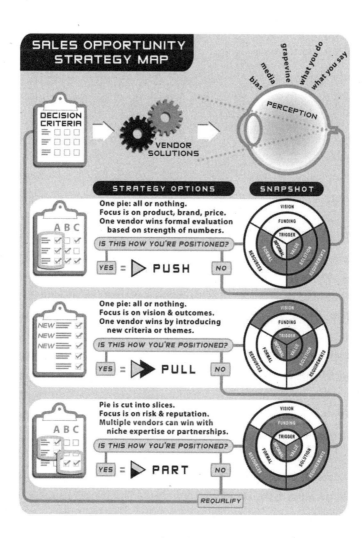

Figure 12.1: An Example of a Strategy Map

that make one sale different from the next, when top sellers describe what their actual sales strategies look like, we thankfully find them boiling down into three versions that are quite simple to understand and execute if you've done the requisite preparation and keep control of your outgoing communications so your strategy shines through.

STRATEGY 1. PUSH

A *Push* strategy requires you to be seen as the biggest gorilla.

You want the customer to perceive that you have a **solution** that will work for them (Snapshot qualification criterion 5) better than anyone else's alternative. They see this based on how well you understand and meet their published **requirements** (criterion 4), how compliant you are with their **formal** decision criterion (criterion 8), and if there's something about your people, your company, products, services, or prices that creates extraordinary **value** (criterion 6) beyond what your competitors bring to the table.

Accordingly, to be ready to launch a Push strategy, you must score high on those corresponding qualification criteria on the Snapshot's assessment wedges (or see a way to make it so by having conversations that drive this perception). Note that in the Strategy Map in Figure 12.1, you can see these same four criteria shaded as strengths on the first example. Having these strengths in place is the minimum muscle required for launching a Push strategy and seeing it succeed. It means you have a relatively strong fit to what the customer is looking for with adequate resources to look like the biggest and best, while making your rivals appear less suited to the task at hand by comparison.

How do you get into this position? Maybe as part of your account management efforts, you were the first person to identify the customer's need, and this led to the assignment of budget and people to explore the idea with you as a Trusted Advisor. Perhaps this makes the sale a one-horse race you can win before any competitor hears of it.

Even if their procurement policy requires them to invite a number of competitive bids, you were the seller to help create the vision, then write and weight the evaluation criteria and time table. Maybe the customer is following actions and dates on a mutual project plan you created for them. You have the advantage of incumbency, or you enjoy thought leader status.

If you *weren't* first to the party and you have been invited to bid for the business along with several other contenders, maybe through your meetings with the customer or through your marketing-at-large, your **company** is perceived as a heavyweight in your industry—their impressions about your size, breadth of resources, longevity in business, stability, or customer service paint you in their eyes as a better, safer choice to be in business with. Or maybe your **product** features, price, upgrade plans, payment terms, case studies, awards, and accolades outclass your rivals' in the customer's eyes.

There was a time when people purchased portable MP3 players from Sony, phones from Nokia, and laptop computers from IBM as separate products. Then Apple released the iPhone, which had all three functions (and more) in one unit. Their product superiority was a Push strategy in action.

VMware, Cisco Systems, and EMC decided to launch a Push strategy against everyone else in the virtual cloud computing market. They formed a joint venture called the VCE Company with an investment in the region of $300 million to converge their technology into modular stacks called Vblocks. Did the investment pay off? In a second quarter 2011 earnings call with analysts, EMC chief executive Joseph Tucci reported: "For sure, Vblocks are proving their value proposition, and we expect Vblock sales to hit the $1 billion run rate mark in the next several quarters."[1]

Airbus built the massive double-decker A380 superjumbo to make Boeing's aging 767 and 777 fleets look redundant as a choice for long-haul flights. Boasting more seats, a range of 15,000 kilometers, cruising speed of Mach 0.85, lower cabin noise, improved comfort, and 20 percent better fuel efficiency, the A380 received a flood of advance orders from airlines that wanted the "latest and greatest" despite its average cost of $375.3 million per unit.[2]

When postal and courier services took days to deliver packages, FedEx coined the slogan, "When it absolutely positively has to be there overnight," focusing on speed as their Push advantage.

When Absolut entered the vodka market, Smirnoff was the bestselling brand. Instead of using pricing parity or trying to win market share with a discount price, Absolut outlandishly pushed its liquor 50 percent higher than Smirnoff, saying that it was first in a new drinks category called "premium vodka." In 1997, Sidney Frank's start-up drinks company Grey Goose launched at a price that was 60 percent higher again than Absolut, creating the "ultimate-premium vodka" category. Seven years later, Frank sold Grey Goose to Bacardi for $2 billion.[3]

Until the A-class car, Mercedes always priced itself at the premium end of the market too, citing that its machine was "engineered like no other car."

Like Madonna before her, Lady Gaga's actual product—her music—is one piece of a much larger package her fans buy into, which includes fashion, fun, activism, and the theme of individuality. The *whole product* of Lady Gaga is pushed as being greater than the sum of its parts.

Apple, VCE, Airbus, FedEx, Grey Goose, Mercedes, and Lady Gaga made themselves into the big gorillas of their industries. Their products, performance, or prestige had pulling power regarded as superior to other choices their consumers could invest their time and money on.

Cast a glance back at the first example on the Strategy Map (Figure 12.1), and you'll see how the Snapshot should look if the landscape of the sale lends itself to your using the Push strategy.

When your buyer believes *your* company, people, experience, products, or prices are the best available, and you can see that at a specific moment of time no competitor comes close to rivaling you, push that perception in all that you do—all the way to the close. Never burst that bubble by letting the customer see you differently! Never admit to weaknesses. Throw all your *best resources* at your sale. Be the embodiment of their expectations. In doing so, seek to make your competitors look small, poorly manned, or unresponsive by comparison. Even better, exhaust them, and erode their resources as they try to keep pace with an agenda that you set.

If the customer wants to buy from a big player, then *look* big: dress the part, flash your Rolex, Cartier, and Mont Blanc. Hand out your specially embossed business cards printed on fine grain stock pulled from a leather holster instead of limp bits of cardboard from a shirt pocket. Never go to meetings alone; instead, wheel in your "big gun resources." Knock the ball out of the park with perfectly staged product demonstrations that leave them awestruck. Spend time giving your documents and presentations the layout flair of a color annual report with saddle stitch binding instead of combs or staples in the corner. Fill the customer's calendar with site visits to your most impressive product installations, to working lunches, golf, or theater (to the extent corporate governance will allow). Be big. Be everywhere. Be seen as the best. Fire on all cylinders. This makes your tactics consistent with the theme of a Push strategy.

If the customer instead prizes buying from a "small and hungry" supplier who will provide greater creativity and responsiveness than an impersonal, monolithic solution vendor, then create a delivery team that's animated by the *best* can-do entrepreneurial attitude. Turn up to meetings at your office with shirtsleeves rolled up. Make sure everyone (from your receptionist to people who *happen* to pass by in the hallway as you walk your guests in) all know the names of those visiting and greet them with reverential comments like: "Oh, so *you're* the customer we lost our guys to for the last few weeks. All they've been doing is talking about you."

Use a meeting room you've dressed with flipcharts on the walls to show how you've been mulling over their needs and designing ideas to present to them, with pizza boxes in the corner as an echo of all the late-night workshops held on their behalf, coffee cup stains on the table, their company literature stacked up in a prominent pile, and a clearly visible note on the door that says *"Their-Company-Name's Solution Lab. Please do not touch"*—dated a month before your meeting with them to show how long you've been laboring on their behalf.

Instead of showing them any preconfigured solution diagrams, entice the customer with a whiteboard or blank flipchart to draw something *with you* that's tailored to their needs. Discover it together, even if it ends up looking a lot like the solution you already decided they need. Involve them in the journey.

Make sure your personal blogs, tweets, or LinkedIn updates during the months you're pursuing these target opportunities reflect thought leadership on the subject matter that's important to the deal. Ask all those involved in the same sale to do the same. Do you think customers today do *not* check each of you out within a day of receiving your business card? Stage-manage press releases to the same end in media located in the cities your customer operates in, to the online magazine channels your customer gets their news through.

Is this deception? No, this is *propaganda*, as mentioned earlier. This is part of your execution of strategy. It's about selling, being a conscious act of persuasion "from opening call to 10 feet tall."

How many late nights do you burn the candle at both ends working on the customer's needs? How many hours drafting presentation slides, editing documents, juggling people, pricing, and resources behind the scenes? Does the customer ever see or give you credit for all the work you do even before they've signed the order form? Rarely. Our hard work is so often an invisible effort because we usually only show them crisp documents, pressed collars, and tidy boardrooms. It's not easy to get credit for what the eye does not see.

The execution of a Push strategy is to make your strengths, your efforts, and your energy clearly *visible*. Let them see your sweat, tears, and toil. What we're doing here is encapsulating all your hard work into a set of concentrated, orchestrated moments to help them recognize how important they are to you, your level of commitment to them, and how you have the biggest, baddest, or best solution they could possibly want.

If you don't feel comfortable creating such "moments of proof," there are two other ways your customer will come to the same knowledge without your help. One is telepathy. The other is when your competitor confesses how awesome you are.

Not likely? Okay then.

To paint your sales campaign with the colors of a Push strategy, you don't need to be the biggest, best, or cheapest by any empirical measure. As long as you can factually deliver what you promise, you need only for the customer to *perceive* that you're the best (Figure 12.2). Beauty is in the eye of the beholder, but sometimes you need to give beauty a helping hand.

	EVALUATION CRITERIA	WHO IS MOST VOCAL FOR THIS?	RANK	YOUR POSITIONING L M H		
1.	Reduce out of stocks in w'house	Bob Coates	1			X
2.	Give real-time inventory	John Horne	2			X
3.	Route nearest van to next job	Sally Jepson	3			X
4.	Reduce reload time at dock	Bob Coates	4			X
5.	Reduce manual calculations	Steve Hansen	5			X

Figure 12.2: An Example of Weighted Decision Criteria When You Are the "Big Gorilla"

Be careful with a Push strategy though because maintaining the halo of being the big gorilla can take its toll on resources and balloon your cost of the sale at the expense of your profits. You must manage that. As soon as you reach a point where it's obvious to everyone you're the choice to run with, the next step *must* be to sign the order and not give your competitors time to imitate you or find partners that equalize the playing field for them. Take the deal off the table! Sun-tzu reminds us:

> *In war, then, let your great object be victory, not lengthy campaigns.*
> (Art of War *2:19*)

What headlines might pepper your presentations, e-mails, and discussions to support a Push strategy? Your words will change from deal to deal depending on what the customer prizes most. But the essence you want to convey goes like this:

- "Our experience is your security."
- "Bigger, better, faster."
- "Easy results. Easy choice."
- "Tomorrow's standards, today."
- "Relentless perfection."
- "Same performance. Half the cost."
- "The gold standard in innovation."
- "When 'almost' isn't an option."
- "Simply brilliant."
- "Success without compromise."
- "Why settle for second-best?"
- "Same cost. Twice the performance."

You get the point. The Push strategy supports the perception that your product, company, people, or service are all hands-down the obvious best choice based on whatever the customer's decision criteria are shaped to satisfy:

If they're budget conscious, be the one with the lowest price or best total cost of ownership.

If they're risk averse, be the one with the best customer success stories and biggest team to support them.

If they're technical buyers, let your product's innovation, credibility, standards, and accolades speak for you.

If they prize intellectual property, show them your "brains trust." Be the biggest gorilla for all the factors they prize.

But be careful. While it is true that the intrinsic value of the 'product or service offering may be what you base a Push strategy on (*if* they want it *and* you have it, flaunt it), if you don't delve deeper into the customer's needs, you can easily find yourself trying to win complex sales armed with little more than the old tactical "feature-advantage-benefit" pitch.

Deciding to adopt a Push strategy doesn't mean you're off the hook from having to dig into the business drivers and the cause-and-effect flow of issues between different stakeholders where the *real* needs are to be found. In our research we found that where this isn't well understood, the Push strategy can quickly become the default approach of product-centric sellers who don't have the curiosity or patience to finesse the sale. Instead, they fire up their laptops with their marketing-designed product pitches, and they call *that* a strategy in the absence of having a *real* strategy.

Launched for the wrong reasons or when focused on the wrong issues to the wrong ears, a Push strategy can be the simplest to adopt (simply bang on about your product or price), and therefore, it can be the simplest to defeat when other more enterprising salespeople from competitor camps actually stop to analyze the sale in greater detail and find a way to paint you as a merchant prattling on about your wares with no thought for the customer's true needs. So be careful with the Push strategy. Like a flaming arrow drawn to the chin before setting it loose, the Push strategy can engulf your enemies in fire under the right circumstances. But used too often, it can also make you blind.

STRATEGY 2. PULL

A *Pull* strategy requires you to be the smartest *guerilla*, not the biggest gorilla.

Let's say you're *not* positioned as being anywhere close to matching the customer's decision criteria, and your Snapshot reveals another company completely outguns you on factual or perceived strength. You've tried to change these perceptions, but it's clear this game is going to play out on a field your competitor totally dominates. What are your options?

1. You might *flog a dead horse* and spend months grinding your way to the end of their buying process, tying up your team in deal

reviews, presentations, and price negotiations for what is already a lost cause on your forecast.

2. You might *flag the deal as lost* so your team members know not to expend resources on it, remove it from your forecast to reflect reality, then go through the motions of staying in the game while keeping your cost of sale as low as possible. This keeps your brand "in play," which you might want to do for three reasons. First, your competitor might slip up, their key supporter might leave, the customer's requirements might change—so it's always good policy to stick around as an understudy in case the lead actor can't finish the show. Second, there's *always* a next time and sometimes buyers rotate through a list of suppliers to be seen as even-handed (especially in sales to government agencies). Third, you need to be seen as being active in the market or people will forget about you.

3. You might *withdraw from the sale* on the grounds of not being in a position to compete, and then you can see if such action provokes the customer to have a candid discussion about your reasons for walking (sometimes you can use such meetings to gain concessions in the decision criteria that improve your position—remember they *need* you in the race to prove they compared offers).

4. Or you can stay in the sale, and roll up your sleeves to *shift the customer's focus* to new or different criteria that play to your strengths (or a partner's strengths), and so avoid being compared on a like-for-like basis—where you would lose because of the other party's long shadow over the landscape.

In a Pull strategy you want the customer to rethink *what* it is they're buying and *why* they're buying it, and thereby see their needs (and you) in a *new category* altogether—a theater of engagement where *you* are the only one offering the right solution for the new mindset. Your intent is to get the customer to add to and then reprioritize their decision criteria so that your competitor's advantage becomes their

	EVALUATION CRITERIA	WHO IS MOST VOCAL FOR THIS?	RANK	YOUR POSITIONING L M H		
1.	Reduce out of stocks in w'house	Bob Coates	5			X
2.	Give real-time inventory	John Horne	6		X	
3.	~~Route nearest van to next job~~	~~Sally Jepson~~	~~9~~	X		
4.	~~Reduce reload time at dock~~	~~Bob Coates~~	~~7~~	X		
5.	~~Reduce manual calculations~~	~~Steve Hansen~~	~~8~~	X		
6.	Steve's team to gain 20 hrs/mth	Steve Hansen	1			X
7.	Andy's team revenue +14%	Mike Steele	2			X
8.	Slow staff churn from 32% to 9%	Gloria vanStrom	3			X
9.	Attract 20 new >$1M clients	Andy Wickett	4			X

Figure 12.3: An Example of Weighted Decision Criteria When You Are Not the "Gorilla" but the "Guerilla"

disadvantage as the new criteria you introduce are ranked as the new must-haves (Figure 12.3).

If you *don't* do this, those competitors who more closely match the decision criteria can apply the Push strategy and hit a home run *without being challenged*.

To drive a Pull strategy, start by examining the customer's **vision** (Snapshot qualification criterion 1), including what is known about each stakeholder's personal agenda. Look for hot topics that don't appear to be overtly served by the current list of requirements your competitors are basing their pitch on. Focus on the issues that are really close to people's hearts but which might have been diluted or not mentioned at all in the technical specification being managed by the evaluation team or procurement officer. If all your competitors are tacticians, they probably won't dig deeper than the official specification list, so you can gain an advantage by being the only one to be seen as getting to the heart of the matter.

Draft a new list of requirements (for your own reference) that focuses on what's important to the hub and spokes players in terms of outcomes, legacies, reputation, trust, security, nostalgia, culture, and enjoyment—all the **informal** decision factors (criterion 9) that are absent from the formal setting but that remain very much a part of the final selection process. Start introducing these themes into your conversations and see who bites.

Show your **solution** (criterion 5) is the stepping-stone to *these* outcomes. Sell the personal and business **value** (criterion 6) of *that*. And to make sure that by introducing new issues you don't simply open the door for your competitors to say all the same things and thereby erode your advantage, you must create some anxiety around the **trigger** (criterion 3) issues so that along with the other changes being made, the decision date is also one of them. Take a deposit. Start a billable discovery phase. Do a paid proof of concept. Lock it down.

Cast a glance back at the second example on the Strategy Map (Figure 12.1), and you'll see how the Snapshot should look if the landscape of the sale lends itself to you using the Pull strategy.

When you succeed in changing the emphasis of the decision, you pull the rug out from under your competitors' feet because their entire approach was based on winning against criteria that are now being reprioritized. After they've staked their resources and reputation on delivering that original solution, it can difficult for them to steer away from that proposition. Their strength can become their weakness.

For this reason, you must be careful about *when* in the sale you announce your Pull strategy. Be assured, as soon as the jungle drums start beating about how the customer is seriously considering new issues, your competition will hear about it from *someone*. Everyone has his or her own little birds, even if you don't see them.

If you adopt the Pull strategy too early in the sales cycle, you give other suppliers time to adapt, and so you lose the element of surprise this strategy might otherwise have granted.

If you adopt the Pull strategy too late, people's hearts and minds might be irrevocably committed and unwilling to entertain new ideas.

So you have to wait until vendors are already explaining their solutions and laying their cards on the table, here in the Business Capital stage of the sales cycle.

Then you say something along the lines of this: "You know, having talked to all of you about how this project started and the issues you're trying to deal with, we wonder if there might be another way to skin this cat. . . ." Better yet, ask your influential supporters to introduce the concept, and let their currency carry it forward, backed by insights and ideas you've prepared and rehearsed with them in advance that make it clear to everyone how they'll achieve their aims plus gain unexpected benefits.

These benefits are usually not based on product alone but on higher-order themes, and they *always* suggest that the customer will receive a profound advantage by embracing the change. It's not good enough to try to move the goalposts simply because you're not winning—there must always be some unit of value exchanged that they won't otherwise experience.

Sometimes you have to base this on intangibles that aren't officially published. Let's say two vendors are toe-to-toe on a large document management systems deal for which the solution will be installed in multiple offices of a large accounting firm. The buying committee sees that each company has common strengths and each has unique capabilities, but in the final analysis they score equal on the vendor evaluation. Both suppliers have professional people and the same caliber of customer case studies. Both will swap out the customer's existing print and copy devices and apply a fair market valuation that will be deducted from their fee. After a round of negotiations, both suppliers are also equal on what this valuation will be, as well as their product and services prices. When the customer can't tell them apart on the formal decision criteria, something else needs to be weighed to break the stalemate. You must decide what this will be, plant the idea through your mentors, and be certain that your competition can't offer the same.

In this case, the account manager at one of these suppliers notices that the accounting firm's stationery includes a byline about being committed to environmental sustainability. They know their rival once faced media controversy about shipping old machines to the technology dumping grounds in Ghana where children walk barefoot across smoking pyres of melted plastic, breathing in carcinogenic clouds as they strip copper wire, gold, and tin from the 50 million tons of electronics discarded each year for collectors who pay them a dollar a week for their effort. Instead of calling attention to their competitor's shady track record, this account manager knows it's enough to simply ask if the customer knows that when his company takes away the old machines, it will go to great lengths to ensure an environmentally responsible method of recycling. The manager also points out how his company plants new forests to offset its carbon footprint. Not once does he mention his rival. He doesn't need to. He's aligned to a core value, interest, or outcome that the customer prizes. The inevitable Google search that the customer will run to compare both suppliers' environmental policies will do the rest. A new decision element will be introduced, and the stalemate will be broken.

When Alamo, Budget, and Hertz were bludgeoning each other's prices in the car rental industry, Avis pulled consumers to a different set of issues with the war cry "We try harder": faster check-in, cleaner cars, and maps of the local area. Their Pull strategy might be summarized as shifting "from price to service."

When Airbus introduced the aforementioned A380 superjumbo (and selected airports had to refit their runways and docking collars to accommodate its size), Boeing hit back by announcing that the new 787 Dreamliner would replace Boeing's 777 flagship. But instead of trying to compete on size and features against "the Goliath of the skies," Boeing pulled the discussion to an altogether different topic: customer convenience. Boeing contended that the A380's size demanded that before international passengers could fly on it, many would first have to board a flight in their home city to reach one of their nation's larger airport hubs before the international leg of their journey could start. In a world where passengers have to remove belts, shoes, clothing, and other vestiges of human dignity, then decant their laptops and run the gauntlet of body scans and pat downs, Boeing decided to offer a jetliner that had a similar range and level of comfort yet could provide long-haul travel from any airport—not just a handful of major hubs. The 787 is a game-changer for the air industry because it offers a solution that wasn't previously available before, and in so doing, it challenges not just how airlines might select the plane as a product but how they might shape their entire carriage strategy. Their Pull strategy might be summarized as shifting "from decadence to convenience."

When Cirque Du Soleil combined the most valued elements of theater and circus (music, thrills, and drama) and eliminated the negatives of both (caged animals, cheap tickets, and expensive infrastructures), it was able to create an alternative that didn't compete with theater shows or circuses because it transcended them as a broader form of entertainment. Their Pull strategy might be summarized as shifting "from predictable to spectacle."

When Nintendo released the Wii, its focus wasn't on convincing hardcore teen gamers that it had better games or controllers. Its focus was on convincing nongaming *families* that the Wii could be a healthy social experience for people of all ages. It released a simplified controller and game titles that encouraged team play from people gathering in the same room, not over a network. Their Pull strategy might be summarized as shifting "from individuality to family."

When Bic introduced the first low-cost plastic disposable razor, it pulled customers away from having to replace safety blades on metal razors and gave them the freedom to simply throw the whole unit out and start over with a sharp one. Their Pull strategy might be summarized as shifting "from maintaining to time-saving."

When *Wikipedia* launched as an online encyclopedia written and edited by a mostly volunteer crew, it pulled the model for information distribution away from publishers creating content that was out-of-date as soon as it was released to *everyone* being able to create the content and update it in real time. Unlike *Encyclopedia Britannica* and *Microsoft Encarta*, this was free of charge and (so far) free of advertising. Their Pull strategy might be summarized as shifting "from buying knowledge to sharing knowledge."

Changing the buyer's perception, then their motivation (and therefore their resulting action), is what a Pull strategy is all about.

If you're not the sort of person who is comfortable networking, challenging the status quo, or coloring outside the lines (all needed to make a Pull strategy work), chances are you'll limit yourself to using a Push strategy most of the time because your repertoire will be skewed toward safe factual conversations about your company, your product, and service or price instead of the more provocative conversations that engage people's emotions on risk, legacy, ego, comfort, moral imperative, or personal status. Working for a big brand or commoditized product may therefore suit you better than working in the arena of solution sales.

Yet can *anyone* learn to talk the language of a Pull strategy? Of course! You can do so by taking a contrarian view in any conversation, just to build the muscles needed to "be different." At lunchtime tomorrow, try arguing in support of a political leader you don't actually believe in. At an upcoming dinner party, speak up in support of a religion you aren't a member of. Next time someone interrupts or upsets you at home, avoid harsh words and instead give the person your full support and take their side. Join a debate club. Sign up with Toastmasters. These ideas might not sound directly related to selling. But they will give your mind the type of creative workout that helps you discuss the road less traveled—a key skill for avoiding herd mentality and seeing how to make a Pull strategy come to life.

In a sales situation you need to concentrate your Pull strategy on people with informal power in the hub and spokes of the Influence Map. This is because at this stage of the buying process, *somebody* with clout inside the customer's organization is going to have to champion modifying those decision criteria everyone already signed off on months before. That can be a major upheaval and not without its politics, so you need the person advocating it to be equal to the task. The changes they suggest must be such that "customer value" is obvious, so that people join this bandwagon, and so when suppliers are assessed against the list, it falls heavily in your favor and fundamentally changes the playing field.

Some customers justify doing so because "new information" has come to light that wasn't available when they first drafted their original specifications list and decision criteria. This is entirely valid and easy for their colleagues to accept. If the person you target has rank *as well as* influence and works in a command-and-control culture where the boss's decisions are rarely challenged, they might choose to simply say the changes are "for strategic reasons" they don't need to fully explain.

STRATEGY 3. PART

Let's say you're not positioned to win on *all* the decision criteria, but:

1. You see that the customer's project plan has a number of clear sequential phases in how it will be deployed.
2. Or the solution they seek could easily be regarded as having several subareas that could be fenced off and handled separately.
3. Or different geographic offices or stakeholders have unique needs and competing concerns.

Let's further surmise that when viewing the project through these eyes, you recognize that if the deal were for just one of those phases, mini-projects, or stakeholders or offices, you'd be the strongest contender to win the work because you're the undisputed leader in that niche, location, or relationship.

In such a case, instead of pursuing the *whole* deal and losing, you might seek to win a slice of the pie.

Think of the *Part* strategy as a Push strategy for a smaller prize.

Of course you'd immediately change your revenue objective in the forecast because you're no longer chasing all of the deal but only a subset of it. Your close date might also change since it may be possible to split off this part of the work, get started, and be paid long before your competitors have finished fighting over the original opportunity.

With this foothold established, your coworkers will be rubbing shoulders with the customer's staff sooner and become privy to opinions, attitudes, and needs that might later help you expand your new incumbency to additional work. You might even be awarded the rest of the project because it's easier for the customer to keep working with your team than educate another supplier.

As with the Pull strategy, you'll need people on the inside as supporters and mentors. To them falls the task of publicly saying their company's goals might be better served by breaking one project into several. You'll need to plant the seed of that idea in the ears of the most influential people for the concept to take root and spread in many camps at once. For the argument to be accepted, you must be sure it's bound by logic for the masses and emotion for the few.

Logic will prove to others why it makes sense to divide the original project pie into different slices. Changing any project plan in midflight carries risk. The people who first framed the plan along with its requirements, timetable, and funding may not like to see their best ideas challenged. They'll push back in favor of maintaining their plan. So the rationale for awarding different components to different suppliers must be wrapped in a compelling argument. It must speak to the virtues of actually *reducing* their risk by allowing experts to do the parts they're best at. This is not a message you can easily deliver from the outside. It is best seeded through those on the inside.

Perhaps the customer's plan is best served by inserting a "validation of needs" exercise for which your company can lend its brand name as a stamp of approval and give a second opinion on areas where you're known experts. Once inside, you make the customer work hard having meetings with you, drilling into details, and having a number of "Eureka moments" that build valuable insight and rapport. Ultimately you want them to wish you would stick around instead of having to start over with a different supplier after your piece is completed.

It might be argued that by the dominant supplier offering a "one-stop shop" for everything on the customer's list of requirements, they might be taking a loss in some areas only to pad out the cost in others—parts you're able to handle more efficiently at a lower cost, or which you can do at the same or greater cost but for a demonstrably lower risk.

Perhaps you see that the customer needs a solution deployed in multiple cities (or cultures) where you are strong on the ground and your rivals are thin in experience.

Maybe you can introduce other companies into the mix that you've worked with before. Their capabilities should fill gaps in your own offering. The trust you've built with the customer should be sufficient for them to see the suggestion of a consortium bid as not just a viable alternative but a very appealing one!

Perhaps your consortium's members might include other best-of-breed vendors who, like you are already in the race but unlikely to win all the work on their own. This is where the enemy of your enemy becomes your friend. Collude to join forces. Each of you takes a part of the project. Suggest that your customer should cherry-pick the best fruit and offer to happily coexist to accommodate that wisdom.

Sure, you're no longer going after the whole pie. But it's better to win 50 percent of something than 100 percent of nothing. Even so, be careful to monitor your cost of sale when using the Part strategy because if the whole pie was worth $200,000 and now you're slicing off a $100,000 portion, you could easily blow your profit on the cost of sale if you use the same resources and time frames as you would

	EVALUATION CRITERIA	WHO IS MOST VOCAL FOR THIS?	RANK	YOUR POSITIONING L M H		
1.	Reduce out of stocks in w'house	Bob Coates	5	X		
2.	Give real-time inventory	John Horne	6	X		
3.	Route nearest van to next job	Sally Jepson	9			X
4.	Reduce reload time at dock	Bob Coates	7			X
5.	Reduce manual calculations	Steve Hansen	8			X
6.	Steve's team to gain 20 hrs/mth	Steve Hansen	1	X		
7.	Andy's team revenue +14%	Mike Steele	2		X	
8.	Slow staff churn from 32% to 9%	Gloria vanStrom	3	X		
9.	Attract 20 new >$1M clients	Andy Wickett	4	X		

Figure 12.4: An Example of Weighted Decision Criteria Where You're Strongest in a Niche Area

for the whole pie. Therefore, "reducing the speed to yes" needs to be considered a measure of whether your Part strategy is working or not (Figure 12.4).

To be in a position to attempt a Part strategy, you must score high around the qualification Snapshot in assessment criterion 2 (the customer must have the ability to carve off a slice of their funding and apply it to the piece of business you want to win); criterion 4 (their requirements list must reveal a logical subset that can be spun out of the main body of work); criterion 6 (the value of breaking the project into separate stages instead of keeping the project intact and awarding it to a single supplier must carry obvious value nobody can easily contest); criterion 7 (you need to have highly credible resources to apply to the niche you want to claim); and criterion 9 (someone on the inside must be willing to stake their reputation on the idea being a sound one for their business—and they must favor you as the company to get the job done).

Cast a glance back at the third example on the Strategy Map (Figure 12.1), and you'll see how the Snapshot should look. As with the previous examples, if you can drive discussions, actions, and perceptions to where your position in a sales opportunity is strong on these parts of the Snapshot, your choice of what strategy and messaging are most available to you becomes clear. Proceed accordingly.

VALIDATION OF INFORMATION

A tip shared by top sellers is to always remember that in the heat of battle it can be difficult to see things objectively. In past times when armies would meet on a field, their commanders would find an elevated position from which to watch proceedings with impassionate objectivity. They would watch movements of the enemy, gauge their own force's progress, and send commands related to direction, speed, and focus down to their troops through a system of flags or drums or horns whose colors and tone all relayed a type of shorthand to the people on the ground.

When all people in your sales force are using a common language and framework to analyze and plan how to proceed in these long, complex sales cycles, it's exactly the same as in armies of old.

You can share your pursuit plan for an opportunity with anyone in your sales team and have them understand (with a minimum of explanation) the status of your sale, your points of leverage, and the risks or gaps that remain. Salespeople who are consistently successful know that it's better to test and improve their sales plan in the company of friends than to have it tested by the competition in front of the customer. Knowing that only the result matters, top sellers are prepared to leave their ego outside their office door and actively ask their peers to help them "test run" and "stress test" the approach they're taking and the meetings they are about to have. They practice, drill, and rehearse.

They don't worry about trying to look like they have all the answers—indeed, they hope to find where they do not, knowing that only by seeing the weaknesses in their approach to winning can weak things be made strong. They note how salespeople who may be less experienced or more egocentric or insecure almost never open up their sales to peer review, or do so only grudgingly and then present pages with text and diagrams doctored to look flawless. They point out how this kind of self-deception wins short-term praise, but it rarely wins revenue.

Top sellers also go one step further in their quest for truth. They validate their views with people in the customer's organization whose word they believe is reliable. If the customer doesn't believe you have a certain strength or weakness, you really don't. It's better to find out early while you can do something about it.

TACTICS AND COUNTERTACTICS

Whether you select Push, Pull, or Part as the most accessible and appropriate strategy for your sale, the intellectual exercise of deciding what label to give your approach is incomplete if you don't design corresponding sales tactics. You see, each strategy choice is like a different kind of music, and each type of music requires different dance steps. You don't dance a waltz when rock 'n' roll is playing, do you? Neither should you mix your tactics when selling.

By watching top sellers define their sales strategies, we observed deliberate and conscious decisions being made about the actions they would then take, and more important, those they avoided. The most strategic sellers don't send mixed signals. If they choose a Pull strategy, their conversations and actions eschew anything that looks like a Push strategy. It takes planning and forethought to do so. I'm going to give you the cliff notes.

In Figure 12.5, the gray panels summarize the direction your tactics could take to bring your choice of strategy to life.

If you recognize that your competitors are using one of these three strategies *against you*, the black panels contain tactics proven to hobble such efforts. Use this chart to guide your efforts when mapping tactics to strategies.

EXECUTING YOUR OWN SALES STRATEGY

If they want to buy 'X', push the impression that you do 'X' bigger, better, faster, safer or cheaper. If you're an incumbent supplier, push how this sale helps leverage their past investment with you. Push them to explore issues where you'll be revealed as strong (or where your competitors are weak).	Pull away from comparisons of 'X', and offer them 'X + Y'. Pull away from comparisons of 'X', and offer them 'Z' instead. Pull the discussion from areas of tangible comparison, to emotive topics you can dominate. Show how awarding you this sale opens the door to broader benefits.	Don't fight the war for all of 'X'; win the battle for 'a piece of X'. Sell the value of splitting the sale into 'best of breed niches', or divide it into a 'phased rollout'. If your solution doesn't meet all the customer's needs, consider splitting the sale with a partner. 50% is better than 0%.
▷ **PUSH**	▷ **PULL**	▷ **PART**
Ask mentors to add and weight criteria that favor your solution. Suggest the client looks closer at issues where competitor weaknesses will be revealed. Fight Push with Push. Project the impression you are biggest or best. Partner with another competitor to bring down a common rival.	Discredit the wisdom of changes to the decision criteria or delays that favor a competitor. Ask mentors to send competitors on low value tangents that dilute and divert their resources. Learn what the customer deems most important or highest risk. Show you're the expert in that area.	Show you can 'do it all', then find advocates of a single supplier (security, convenience, leverage). Paint the competitor's niche area as something you'll bundle into your solution at little or no cost. Ask mentors to ensure your rivals win low-profit work that is doomed to be political or problematic.

WHEN A COMPETITOR USES EACH STRATEGY

Figure 12.5: Tactics and Countertactics

Now let me pose some questions for sales managers to consider. Let's say you've run an opportunity review for a significant deal in your forecast. As a result of this analysis, everyone agrees the approach most likely to lead to revenue being attained is to adopt the Part strategy. The review team spent 30-minutes developing "scripts" for the sort of conversations your salesperson should now go and have with specific people in order to move their thinking to a place where the Part strategy has a hope of succeeding.

All of the people involved with the sale are pumped up and certain that with this sales plan, they're backing the right horse. You agree the salesperson can adjust their forecast to reflect the smaller piece of the pie they're now going after. Let's also say that if you could look into a crystal ball and see the future, it's true that if they do the things they've planned, they are certain of victory.

Now here's the rub—as the manager for this team, you know the rep in charge of the deal is not particularly skilled doing the things that success is now hinging on. You've been out on customer calls with them many times, and you know deep in your bones that they're the type of salesperson who likes to be social, needs to be liked, and easily gets lost in the thick of thin discussions rather than call the customer's attention to anything that might be controversial or challenging. They're an order taker more than an *order maker*. Is this rep really the right person to drive a Part strategy when its very essence demands they shake things up? Left to their own devices, they won't do it. And so no matter how much care is put into deciding which strategy to run with, it will all come undone in the execution of it.

This is where the sales manager plays a crucial role in giving that salesperson focused coaching to develop the skills each sales strategy requires of them. Where sales managers don't spend a large part of their time observing their reps in action, spotting their skill gaps, and training them to be all-rounders, those same managers become the weakest links in their company's drive to sell more strategically. You see, sales strategy is certainly about analysis and planning, but that alone doesn't win the day. It's only with the execution of the strategy that the tide can turn—and that requires people to not just do the right things but to do those things right.

It is the sales manager heading each sales team who ultimately turns good sales strategy into results. But they don't do this by selling for the team, even if being a top rainmaker was what they built their reputation on to win the manager's chair in the first place. No, the best sales managers understand their job is to create results *through* others. They focus on identifying each salesperson's development needs and then on coaching their staff so the skills needed to execute their sales strategies become self-sustaining.

It's a weak sales manager who ignores this part of their job description, and it's a weak HR manager who doesn't insist that the sales manager's key performance measures should include how much they increase the selling skills of their team each year.

WHICH SALES STRATEGY IS BEST?

I'm sometimes asked by sales directors to offer an opinion about which competitive sales strategy has the highest win rate. Unfortunately there is no silver bullet. Every sale has different dynamics, different stakeholder opinions, and different competitors. As such you *must* complete your due diligence to examine each sale, each time, and avoid the trap of using one approach.

The **Push strategy** can be the most easily defeated when it is used as a default behavior. This happens when "product, brand, price, or reputation" is the arrow you load into your bow every time you go hunting, without examining each sale on its merits. It's a lazy approach to selling, bereft of curiosity about what makes the customer tick, and it is highly predictable (hence easily countered). If the customer doesn't share the view that you're superior but you sell that way because *you* believe it, you might find yourself being regarded as akin to this fine Texan phrase: "Those guys are all hat and no cattle."

The **Pull strategy** relies on getting buyers talking about decision criteria that are different from what they have already thought of. You have to do your homework to know what the right issues and who the right people are to find the fertile ground for this. You need the courage to take a contrarian path, stand out from the pack, and make a difference. There is some anecdotal evidence from reviews of thousands of opportunity plans that a Pull strategy wins better than half the time (62 percent) when applied under appropriate circumstances and when it is followed through with conversations and actions that reinforce the theme of the strategy. Likely this success is due to the implicit requirement of researching the customer, which results in the sales rep being better prepared to have deeper business discussions with them.

The **Part strategy** also appears to have a higher-than-average success rate (71 percent) for smaller companies going up against the big guys and also for large companies that want to make sure they hold the most profitable chunks of hotly contested projects. In a risk-averse financial or legislative environment, clients value approaches that allow them to start projects faster at a lower cost or that create opportunities for partnering between suppliers, leading to efficiencies and economies of scale.

But before you pledge to use the Part strategy *all the time* because of its win rate, remember that by definition the Part strategy means you're going after smaller deals—so your company is well advised to redesign its measurements and reward system around time to closure or profitability of sale instead of just top-line revenue. If you don't revise your governance safeguards, you could easily bankrupt your sales effort by spending too much time and money chasing deals for lower revenue. So be careful.

ARE THERE MORE THAN THREE STRATEGIES?

Some sales training lectures imply that more than three strategies exist such as these: *defending* existing contracts against competitors trying to break into the account; citing a pending product release or price change to *delay* a decision that's sliding to a competitor; or *developing* ideas that create demand so an opportunity cycle can commence and find funding. Such notions confuse "account management tactics" with "opportunity strategy."

Where your customer has a vision, funding, and a trigger to act, the situation is a "live" opportunity. For these sales opportunities, if you focus on selecting and executing the Push, Pull, or Part strategies, you'll be more focused, on message, and successful. We'll consign any discussion about the other strategies to a book on account management, for another time.

With your competitive analysis complete and your strategy and positioning in place as a result of effective polling, positioning, and propaganda, we're ready to talk about how you establish Proof that you can deliver what you promise. Turn the page and we'll get started.

Chapter 13

Establish Your Proof

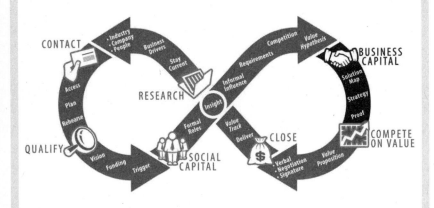

The Sales Expansion Loop: Business Capital—Proof

Did you know that buyer psychology changes in each trimester of the sale?

Early in a sale, prospects are keen to define their **needs** and crystallize their vision. Sometimes you help them do this.

By the middle of the sale, the buyers' focus moves to assessing the **credibility** and fit of potential suppliers, which is a subjective exercise that creates emotional favorites and factual frontrunners.

At the closing stages of a sale (as they get closer to staking their reputation on a decision), their internal compass rotates to a different concern you must satisfy: **value versus risk**.

As a result of the changes in the psychology throughout the sale, your discussions need to take on a different emphasis in this final trimester of the sale. You need to focus on proving *why they can't lose* if they buy from you.

How do top sellers achieve this?

CASE STUDIES

It builds prospect confidence when buyers can read how other customers solved similar problems using your solution. Most people minimize risk by moving in herds, so every account manager should revisit each customer after a solution is in place and work with them to track how well all the promises made during the sale were actually delivered. This is where reference stories and case studies come from.

If the rep used PRECISION Questions during the initial sales campaign, it's easy to dust off those F2F Meeting Plans to see what the issues were and then revisit the customer months after the solution was implemented to examine the extent to which those issues were resolved. How have the customer's performance metrics changed? How far did the needle move? How satisfied are people with the changes in their world?

An ongoing cycle of promise-deliver-measure is a best practice in account management—and it's no coincidence the Sales Expansion

Loop is shaped like the infinity symbol with this principle in mind. Not only do you get testimonials to use in future sales elsewhere but the very fact that you care enough to follow your own work and check on results can also prime the pump for new sales, both to the same account and to others you inspire with the case study you gain.

Interview each key stakeholder, especially those who served as supporters and mentors. Format your findings as stories that tell a narrative future prospects will relate to.

Here's how to write the case study:

- **Problems.** Start by explaining in simple terms what the customer's problem, need, or vision was (get this information from the PRECISION notes you made on your F2F Meeting Plans as you met each stakeholder when the sale was in progress). State what industry the customer's company operates in, what role or job title each stakeholder plays, and what vision, triggers, pains, or business drivers were behind the need to change. This establishes the background to the story; it describes a situation future prospects will relate to because it's their world too. Using these tag words helps catalog case studies on your server or archive system so you can browse cases by industry, company, job, or problem when seeking relevant stories to use with future prospects.
- **Concerns.** Next, the case study should include statements from the customer about what their doubts and biggest concerns were. You can learn much from this to apply in future sales. For your case studies, these personal anecdotes lend a degree of authenticity that these are real people with familiar needs and legitimate concerns— possibly the same unstated risks that are going through your new prospect's mind as they read the case study about a past customer.
- **Solution.** Next, the case study should explain what the solution was, how it was put in place, and how your company helped make it work.
- **Impact.** Add customer-validated metrics about savings, improvements, and uplifts to productivity wherever you can. As stated

above, if you do your job collecting the "before" picture during the sale, it's easier for the customer to measure those same things for you to collect the "after" picture several months after closing the deal and putting the solution in place.

Some sales managers view revisiting the customer and writing the case study as too important a task to leave to their marketing departments, who are strangers in the account. So they mandate that their salespeople collect a minimum number of case studies each year based on the deals they closed the year before. Some even award points for extracting these cases from multiple job titles and different needs. Marketing copywriters and layout artists then wordsmith these into properly formatted documents.

This is how companies amass a library of up-to-date case studies for all the situations, industries, roles, and solutions that apply to new prospects. Being able to show a relevant example of your track record goes a long way to ameliorating a prospect's fears and doubts. Being able to produce a thick sheaf of relevant stories only strengthens your case.

So ask yourself: When was the last time I revisited a past sale to extract a customer case study? Last month? Last quarter? Last year? Never? How much more ammunition would I have if *everyone* on my sales team completed this task in the next 30 days?

Can you see how these case studies could be game-changers in your market? So go do it. Get the ball rolling by making the suggestion in your next sales meeting.

REFERENCES

Customer references are requested when buyers want to talk to people who will vouch for the quality of your work. Why do customers ask for these? In simpler times when people lived and worked in the same suburb and all their clientele were local and probably knew each other, the community grapevine of references held value. It's like the word of mouth you seek when you're selecting a local builder, plumber, or babysitter from your neighborhood.

But when prospects raise the same request in the corporate setting, they're probably doing so out of instinct without thinking. If they stop to examine the logic of these requests, they'd see that you're only ever going to put them in touch with people who will endorse you and that you'll already have coached them on what to say. Unless the referee is someone they've heard of and respect, their word won't carry much more weight than yours.

Such requests are therefore questionable in the value they give to the prospect (other than validating that you have at least one other customer). Furthermore, gaining agreement and scheduling these calls can be a pain for you to set up, for too little return.

So why play this game?

Well, it can work out pretty well if there's a specific case study they've already read, one that they'd like to ask that customer some specific questions about. That actually makes sense. But even your most ardent fans will eventually tire of calls from your prospects—they have their own job to do without being your public relations agent.

So do everyone a favor: film your referees on video giving their testimonials, and get their signatures on a transcript of the video, printed on their company letterhead. Then split an audio clip off the video and make an MP3 file. This way you have three different forms of reference on tap from the same customer, and you can easily mail these assets as attachments in whatever format your latest prospect prefers. In most cases, hearing, watching, or reading such a reference will satisfy these requests better than talking to a live person.

SITE VISITS

If you're already installed at a "golden customer," showcase site, or Center of Excellence where a community outreach or public relations program means they're happy to show your products and services in action as part of a larger tour, these are places to take prospects who feel "seeing is believing."

Perhaps the company is proud of what they've achieved in their automated manufacturing, efficient logistics, state-of-the-art computer center, "green" office layout, engaged and motivated staff, or some other aspect of business that is unique and praiseworthy.

You can benefit from that sentiment by taking new prospects to see your solutions working in a real environment, where they can ask questions of company officers who hold the same job title.

Top sellers place a price on such a premium activity, especially if they're funding the lunch, flights, and hotels. They know it holds tremendous value for the prospect and that to give it away for free sends the wrong message. You must treat it as a rare and precious VIP event reserved for the privileged few. Failure to attach a value to the activity can lead to the visiting prospect seeing it as a junket on your dime. Activities that hold value must always be *traded*.

You might make it a billable activity that you'll give a partial credit for when they sign the contract. Perhaps you'll negotiate something you want—like a verbal commitment or signature—in return for a successful site visit. To that end, you must establish in advance a list of the concerns and questions they want to satisfy at the site (their business reason for going), and get them to explain exactly how these specific answers will better help them take action that advances the sale.

Once you know this, you have the foundation for trading their satisfaction into a commitment of some kind. Never waste an opportunity to gain commitment. There's no need to be sheepish about this being your aim when taking them on site. They know the game being played.

Their answers to such questions also frequently reveal wonderful competitive intelligence about where gaps appear in each vendor's offer and where the prospect's concerns are focused. Fill those gaps. Be the stepping-stone to their goals.

DEMONSTRATIONS

At the prospect's premises, at a customer demo site, or on your own factory floor, showing your product in action can be a potent lure. This is why late-night television abounds with so many infomercial channels. What are they doing? They're *demonstrating* their product! And they make millions of dollars every night from people who want to experience the same ease, utility, prestige, or comfort as the people they see enjoying those products already. So when you know what functions and features most interest them—especially those that are weighted as priorities by the people whose formal vote or informal influence is key to success—giving a demonstration of these and allowing the prospect to get hands-on experience with them is a great step forward.

Demonstrations begin by asking what the prospect is most curious to see, and why. Always get the "why." Ask how it relates to what they've already told you about their Problems and Reasons or their existing Ideas for what a solution should look like, as gleaned from your use of PRECISION Questions in each meeting to date.

Before the demo, pause to help the customer paint a picture in their mind about how their business or daily routine will change if they can put in place the capabilities they're most interested in. Ask what it will mean to them in terms of time saved or raised productivity. What will they do with that extra time or quality or profit? Help them picture themselves in that future state before you show them anything. The vision will always appeal more than the product you're about to demo, so always make certain the vision is stirring in their heart and mind before the demo begins. Your goal is then to sell how your product delivers that vision.

If you've heard the saying, "You don't sell the steak, you sell the sizzle," this predemo discussion is where you marinate that steak in juices and rich dark sauces so when you throw it onto the grill, the sound and aroma will fill the prospect's senses and get them salivating faster than Pavlov's dogs. Too many salespeople rush past this preparation, to their detriment. Helping your prospect visualize the future utility of your product is a key step in baiting the hook so they swallow it up to the gullet—hook, line, and sinker.

When you turn on your product, it's the equivalent of firing up the grill. Start by showing how it works on those functions you know they already enjoy today. It's important to show that your product is at least equal to the things they already appreciate about their old product, to alleviate any unvoiced concerns about what capabilities they might miss out on if they change suppliers. As you do this, the hot plate heats up nicely one degree at a time. You're almost ready to throw on your juicy sirloin.

The time will come to show the new capabilities your product offers. Make something of a fanfare when you place this meat on the grill. That first burst of wet sizzling as its juices are locked inside is a sound that's seared into the memory of anyone who's ever stood around a hot plate or campfire. So use your demo to start with the *most important* feature, the thing everyone came to see. Sear it into their memory first. Seal in those juices. Show how it works, and before moving to the next feature, ask them to confirm that if they had this capability, it would bring them closer to their vision. Sell the sizzle.

Next, it's time to drizzle on some glaze and toss on a handful of salt, a grind of pepper, or a sprig of fresh herbs. These are the *next most important* features and capabilities on the prospect's list, and as before, you pause to answer questions and then confirm that these also bring them closer to that vision they can now smell and taste as being within their grasp.

By now your steak is showing dark grill lines as the skin gives off the tangy aroma of your marinade. Locked inside, the pink meat is bubbling in its own juices, turning darker and tastier by the second. But only on one side: it's time to turn it over. So take your barbecue tongs and hand them to your prospect. Let them turn the meat. This is where you give them hands-on experience with your product. You remind them of a specific function they do today with their aging product (or the manual process they follow if they have no solution in place), and you ask what they want to improve about that experience. Then you get them pressing the buttons, pulling the gears, or viewing the screens of your product so they see the difference. It's faster, it's easier, it's more accurate—all the things they dream of.

Once the other side of the steak hits the grill, it gives off another crackle that surprises them in its intensity, the rich tangy smoke curling up their nose and making them hungrier than ever. With their hands now touching your solution, they can imagine how this steak is going to taste as they tend to it on the grill with their tongs, lovingly nudging it to perfection, eager to serve it up. This is no longer your steak. It belongs to them now. They're already thinking of what drink they'll serve with it.

"Is this what you want?" you ask. Knife and fork in hand, they reply: "Serve it up. I'm starving!"

I've given you the five-step model top sellers use for demonstrations:

1. Connect to the prospect's vision and let it marinate.
2. Make yourself equal to what they have today as you turn up the heat and tease their expectations.
3. Show how you solve their biggest unanswered questions first, and sear the sizzle into their memory.
4. Garnish with additional unique capabilities.
5. Hand over the tongs, and let them produce the next burst of sound and flavor. Let them turn the steak until they own it.

Can you smell the salt and pepper seasoning and taste the tangy dark barbecue flavor we left the meat soaking in while the grill grew searing hot? Can you smell the smoke up your nose, see the mirage-inducing heat as you stand around the cooker, and hear the sound of metal scraping the grill as you turn the meat over? You know those sounds, smells, and tastes, right? I'm pulling you in, aren't I?

This is a book made of paper, yet its words have the power to stimulate all five senses. So can *your* words when you stage a demo the right way.

Chapter 14

Compete on Value

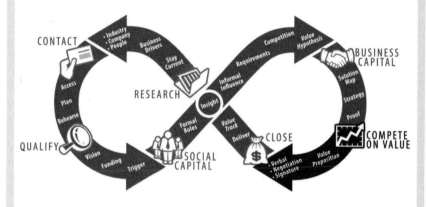

The Sales Expansion Loop: Compete on Value

At the end stages of the sale there may be a final presentation, a ritual wrap-up to summarize what all parties have agreed to in past meetings, discussing what you'll deliver, and how they'll benefit. Part of your final presentation will focus on the value proposition that has been codeveloped (and hopefully copresented) with customer stakeholders around the table. This will all be documented in a formal proposal you write.

All these calendared steps should be featured in the Mutual Project Plan you agreed to long ago, which even now at the end of the sales cycle should still be giving you the upper hand. You can expect a knee-jerk attempt at negotiation. But once this is completed to everyone's satisfaction, triumphantly you'll emerge with a signed contract.

Amid all this activity, the one thing top sellers agree to as a critical success factor is to compete on value, not sell on price. In this chapter we're going to explore that concept, including how to turn the *value hypothesis* you've been working on with different people into a *value proposition* your customers can get excited about.

DECIDING WHAT VALUE LOOKS LIKE

The first thing to consider is that value is in the eye of the beholder. It may look slightly different to each person you meet in the customer's organization. While they may all agree on the group outcomes they hope this purchase or investment will deliver, they're also hoping their unique departmental or personal agendas can piggyback the project.

This means there will be one bundle of value that will be featured in public discussion, plus other propositions that matter to people in ways that might not be shared in common. It's your job to know what these are and to show relevant people that these outcomes will flow not from just any supplier but only from you.

Once you embrace this reality, it can be like a lightning bolt. This is the flash that illuminates the vision of top sellers the world over and helps them see clearly what others only strain at in darkness: it's not good enough to present *one* value proposition in your meetings and proposal document—you need a separate value proposition for *each key person*, as well as for the organization as a whole. That's the secret most other salespeople miss.

As you use PRECISION Questions to drill into the triggers, problems, and opportunities behind the customer's vision, you collect a list of core needs people have. Each time you run a call using a F2F Meeting Planner, you collect descriptions of these needs using the customer's own language, jargon, and measurements. The more people you meet, the more questions you can ask. The more questions you ask, the more meeting notes and measures you collect. The more meeting notes and measures you collect, the more accurate your Solution Maps will be and the more accurate and compelling your value propositions become.

In Figure 14.1, you'll note that there are multiple F2F Meeting Planners collected throughout the sale. These come from each visit, from multiple people you meet between "Hi" and "Buy."

Being able to collect such a wealth of information about people and their vision, attitudes, and objections is the value of planning each call. If you've been writing a plan for each meeting and making notes on those sheets about what people say in response to your PRECISION Questions and presentations (especially where you collected the *how much*, *how soon*, *how many*, *how often*, or *how far* measurements of their problems, reasons, impact points, and ideas), all this becomes an important archival asset. These records are the building blocks for your value proposition.

You'll find some needs may be common across departments (*corporate value*). Others will be unique to specific roles or groups (*department value*). Sometimes making a change, networking, or gaining visibility on a project team serves people's personal ambitions (*personal value*). High performers are careful to show customers they understand and can deliver these three levels of value. For this reason you see these phrases listed under the Value column of the F2F Meeting Plan.

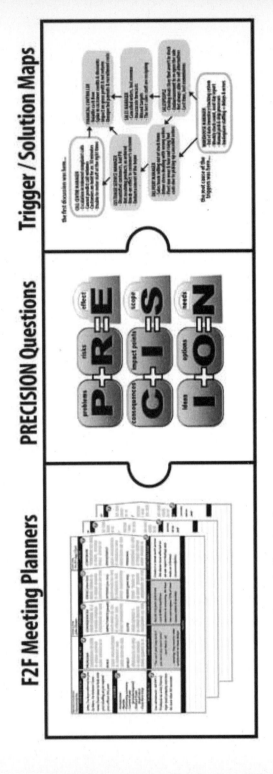

Figure 14.1: The Building Blocks of Value

Where you have captured specific phrases and jargon the customer uses to describe their world, you'll need to present your value proposition using those same terms. For example, airlines use metrics like "breakeven load factors" and "available seat miles." Banks use metrics like "return on equity," "gearing," and "cost to income." Telcos use metrics like "client churn," "wireless revenue share," and "network performance." Web marketers talk about "caching," "eyeballs," "click-through rates," and "avatars."

Make sure your value proposition includes the language of your prospect's world and describes how your solution will change the way people conduct themselves on the job and how they achieve or surpass their measures of success.

Try coming up with three sets of measures for each key role, department, or user community in the business:

1. **Their current performance.** Tell typical, day-in-the-life stories of how people in certain roles do their job. Include measurements for how long, how well, how accurate, and how effective their experience or outputs are today. Describe what frustrates them about the status quo. Use people's names wherever possible so your audience hears you talking about peers they know and see in the office or plant every day—this helps them visualize what "now" looks like.

2. **Their desired performance.** Repeat what people have told you about their vision and how much faster, easier, or better their job or outputs could be. What positive events or results will they get more of? What negative events or results will they see less of? Confirm the sources that say these results are possible or are already being enjoyed by other people who do the same job elsewhere (case studies). Include how making these changes will make people feel (in their own words where possible). Continue using the names of people you are talking about so your audience visualizes how people they work with will benefit in the future. Be sure to explain

the ripple effects of these benefits to other departments or functions, as shown in your Trigger Map.

3. **What's possible with your solution.** The first thing is to show the delta between current performance and desired performance. This answers "Why do this now?" The next thing is to show where the products, company, people, partners, or other deliverables on your Solution Map will enable the prospect to achieve the desired delta with less risk, greater ease, convenience, or speed. You present this in words consistent with your choice of a Push, Pull, or Part strategy, and you show how it's possible by citing case studies or other credible testimony. In essence, what you're saying is this:

> You told us what you thought was possible, but we know a way to achieve results even better than you have been hoping for. Here's how we will do it. We're the only source for the blend of people, experience, and circumstances needed to do this.

Don't wait until a final presentation to share your personalized value proposition with individuals within the company. They should already have heard this from you in private chambers, and they should already have commented on it so you can refine it. When they see it again in a group presentation or written into the pages of a proposal, it should come as no surprise. It should be a reflection of something already agreed to.

In fact, star salespeople depend on the value hypotheses of key people having been explored, challenged, tweaked with metrics, and turned into true value propositions before they are disclosed in a group setting. Having had these discussions privately is one of the ways they get people off the fence and turn them from neutral people to supporters or mentors who see you are taking an interest in how they benefit. The earlier you make those connections the better.

Even after you've made these connections with people, their purchasing process may still require that you attend a day of presentations to a panel of evaluators, a decision maker, and approvers. Inexperienced sellers think these days are their "big chance." But you know better. You don't leave it to this late in the process. Like a chess master, you made certain of success several moves earlier by having the right conversations with the right people about the right value. In connecting to people in the spokes of the business, you've achieved high signal strength with them as well as those in the hub. Even if you haven't met people in the hub directly, they've heard good things about you from their lieutenants.

But the canniest sales pros admit they don't always get the time or the connections to cover everyone. There can still be people who help make the contracting decision who emerge from their stronghold only late in the game. Therefore, it pays to make the best impression in a final presentation, even if you think you have the deal all sewn up. Here are some tips.

THE BEST TIME TO GIVE A PRESENTATION

When a prospect is lining up vendors for a competition, does it matter what slot you get on the calendar? It turns out it does! Research at universities and clinics into energy levels, concentration, and receptivity[1] conclude that there's a specific window of time to make the best impression.

Between 9 a.m. and 11 a.m. following the routines of waking from sleep and starting the workday, the brain holds moderate levels of the stress hormone *cortisol*, which helps the mind focus, says Sung Lee, MD, secretary of the International Brain Education Association. Customers are primed for learning and are more able to process tasks that require analysis and concentration. This is a good time of day for anyone giving or receiving a technically oriented, game-changing, or detailed presentation to challenge preconceived ideas (such as when your sale is using a Pull or Part strategy).

From 11 a.m. to 2 p.m. levels of the sleep hormone *melatonin* are lowest, and people's mental agility is high, best suited to working through sequential work where they can tick one box after another,[2] according to René Marois, PhD, director of the Human Information Processing Laboratory at Vanderbilt University. This is a good time of day for anyone giving or receiving a product- or services-focused presentation when your compliance to a list of requirements is being judged (such as when your sale is using a Push strategy).

Avoid the "dead zone" between 2 p.m. to 6 p.m. When people digest their lunch between 2 p.m. to 3 p.m., the stomach draws blood away from the brain. The body's circadian rhythm that regulates sleep and wakefulness powers down. It's no coincidence that phone texts, e-mails, and tweets surge at this time[3] as people seek undemanding tasks they can complete on automatic pilot.

If you're stuck having to present at this time of day, get people on their feet, moving and drinking water to increase vascular volume and circulation to drive blood back to the brain. After 3 p.m. the brain is getting quite fatigued. People are more easygoing, but they're not as sharp; therefore, they see complex details through a fog. Expecting your proposal to resonate when presented late in the day is a long shot.

Are the days of the week similarly stacked for success or failure?

Some books and articles suggest that Tuesdays are best for presentations (paraphrasing): "People use Monday to get into gear for the week, then start sliding back into 'weekend mode' from Wednesday onward."[4] Not convinced? Neither was I. Such conclusions don't sound very scientific.

So in seeking the opinion of top sellers, we were reminded that we live in an age when the pervasiveness of social media crosses the work-life divide, meaning that people stay connected to the online world at work as much as at home. If we could spot patterns for the times of the week when people are tuning out during work hours to instead lose themselves in social media like Facebook, SMS, and Twitter, we might infer that these are times when people are *least* focused on business.

Such a test could only be meaningful if the sample were broad and significant and if high and low usage points showed a dramatic contrast. Enter Dan Zarrella at *Hubspot*. Dan dug into a giant data set of over 9.5 *billion* instances of online traffic monitored by Mailchimp. What he learned was that all around the world, Thursdays show the week's lowest ebb in people doing housekeeping of their online subscriptions. Furthermore, Thursdays show the lowest workday level of socializing on Facebook.[5]

The data implies that people are most "in the zone" for business on Thursdays, having used the earlier days of the week to play catch-up, clear backlogs, reset priorities, and rally focus. By contrast, Tuesdays are when online social activities peak each week, implying that people are least in tune with business concerns that day.

In a separate study reported in the *Marketing Watchdog Journal*,[6] researcher Ken Molay wanted to know which day of the week has the highest response rate for businesspeople joining webinars. It turns out that Thursdays are again reported as the day audiences respond most favorably to presenters. The day of least appeal? Tuesdays.

A pattern emerges.

A poll by Robert Half International, a recruiting firm, asked 150 senior executives their thoughts on this topic. "In addition to serving as a catch-up day after the weekend, Monday is when many regularly scheduled meetings occur, which can decrease the time available to complete tasks," says Max Messmer,[7] chairman of subsidiary Accountemps. "Many view Tuesday as an opportunity to focus their efforts and establish momentum for the rest of the week." It appears early in the week is when 69 percent of senior managers focus on internal planning and housekeeping. Not surprisingly, Friday is reported as a write-off by 97 percent of managers in the study. This leaves Wednesday and Thursday when managers flip their mental process from working "on the business" to working "in the business." This timing is ideal for delivering sales presentations to your audience.

Therefore, if you're given a choice of when to stage your most important presentations and pitch your value, the sweet spot is mid-week (with a preference for Thursday), from 9 a.m. to 2 p.m. when you and your audience will be most alert and engaged. That's not to say you should refuse an opportunity to present at other times. But if a procurement officer or secretary books you in for 9 a.m. Monday or 4 p.m. Friday, think twice. You can do better.

PREPARING TO PRESENT

A search on Amazon.com for books on presentation skills returns 10,000 hits. A Google search returns nearly 80 million blogs and slideshows. It's safe to say that if you want to know how to prepare and deliver an effective presentation, the answers are a click away. But having conducted hundreds of interviews of C-level executives and revenue leaders, we began to see trends in what buyers look for and top sellers do most often that are valuable because they're not generally known. These insights are brief, but they're poignant.

When preparing to pitch your value in a major presentation, involve your customer. Seek out those with whom you have the strongest signal strength (refer to your Influence Map), and enlist their support. This begins *several weeks before* the big day. Meet with them and agree on what your presentation should achieve and what presentation medium you should use based on which people are attending from their company. For example, if the most important decision influencers in the room are known to be fans of whiteboard discussions and opponents of boilerplate slide presentations, that would be helpful for you to get straight.

Rehearse your presentation with them. Share your Trigger Map and Solution Map, show how you're touching on all the right themes to the people you think matter most, and ask for feedback on how your presentation resonates.

Do this with several people. Make sure they see the value to them and their department shining through. Ask for a verbal commitment that they will support your solution as the front-runner.

Book your own team to agree on what will be in your presentation. Decide which people should present different topics so that nobody is seen to attend without a clear purpose. Agree on how you will each introduce yourselves in a way that makes it clear why each person is attending, the value they add by being there, and what they want to gain. Lead the customer to reciprocate with the same quality of information, as explained earlier in the book. Decide how long individuals should talk before they need to pause and solicit feedback and discussion. Make it as interactive as possible to engage your audience.

A week before the presentation, recheck the list of people attending. Decide if there are any people on your side who are better known or liked by the customer's staff. Plan to seat them closest to the customer's people and to be the individuals who "own" giving the answers to these people (unless the answers are obviously more appropriate coming from a different person on your team).

If your presentation is going to include a break for lunch, make sure your team members agree on a set of safe discussion topics they will stick to. Anticipate what questions the customer might ask each of you after they divide you up (such as "How many references do you really have for this solution?" "Which ones are most like our company, and what was their result?" "What could go wrong?" or "Just between us, what's your best price?"). Design answers to these questions so everyone on your team provides consistent information. Lunchtime can be where you're tested the most.

Double-check the logistics around the location, the time and equipment needed for your presentation, and if there are any late-breaking adjustments your supporters suggest.

Agree on a covert "control signal" you will use with your supporters if you need them to jump in and take control of the discussion. For example, if someone on their team gives you a difficult time or acts unreasonably, it is more effective for a peer in the customer's company to call it out and restore order than for you to attempt it.

Be clear about what commitments you will ask for at the end of your presentation, and check with your supporters that these are reasonable.

Always plan to ask for their verbal commitment to move forward. Your Mutual Project Plan should show what the next step is. If it's to win the order, ask your supporters and mentors if doing so is appropriate for your meeting.

Seek your supporters' agreement to talk the day after your presentation and debrief their colleagues' reactions to your presentation compared to others they've seen.

Meanwhile, rehearse, rehearse, rehearse. Directors of theater productions know that customers who pay for a ticket expect a flawless performance. Their troupes might rehearse five times a week for four weeks before they go live with an audience. That's 20 practice runs and dress rehearsals. Film directors calculate that their actors perform one hour for every minute of finished footage. Salespeople don't have anywhere near that amount of time available, but the lesson is still clear: practice makes perfect.

The day after your presentation, ask your supporters separately, "What resonated?" "What didn't?" "Who is being vocal in their support, and why?" "Who is backing a different horse, and why?" Triangulate what people tell you. These insights will be invaluable for your follow-up, negotiation, and close. You may learn that people are buzzing about what they heard from you. Maybe the day after your presentation is the right time to ask for a verbal commitment or signed order. Strike while the iron is hot. Without a mentor on the inside feeding back to you what people's reactions actually are, it's impossible to guess the climate from the outside. You don't want to miss the opportunity to close a deal while emotions and excitement are high just because you never thought to set up a way to take the customer's temperature.

ISN'T VALUE JUST ABOUT NUMBERS?

When we hear the term "value proposition," it's common to think about spreadsheets of financial data and proposals lit up with line graphs and bar charts. A vibrant industry led by companies that include Qvidian, Solution Matrix, and Shark Finesse exists to train salespeople in the language of finance and business acumen, and these companies sell us software to make the task easier.

For salespeople who regularly present cases to purchasing agents and financial managers for budget approval, using this type of software makes abundant sense, as does gaining a working knowledge of finance to hold a cogent discussion with these buyers. They might not get excited about pledges of partnership and synergy, but CFOs all crack a smile for a sound financial case—especially where you outline how reductions in cost, increases in gains (and the speed to achieve said gains) impact their cash flow over time (as shown in Figure 14.2).

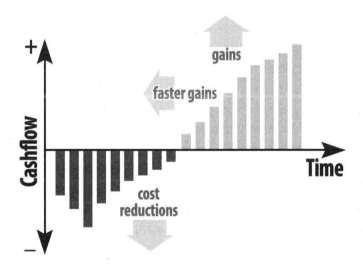

Figure 14.2: An Example of a Cash Flow Chart

Other financial terms may be expected in your proposal, like the *net present value* (the difference between the value of cash outflows and inflows now and in the future, based on the time-value of money); *internal rate of return* (the rate of growth a project is expected to generate); *payback* (the length of time required to recover the cost of the investment); and *return on investment* (the projected benefit of an investment divided by the cost of the investment, based on the business case). These calculations provide accountants with objective, unemotional comparison of one investment against another, which guides them to spend funds on projects that are most attractive. Most accountants are risk averse. Numbers don't lie. There's safety in numbers.

Finance managers and senior executives who come from an economics background are often left-brain thinkers (who focus on logic, data, and structure). They value and know how to interpret financial information. Most salespeople, however, are right-brainers (creativity, connections, flexibility) for whom complex calculations don't always come easily.

Top sellers recognize this, and they are advocates of outsourcing left-brain tasks to software that can do the heavy lifting for them. If they expect that a meeting will require a financial discussion that goes deeper than they're comfortable with, they invite someone from their own finance department to field those questions instead of bluffing their way through and losing credibility.

This is an interesting finding because it is commonly assumed the top salespeople in the world are fluent in the language of the boardroom. It's not uncommon for salespeople who have never studied commerce or economics to believe this, and they consider their lack of financial education to be a handicap blocking them from calling on senior buyers.

Yet the truth is that while having some level of comfort with these themes is an advantage, even heavy hitter salespeople use sales aides to arrive at the numbers. The time they spend discussing rates of return and economic value added is tiny compared to the time they spend applying their charisma and right-brain skills to emote, create, inspire, and connect with nonfinancial stakeholders.

So while business cases and calculations have a place in your value proposition, they are only one dimension of it. The *majority* of people you sell to are more interested in the change you're proposing and the emotions you create when explaining it.

As stated earlier, it pays to approach each stakeholder who has formal and informal power and sell a personal value proposition before making your blanket case of company-to-company value. Personalize your final presentation and the pages of your proposal document. Tell a story about each department's "before and after." Describe how the experience of completing certain tasks will change (and what this means for the people who do those tasks today). Doing so pays huge dividends.

As a result, a truly effective value proposition isn't based only on the cool calculation of left-brain logic that appeals to financial minds. Instead, it includes right-brain emotion and persuasion.

You may have heard the axiom, "People buy on emotion, *then* justify with logic." It's a concept scientists have been investigating in a branch of science called *neuroeconomics*, where the brain's role in buying and selling is studied. A landmark brain-imaging study led by Benedetto De Martino at University College London has proven that emotions rule decisions almost completely.[8]

Subjects underwent brain scans while being asked to gamble or refrain. They were given a pot of money. When one group of participants was told they would "keep" 40 percent of their money if they didn't gamble, the prefrontal cortex that commands logic fired up, and they chose to gamble only 43 percent of the time. Interestingly, the part of the brain that controls emotion, the amygdala, *also* activated.

When the question was framed that they could "lose" 60 percent of their money if they didn't gamble, the amygdala triggered, and they rolled the dice 62 percent of the time—44 percent more often when logic was not invoked. De Martino recalls, "We found everyone showed emotional biases; no one was totally free of them."

Another way of saying this is that the brain's emotional center engages in *all* decisions, but when propositions of logic are relied on, the discussion becomes 44 percent *less compelling* than if left to emotion alone.

This is a bombshell for sellers.

It's an insight in line with what our star performers revealed. They provide a financial value proposition (to satisfy a customer hygiene factor that requires they show one), but the secret of their success is in creating emotional connections around the advantages each person will enjoy: *personalized value propositions.*

In this revelation about emotion versus logic, I'm reminded of a scandalous hidden camera show by masters of misdirection Penn & Teller. Diners attended an upscale restaurant where a "water steward" appeared at their table before the food was served to offer various boutique bottles of water purportedly from rainforests, volcanoes, and glacial rivers.[9] One label clearly stated the water was from a "municipal supply," another was titled *L'eau du Robinet* (French for "tap water"), and a third was even called *Aqua de Culo* (Spanish for "ass water")!

Yet because of the *emotions* the sales pitch had stirred in them, customers couldn't see through logical eyes. They were happy to pay prices more outrageous than gasoline, and they waxed lyrical about the various tastes and feelings each sample of water evoked. The catch was this: all those bottles were filled from the same garden hose in the back room.

The message is clear: logic lacks the power people ascribe to it. Forget the "Ben Franklin Close" of using two columns to weigh up the pros and cons—science doesn't really support such a basic approach when selling to Ideas Buyers. Even when people think they're being logical in their decision making, it's *always* emotion at the core.

This is why rational people are happy to pay a high price and love the purchase *if they think the product is worth it.* A lot of this belief comes down to how convincingly the value is presented to them and how persuaded they are by your passion. This is such an important element that some sales managers have been heard to shout the war cry: "If you don't execute passionately, you'll be passionately executed!"

Maybe this is why superstar salespeople start by painting a vision, drive it with triggers, sell the value, and work across all the points of influence as they methodically complete the Sales Expansion Loop.

Each of these is a reinforcing element. They all build belief. They all lead to "Yes!"

"YOU'RE JUST TOO EXPENSIVE"

How do top performers handle price objections? Here's an amalgam of ideas from the best and brightest.

First, an Interest-Creating Remark

> I find what you're saying interesting. I appreciate it. And it reminds me of something one of the richest men in the world once pointed out. Warren Buffett said: "I try to buy stock in businesses that are so wonderful that an idiot can run them. Because sooner or later, one will." What I'm asking you to do today is invest in *my* business. We might not have the cheapest price, but the way we run our business means more than that.

Next, a Credibility Builder

We're stable and have the bugs worked out. Everything about our business just works. As Buffett says, any idiot can run us. We're profitable. We reinvest in our business to create new ideas and bring new value to our customers. We're growing in this market while others are not.

Now, Translate This into Their Language

What this means to you is that you don't have to worry about whether we'll still be here five years from now, or if we really know how to deliver our promises. Customer satisfaction is important to us. And because of our past investment and experience, you'll start enjoying the benefits right away. There are smaller, newer, or cheaper companies you could buy from, where you might be one of the first customers they've attempted this kind of solution at—a guinea pig where they're learning how to get things right at your expense, with hidden costs around every corner. You get none of those problems with us—just ease of use.

Next Comes the Price Justification

That's why our price is a little higher: your peace of mind is worth something to us, and I'm sure it's worth something to you too, isn't it?

Always wait for the customer to agree. Now you're on the same page again, and you can move forward from here with another attempt at closing. However, some pros prefer to drive home the idea of how farcical it is to ask for a discount, to safeguard against the price objection being raised again. A lighthearted metaphor will do:

> When you go out for a high-class meal, do you ever ask them to knock 20 percent off the price when the bill comes and use McDonald's as a benchmark to justify such a request? Can you imagine telling the waiter: "Hey, you know I had a choice when I came out tonight. I could have taken my family or work colleagues out for McDonald's burgers or Pizza Hut instead of coming to the Ritz. But we chose to eat here instead. We've enjoyed it, but we think you should knock some numbers off this bill as a reward for choosing you." Would either of us do that? Of course not! In fact, we usually leave a 10 to 15 percent tip on top of what we're charged for the meal! We don't mind paying more . . . if it's worth it.

Shift Gears and Make a Rational Argument

> So it seems that what we need to establish today is why my offer is worth the asking price, or if you'd like to order less from our menu and reduce your price that way. We need to decide if you want to eat a full-course meal at the Ritz, or if you want a smaller-sized serving from McDonald's. But the one thing I've learned from having more business lunches than I care to remember is that there's no such thing as eating at the Ritz for McDonald's prices. That's an unrealistic expectation.

Now, Classify the Reasons for the Price Objection

> To get started, can you help me understand if you're facing real budget constraints and don't actually have the money to afford the right solution, or if this price sensitivity I'm feeling from you today is part of your buying policy to shave something off every supplier's ticket price?

How Much Is "Too Much"?

> I certainly have mechanisms at my disposal to lower my price, and I would be happy to work with you on that. Let's start by agreeing how far you want the price lowered, and your reasons why.

Collecting this information reveals volumes.

Classify the Reason

It may help if you suggest what their reasons might be. This gives you control when answering them. The following are suggestions:

1. **"Maybe you're asking for a lower price because you physically don't have enough money in your budget. Is that what's happened? Can I ask what funding you actually have available?"** Funding should have been qualified on your Opportunity Snapshot in the first trimester, but if you learn their true budget only late in the sale, you should explain that this new information requires that your solution be rescoped. Ask them to help you prioritize must-haves from nice-to-haves, and agree that if you go to the trouble of reworking your offer, they're truly in a position to go ahead with no other surprises or delays.

2. **"Maybe you're asking for a lower price because you have a cap on how much you're authorized to spend before the decision goes up to someone else. Is that what's happened?"** In these cases ask what level they *are* authorized to spend and what steps they need to take to approve investments above that limit. Offer to work with them to build a business case they can present internally, or better yet, invite them to set up a meeting for you both to meet with the powers that be.

3. **"Maybe you're asking for a lower price because you came to this discussion with a preconceived idea of what the price range should be, and I'm outside that frame of reference. Is that what's happened?"** Ask what they thought the solution was going to cost, and what sources created that impression. They may have underestimated what was needed or scoped their own needs incorrectly (a common problem when customers prescribe their budget before diagnosing their need). Or they might have received bargain basement pricing from a vendor selling a far inferior approach to the one you're advocating. Or they might have simply guessed with no foundation to their logic at all. You have a right to know. So ask. Then process it carefully so they don't feel embarrassed. Let them know you understand how they came to their conclusions. Point out whether their conclusions are based on reasonable assumptions as something you're able to work with or if they've been misinformed and the gulf is too great to cross.

4. **"Maybe you're asking for a lower price because your procurement process has a step in it that says you always have to ask for a discount. Is that really what's going on?"** If the price objection is just for the sake of ticking a box and not a material objection to your offer, you need this called out right away. Some buyers are measured and rewarded on the difference between a supplier's proposal price and the price on the final contract. They don't want to look bad to whomever they report to. If this is what's really on their mind, you could suggest some mutual back scratching wherein you each

walk away with a win after some negotiation that agrees on terms you can each live with.

5. **"Maybe you're asking for a lower price because you don't think my company will really deliver the value we've promised. Is your request really an exercise in risk mitigation?"** Here it helps to isolate exactly what it is they have doubts about, and why. It could be a misunderstanding that requires some reeducation. That's easily resolved. Perhaps they're concerned about *their own company's ability* to make your solution work, in which case you may find an opportunity to sell additional support services they're happy to pay extra for to reduce the risk they sense. Many an outsourcing deal has been won on this premise. Or maybe they simply need you to look them square in the eye and say you won't let them down.

NEGOTIATE VALUE

Most times it's not the key stakeholders you've spent weeks or months establishing your value to who eventually crush you on price but someone else whose job it is to come in as a neutral party and lower the decimals on the ticket. Professional purchasing managers, consultants, project leaders, or financial or contracts officers may try this stunt.

Top sellers make it clear to the prospect that a reduction in price can be achieved . . . but only by stripping the solution's components. If the prospect wants a chocolate cake with jam filling, butter icing, and candles but can't afford it, maybe they can do without the candles. But they can't have all the cake for a price that only buys a slice.

When going into a price negotiation, it helps if you bring a friend with you. That friend should be a mentor from inside the customer's organization who can stare down the price objector and ensure that the price discussion is had one time only and that it is resolved the same day rather than being something that drags you through weeks or months of negotiation. Ideally the mentor would attend with you, like a lawyer who argues your case in front of a judge, and say something like this:

> Look, we're happy with the price and just want to get started with this supplier. They're the ones we want to work with. In the time it takes you to wring a few points off the top, we could already have the solution in place. So let's just pay them to do their job the way they know works best, for the price we agree is fair, and move forward.

Someone you've built social capital with who believes in the business value of your solution should be willing to do this for you. The closer they are to the hub and spokes, the better. All you need do is ask.

Your intent is to help their company move forward and start enjoying the benefits of ownership without stalling the process by having to unbundle the perfect solution and remove parts just to hit an artificial price point. No serious businessperson thinks that putting his outcome at risk is a smart move. So get the customer's own most serious businesspeople arguing on your behalf. Let it become their debate. After all, they're the ones who need the solution, believe in it, and want to work with you. This is *their* opportunity to show how invested they are in that proposition.

The price objector's power is reduced when you use this approach because their strategy to hobble the price of a vendor transforms into a debate about which fingers they want to cut off their own hand.

Let them know you don't think it's a good idea to dismantle, unbundle, or otherwise mess with the plumbing shown on your Solution Map, but if they want to do so, you'll support them. But let the cuts be *their* decision, and with each proposed cut, let them know which results you'll no longer be in a position to promise or guarantee. Help them appreciate that there are consequences to each concession they ask for.

This is important because it reinforces that you didn't bloat your price to begin with and that each element in your solution has a purpose and an outcome, like cogs in a machine. Remove one cog and the machine will no longer run the same way.

Imagine how it looks when they're having a serious cause-and-effect discussion with you in response to a discount request, while your competitors are giddily slashing their price without a fight. Which supplier looks like they really know the customer's business? Who looks like they offered a solution that has a deliberate design backing it, not easily changed? Which supplier looks like they're prepared to debate the discount in the name of what's going to work best for the customer?

That's right, it will be you.

So stand your ground, do the right thing, and let the consequence follow. Customers who buy value and want a real partnership will meet you there. Their compass is pointing to true north.

Customers that want only a cheap transaction might not go forward with you at this point, but that may be a blessing in disguise—if they're fickle now, they're likely to *always* be looking for a better deal somewhere else; they are unlikely to give you any brand loyalty; their repeat business may come at a high cost of sale each time; and they're unlikely to yield good quality references if business outcomes aren't their primary drivers. If they don't buy for the right reasons, they won't measure success the right way.

I'm reminded of two interesting stories that were shared by sellers at the top of their game while doing this book's research interviews. The question asked was this: "How do you help price-sensitive customers shift to thinking about value?" Their answers were illuminating and colorful.

Example 1 of 2: A Mountain of Cash

One account manager always goes into negotiation meetings with a briefcase filled with bundles of "cash" that he has Photoshopped with his picture or company logo onto the bills with the words "not legal tender . . . yet" printed along the margin (to avoid being confused with an attempt at counterfeiting). Other than these cosmetic changes, each note looks like a genuine replica of his country's currency. And the briefcase is stuffed with them. The sum of paper-banded wads in the case is always equal to 10 percent of whatever cash flow he calculates his prospect will gain in the first 6 to 12 months of using his company's solution.

Tucked into a pocket in the case is always a real $10 bill. All this is hidden from sight inside the case, which he always places on the table but doesn't open until the time is right. Sometimes in a display of added theatrics, he enters these meetings with the briefcase handcuffed to his left wrist (so he can still shake hands with his right hand). He draws no other attention to the mystery case as he unlocks the cuffs at the start of the meeting. But the customer sees it and is immediately curious. If they ask about it, he downplays it and says, "We'll touch on it later."

At an appropriate time in the negotiation, he asks the customer to produce a $10 note from their wallet. Most people have this amount in their pocket. He then tells them the closed briefcase contains a lot of money—in fact, an amount equal to their projected gains for every $10 he is asking them to invest in his solution. He asks if they'd like to see how much money that is. Everyone wants to see what's in the case. The catch is they have to hand over their $10 note as the price of admission.

Someone always produces the money (which goes ceremoniously into the account manager's shirt pocket), at which point, he unsnaps the locks, spins the case around to face them, and then opens and closes it quickly so the customer gets a glimpse of what's inside but not long enough to pull any money out. It looks like a case full of money.

The seller then goes into a short verbal presentation about how you need to spend money to make money. His proposal isn't a cost, but an investment. The reason he's talking to them is that he is offering a proven way to exponentially increase their returns. A small investment now will yield big returns within the first 12 months (or however long he calculates it will be). He asks if they have ever bought property or company stock knowing with any certainty what it would be worth a year later. Most say they hope the value will go up, but they never know for sure. He points out that they're describing a gamble, a leap of faith. This level of risk is what they're willing to accept *when they spend their own money.*

He explains his company has been doing the type of work they do for so long, with so many customer cases, that they've taken most of the risk out of the equation. They know their clients will make a return. And today he's offering them the chance to take a "managed leap of faith" with him, to multiply every $10 they invest into a sum equal to the wads of cash in the case. He then upturns the briefcase and spills the banded cubes onto the table, making a small pile, and slides out the real $10 hidden in the case, which he places onto the pile like a cherry topping a sundae. This is so the customer who donated $10 to his shirt pocket doesn't feel like they've lost anything in the discussion.

His point is made. The customer is left with two impressions: "This decision is about value, not cost," and "This supplier is confident enough to show us a calculation about the money we'll make." Good luck to the competitors that follow his presentation. Even if they provide spreadsheets and bar graphs about economic value added, rate of return, or return on investment, it is the guy who dumped piles of cash on their boardroom table that everyone will be telling their friends and colleagues about that night.

Example 2 of 2: A Reference from the Future

The other standout story we were told goes like this. It's an interesting exercise where you write two different versions of a "typical reference story" before attending the meeting and tell your prospect that a year from now you hope they'll be in a position to put their signature on one of them. They need to decide which one it will be.

The two sheets are properly formatted with your company logo, are laser printed onto 100-gsm glossy paper, and look like they're ready to drop into the pages of a magazine. Each one has a blank signature line at the end, over a printout of your contact person's name and job title.

Hand the first reference story out. Only when they finish reading that do you hand out the second reference story. You tell them that you want them to decide which one they want to see themselves signing in a year's time.

In the following examples, the words in brackets would be replaced with real information you have collected about the customer you are selling to. The first reference story you hand out is along the lines of this:

> We signed on with [company] a year ago. Our reason for doing so was that we needed to achieve [vision]. Our reason for making the change was [trigger]. We paid a bit more to work with them, but it was worth it. In the past year their people and ours have worked like a well-oiled machine. It wasn't always easy to achieve the promised results, but [company] demonstrated a flexible and innovative approach to problem solving. Their [solution] worked. In my department we achieved [quantified results]. We also enjoyed the added benefits of [qualitative results]. We have no hesitation recommending this supplier.

The second reference story you hand them says this:

> We signed on with [company] a year ago. Our reason for looking for a supplier was that we needed to achieve [vision]. Before we went ahead, we told them we were sure 10 to 20 percent of the solution wasn't really necessary. Instead of pointing out the risks this would create for us, they cut their proposal and dropped their price. They were desperate to get our business at any cost, even if it meant selling us an incomplete solution. While we cannot give [company] a positive reference about the results we achieved, we can endorse them for being cheap.

The sellers who use this type of approach agree it cuts close to the bone. But that's the point. They see a look pass across the customer's face as they finish reading the second reference. They might look confused, guilty, appreciative, or a combination of all three.

This is where you speak first:

> There's only one type of supplier we're willing to be. You see, our reputation is on the line, and that means as much to us as something else that's core to our company values—making sure we deliver to you a solution we're able to stand behind in full confidence that it will deliver everything you ask for. It seems to me that what we need to agree on in this meeting is what type of customer you want to be. We can succeed together, or we can fail together. So which of these two references is closer to the one you want to be signing your name to a year from now?

This is where you stay silent until you have an answer. Embrace that silence. Don't fill the void with your own voice. Give them time to think about it. If they take the high road as you hope they will, trial close them with this:

> I'm glad to hear you say that.

Lean in to them for a handshake:

> You've made a wise decision.

That statement shifts the "threshold of the close" to the *past tense* and telegraphs to the customer that they've *already made the decision to buy*:

> In order for you to be signing that positive reference story for me a year from now, I need you to sign this for me today . . .

You then slide the signature page of your proposal or contract in front of them and hand them your pen. This is where you stay silent, smile, and cock your head in polite expectation. And again, you keep your mouth shut. Embrace the silence.

If they endorse your offer with their signature, shake hands, don't talk past the close, and wrap up the meeting with a promise of appropriate documentation to follow.

If they walk the low road, refuse to sign, or raise more objections, stall tactics, or hidden concerns, process these by asking for full disclosure of their entire list before dealing with them. Get their concerns out in the open to avoid dealing with one issue only to see another take its place.

These two approaches are colorful and creative. But they're not the only ones top sellers use.

Some hand out Rubik's Cubes with custom printed panels, which the customer can twist until a jumble of fragmented images turns into clear messages printed across each face of the cube. The metaphor served is: "We turn complexity into clarity."

Some begin a presentation by turning out the lights in an enclosed room, and in the darkness that follows they cast dim flashlights at flipcharts about how the customer runs their business today. Then they turn the lights on full blaze when the flipcharts show their solution. The metaphor is: "You're running your business in the dark. We bring you the light."

Be creative. Be dramatic. Be different. Be memorable.

It's an undeniable trend observed in high sales performers that they distinguish themselves by peppering meetings with memorable visual aids designed to make people think and get them talking. The more they're telling other people in the office and at home about something different they experienced in your meeting, the more you get under their skin; the more you are seen as part of their world; the less time your competitors will occupy their thought process. Even if it means being controversial, these tactics are designed to boost your signal strength and bring people back to focusing on value instead of cost. However, always temper your enthusiasm by asking if the visual aid or stunt you plan is going to come across as "cheesy," "kitsch," or "amateurish" by your audience. There's nothing worse than attempting to kick a goal and tripping on your bootlaces.

An even simpler (and often used) response to the customer who says, "I can't believe your price," is to respond wide-eyed along the lines of:

> I know! Cheap isn't it? You've told me this problem is costing you time, productivity, and risk equal to $100 million a year . . . and you get to solve all that for just 20 percent of what the problem is costing you. The approaches you've been using up until now are part of this problem, which is why you've come to me to fix it—which I will. Honestly, I can't believe our price either—a fee of $20 million to turn things around is a bargain.

Then they ask for a verbal commitment to proceed. Star salespeople know to embrace the silence that follows and wait patiently for the customer to speak. Serious buyers will lean back, scratch their chin, and say, "Okay, let's talk." Even if they're not ready to commit yet, any negotiation that follows will be based on *your* paradigm of where the price should be set, not theirs.

But if the customer's reply is to again complain about price as a gambit to lock you into a relationship of transactional bondage, you may need to have the stones to politely smile, stand, and extend your hand to conclude the meeting. The bewilderment that follows as the customer asks *"What are you doing?"* returns control of the meeting to you, where it belongs.

The message you're sending is clear. You're a busy businessperson. You know the value of your offering. If the customer can't see it, you've got other places to be. You need guts to do this. But you'll be amazed how many times the customer will pacify you to stay at the table.

Remember, they *need* you. Sometimes you need to show them when they've pushed the price game too far. Otherwise they'll keep nipping for discounts.

A common formula I hear top sellers citing is this: if they're solving a problem that's costing the customer a 9-digit sum (i.e., a

$200,000,000 problem), their solution needs to be at least 8 digits (i.e., $40,000,000) to have any credibility with senior buyers. An 8-digit problem (i.e., $10,000,000) gets a 7-digit solution (i.e., $2,000,000), and so on. A problem-to-price ratio of 20 to 30 percent is common. It's as if all those zeroes on the end of your price add to the potency of your solution. For this reason, some companies have stopped printing price lists altogether and instead encourage their salespeople to adopt an approach of "value pricing" where they quantify the customer's annual pain and price their offer one decimal lower.

You can do this if you've followed the steps in the Sales Expansion Loop that serve as due diligence when selling to Ideas Buyers. You'll know what, why, who, and how much. But if you haven't followed the process and have instead jumped straight from "Hello" to "Here's my pitch," should you be surprised when the customer responds like a Price Buyer and you have no ammunition to fight back? You create your own reality by the way you sell. Salespeople who face massive price objections at the end of the sale need only look at how they've managed the previous steps to explain why they're in such a mess.

Never Give Unless You Get

At some point you will enter the realm of negotiating the terms of the final deal.

There are so many volumes of books and training and video courses on this aspect of selling that I won't attempt to summarize it fully in this chapter. You can find a lot of information on YouTube for free. But I will share three highlights of what the successful salespeople we interviewed or rode along with told us works most often, in any culture, all around the world.

First, make sure the person you negotiate with is the final arbiter. The last thing you want to do is go through one round of negotiating and give things away, only to be told at the conclusion that it was just the first step and now you're being sent up the line to start over with someone else. Here your end point with Person 1 becomes the starting point for negotiations with Person 2. This sharp practice will go on several rounds if you let it. The buyers have nothing to lose. Their job is to trim the fat, and they'll keep cutting until you cry out and they know they've hit bone. You can avoid this abuse by establishing the rules up front, making sure there will be only one round of negotiations, and that the person sitting across the table has the authority to approve the deal you strike. If not, then don't play. Also, know when to cry out that they've gone too far. Set yourself a floor limit you won't go below.

Next, be aware that it's a favored buyer's tactic to wear sellers down with a seemingly endless stream of requests, knowing that the longer they can drag things out, the more likely we are to give things away just to end the pain. Some observers of professional negotiations note that 80 percent of concessions are given away in the last 20 percent of the meeting because people get emotionally worn out. Buyers try to negotiate each item separately, to get maximum advantage. Then they might look at the item they gained the best concession on, turn it into a benchmark, and say they'd be happy to go ahead if you apply the same percentage across all the items you've just negotiated settlements on. Your first defense is to get all their doubts and requests on the table, then negotiate matters as a whole instead of one by one.

Your next bastion is to always ask for something in return before giving anything away. If they see that every time they ask for something, you're going to ask for reciprocity instead of granting all their requests for free, it gives them pause and stops them grinding you down for more. The more you give, the more they'll take—unless you draw the line. By asking for something in return, you elevate the value of any concession you *do* give. It's only fair to insist on this, and to do so you need to have a list of your own requests prepared before such a discussion takes place.

You can likely anticipate that the customer will hit you for concessions on lower prices, longer payment terms, free trials or support, payment in return for results, buy-back schemes, and similar gains. So what can you ask for of equivalent value from them?

Items favored by top sellers include asking for upfront deposits; shorter payment terms; having the customer agree to buy older models to clear backstocked inventory; being given access to use resources or services in the customer's organization (like their granting you security passes, a cubicle, and lunch vouchers when you visit their office, or having them agree to book and pay for your travel to their sites); being given access to a network of people or groups you can benefit from knowing; their granting positive testimonials on a preplanned release schedule; extended contract periods to keep competitors in the cold longer; and even guarantees to be awarded other contracts that may already or soon be in play in the market.

If you don't know what's possible to ask for, put the shoe on the customer's foot. Master negotiator Roger Dawson promotes simply asking: "If I do that for you, what will you do for me?" He says this:

> *When you ask what they will give you in return, they may say, "Not a darn thing," or "You get to keep our business, that's what you get." That's fine, because you had everything to gain by asking and you haven't lost anything. You can always revert to a position of insisting on a trade-off by saying: "I don't think I can get my people to agree to that unless you're prepared to accept a charge for expedited shipping or move up the payment date."[10]*

As the old adage goes: "If you don't ask, you don't get."

That's why throughout this book I've been advocating that you ask for verbal commitments on small points and create a pattern of the customer telling you *Yes*. Here at the close of the sale is where this behavioral conditioning pays off. You're now on the threshold of winning. Everything you've done in the sales process has led you inexorably to this point.

It's like 6 p.m. on a Friday after a busy week. The sun is shining, you've got the top down on your sports car, sunglasses on, radio cranked up, and you're ready to cruise to your weekend getaway. But one last barrier remains before you can slip onto the freeway. You're at a tollbooth, and it's asking you to feed three "tokens of commitment" into the slot.

The first token is to gain the customer's *verbal* agreement. The second token is to *negotiate* price, terms, and objections. The third token is to secure their *signature* on your contract. With these three tokens fed into the machine, the barrier lifts, the freeway beckons, and you're ready to join the fast lane.

Being able to rise to the challenge of *asking the customer to do something* as a result of your time with them (as though you fully expect them to comply) and getting ink on paper is one of the distinguishing features of an expert seller. You are paid to close deals. The customer expects it. Whether you call it closure, completion, or climax, every long game of seduction ends with somebody making a move.

That's where we go in the next chapter.

Chapter 15

Closing . . . and Opening

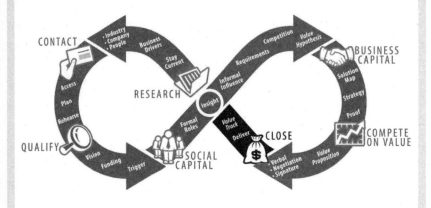

The Sales Expansion Loop: Close

One of the distinguishing features of the Sales Expansion Loop compared to a linear sales funnel is it doesn't have an end point. The "close" is not where we finish our sales activity. It's not where we stop measuring salespeople's success, and it's certainly not where we cease having intriguing dialogue with the stakeholders we just spent weeks, months, or years getting to know. So why do we call this step a "close"?

As a quick recap, the Sales Expansion Loop came to light after watching what today's top solution sellers do the same as each other when pulling complex sales campaigns together. I didn't invent it, but I did give it a name and captured its essence and ethos in visual form. Some people "get it" and readily embrace the need for a new model to sell by. Others defend the ubiquitous wedge shape of the sales funnel as something so familiar, so intrinsic to how they've been raised to sell, that it shouldn't be changed. As outlined earlier in this book, it's a matter of choice.

But making the wrong choice is why some companies burn through successive generations of sales managers and never transform their culture, despite people's best efforts. One after another they join a new employer or get promoted from within to a senior role and proclaim: "*This* is the year we adopt a solution sales culture!" or "*This* is the year we become more customer centric!" They initiate change programs and buy new sales training courses.

You've seen it.

Then like waves crashing on the rocks of reality, they foam and fizz with good intentions until they are spent. The tide takes them back out to sea, then their replacements arrive to do the same thing. Sounds familiar, right?

Having consulted to companies of all sizes in most countries of the world for 25 years, I've seen this as a common pantomime that plays out again and again. Part of the reason is that the underlying physics of how sales organizations plan, manage, measure, and communicate their activity is still stuck in the 1950s models of that old transactional sales funnel and the culture that comes with it. The funnel is so ubiquitous on spreadsheets and CRM screens that nobody challenges its utility. Until now.

It wasn't until we looked at what Hall of Famers are really doing differently that the Loop revealed itself.

I'll assume you've read this far because the kernel of this idea has struck a chord and started to grow within you. So allow me one small indulgence before we dive wholeheartedly into the "how" of closing, because we first need to be clear what *closing* really means. Ask yourself if you've ever stopped to think about where we get the word *closing* from, and why it's associated with the sales profession you work in.

Some people say it comes from the real estate industry, where the *closing date* for a transaction is when buyers transfer funds from their bank to the agent and settle the paperwork in return for the deed and keys. They "close off" the selling discussions so ownership can begin.

Other people say *closing* comes from the legal profession, where attorneys for the plaintiff and defendant take turns delivering their *closing arguments* and summaries of important evidence to a jury, without adding any new information.

Closing time is when a business shuts its doors for the day, when a bar takes "last orders," or when the stock market rings a bell on its last trade. Pulling all our money out of the bank or paying off a credit card, loan, or mortgage is when we *close* our account.

The truth is, nobody remembers exactly what the etymology of *closing* is. But what we see in these examples tells us something about the culture so often associated with *closing*: enemy combatants, judges and juries, transactional exchanges, and money changing hands between people whose job is part merchant, part mercenary.

Is that who you are?

Is that what closing is? Rainmakers the world over say it's more than that.

SO WHAT IS CLOSING, REALLY?

With a Mutual Project Plan (Close Plan) agreed on long ago, the date for the customer to "own" your solution has been etched in stone for some time. Even if they didn't agree to follow your evaluation criteria and timeline suggestion, they still have a date in mind for putting a solution in place. To reach that point, money will need to change hands, and paperwork will need to be completed. And to reach *that* point, someone has to say "Yes." We all know that getting to "Yes" is part of what we call *closing*.

But this is where top sellers start to think differently. In their mind, the customer has already said yes.

They said yes when they listened to your first phone call and agreed to meet; when they confirmed that you understood their vision and the triggers driving a need to change; when they sat back in one of those early meetings and said, "You've really given me something to think about!"

They said yes when every time you met a new person and processed them through the PRECISION Questions, they agreed on the Effect they needed a supplier to have, the full Scope of people affected by this decision, and what they really Need to satisfy all the factors and people involved.

They said yes when they put pen to paper and modified your hand-drawn Trigger Map, then again when they moved sticky notes around on a whiteboard session to agree on what a Solution Map might look like.

They said yes when people on the Influence Map started introducing you to new contacts in the spokes and then in the hub; when they explained their internal decision-making process after you asked about it; when they clarified how they get funding approval for unbudgeted projects or expenditures above their authorization level.

They said yes when the value hypothesis you presented to different people was debated, changed, and reworded to the point that they agreed it was realistic, doable, and desirable; and then again when they provided you with metrics about how they do their job today, how long things take, where the costs and risks and deficiencies occur, and how improving this would give them more time, profit, reputation, and so forth—the seeds that later grew into your value proposition.

They said yes when every time you asked people for something small, like an updated organization chart, copy of their five-year plan, glass of water, or directions to a good restaurant, they invested part of themselves in you and a connection was made; when every time you shared a draft of anything to ask for their input, they actually took the time to do so.

They said yes when they agreed to trade something you want in exchange for something they want, a win-win negotiation was successfully concluded, and they found themselves thinking, "These guys are firm but fair. I'm in good hands. I can do business with them."

They said yes when all through the sale you asked dozens of times, "Does that sound good to you?" "Is that fair?" "Do you understand what I mean?" "Does this sound like what you're looking for?" "Shall we move ahead on that basis?" "Shall we discuss this over a working lunch?" "Will you bring a copy of that to our meeting tomorrow?" "Will you share this with your boss?"

I didn't wait till I was at the altar before I told my bride I loved her. There were thousands of occasions in ways small and great where this built over time. It began with a look, which became a feeling, that turned into lunch and other shared pursuits, then various levels of "let's hang out," "this feels right," "let's keep this forever."

Every relationship begins with "Yes." It's built with yes. It continues with yes. Sometimes I think the letters in *yes* mean *you're equally striving*—heading in the same direction, chasing after the same goal. When *negative opinion* shows its face (it always will), you need enough yes stored up to protect you from no.

So in every sale, whether it takes three months or three years to go from handshake to handshake, there are literally hundreds of opportunities to make yes happen. When you do this, you don't have to worry about the close. It's just another yes.

YOURS FOR THE ASKING

As stated, high performers don't see "the close" as a single event but as a step in a longer journey. Not the last step. Just another one of many.

However, change doesn't happen without a nudge in the right direction. So to win the deal after all the effort invested in prospecting, preparing, planning, and pitching, you now need to ask for a commitment. Don't expect the customer to lead the way.

This is what you're paid to do. Be a leader.

Later in this chapter, I'll share the conversations top solution sellers use. If you want to develop a broader set of skills, there are many books written on closing you might choose to read. Google can show them to you. Just be mindful as you read these to keep one eye open for the transactional techniques that lie in wait. You're likely to read some wonderful wisdom mixed with other techniques that frankly border on coercion and manipulation. I suggest you avoid all of that. You don't want all your hard work to come undone at the finish line because of a clumsy tackle.

Before we look at what you might say to win the sale and ring the bell, let me first share with you something noteworthy the top sellers said about this part of the sale. It has to do with their ideas on why some customers don't buy.

They point out there are three versions: the customer who buys from nobody after talking to everybody; the customer who buys but only after long delays; and the customer who goes ahead but buys from your competitor (or finds an internal solution).

Each of these outcomes can be traced back to inadequate qualification, a lack of motivation, or an absence of belief earlier in the sales process. This is one of the reasons why the clarity you get from writing down your plan and reviewing your progress with others is so important to cultivate often as you pass from one stage of the sale to the next. But behind all these reasons for the sale stalling or going elsewhere is something else: fear of change.

There's a growing opinion in the ranks of the sales elite that our role is transitioning from "sales agent" to "change agent." As the business challenges we're called in to solve become more complex; as our own companies struggle to remain relevant, competitive, and lean; as customers expand or pull back, with the technological, cultural, financial, and operational challenges that follow, so complexity and the pace of change accelerate for everyone. People can hit the wall and disengage due to so much "change fatigue" that they're paralyzed from moving ahead with *anything*.

In 2009 SalesLabs partnered with Johnson & Johnson's Human Performance Institute (creators of the popular *Corporate Athlete* program) at a time when America was in a dark place. Banks were failing, companies were going under, homes and savings were being lost. Our project was to conduct deep research to learn the extent to which these woes were impacting the productivity and motivation of America's workforce.

Two white papers were produced from those findings. *Building Resiliency: The New Business Imperative* (April 2010) and *Engagement Is the Keystone of Employee Productivity* (June 2010).[1] Together our analysts learned that more than 65 percent of workers felt disengaged and burned out because rising corporate expectations had eroded their work-life balance, which in turn was causing an alarming rise in chronic illness, errors, and absenteeism, costing companies billions of dollars in medical costs and lost productivity. This isn't isolated to America; the same story unfolds anywhere as economies sputter.

So risk aversion, burnout, and change reluctance are other dimensions we need to understand when we try to close sales.

Have you ever managed a sale perfectly, confirmed budget and authority, nailed your presentation, seen everyone nodding their heads in agreement that your proposition is brilliant, but then the customer does nothing about it? You drive away from their office ranting, "What's wrong with these people? Are they thick or something?" We've all faced bewilderment in that situation.

Let's look at four reasons it happens and some simple change management practices to handle each:

1. **They were happy to "go with the flow" when nothing was required of them, but when asked to take action, they _lacked the will_ to engage.** This may be due to skepticism or exhaustion, and it can manifest as passive resistance to _anything_. If your implementation plan has 10 steps, you need to show it has only 3 steps—which someone else will do for them. Make the workload simple, so all they need to do is nod their head when you invite them to move forward. Ease their burden. Make it easy for them to say yes.

2. **They retain strong emotional connections or _nostalgia_ for the people who established the current way of doing things, want to preserve their memory, and avoid taking action that feels disloyal.** This bond can be very strong. So find the person who introduced the changes people now cling to and get their endorsement. Ask what people like most about the way things are, and build awareness of how your solution embraces all the things they already enjoy, plus a few updates. Deemphasize how "new" you are, and reemphasize how much the "same" you are.

   When Kellogg's releases new versions of its cornflake, it doesn't put big red letters on the box that say "New." They say "Improved." People don't always like new. They prefer what they have. After all, look at what happened to Coca-Cola when it released "New Coke"—the world was in an uproar and Pepsi claimed their market share!

   So explain how your solution is an evolution, not a revolution, where everything they enjoy will be the same, with a few changes. Then ask again for their commitment.

3. **They _fear_ losing the security of routines, tools, or work practices they understand, or they fear that the changes will shift the balance of power to others and thereby disadvantage them.** Fear, uncertainty, and doubt are highly emotional triggers, best handled with open communication to resolve their concerns. This begins with: "I understand . . . ," moves to "Tell me how you feel about . . . ," and includes "What do you need to see happen so you can get behind this?" Give _them_ the power.

You'll need to use short sentences and straight talk with no hint of slickness. Be prepared to listen. Deal with one concern at a time.

If they fear your solution will give others an advantage, you're looking at internal politics in play. It's best to ask someone else in the customer's business with whom you have good rapport to help you understand the dynamic of what's going on. There may be territorial or historic rivalry. As an outsider, you can't resolve any of that. But you can give them a chance to air their concerns and to agree on what you have the power to change, with care to make clear what's beyond your control.

Sometimes allowing them to air their grievances is enough. By talking about things, they may resolve their own fears. At other times you may need to write down a plan of items they need to hear or see to overcome their fears. Gain their tacit agreement that if you make those things happen, they'll move ahead. Remember to negotiate action in return for resolution.

4. **They doubt they have the skills or time to lead the change or that their company will adequately support them. It's less *risky* for them to do nothing than to be set up to fail.** This comes from a lack of belief in themselves, their team, or the people they work for. If you're selling a corporate solution that affects different departments, you may need to find a new sponsor and get the responsibility (and the risk) to change hands to someone more likely to go the distance. If you're selling something into one department only, enlist help from other people who want to see their company move forward. Help the person who feels the most risk see that they can be trained in the skills or knowledge they need or that tasks can be delegated and that responsibility for success can be shared.

Beyond these reasons for delay, there's nothing else stopping you from asking for the business, except the fear of hearing "No." So again, if you've built up a credit of "Yes" throughout the sale, this should be easy to ask for.

SELF-BELIEF

But are you the sort of person who believes you're worth saying yes to? Do you ask for the things you want as if you fully expect people to give them to you in every facet of your life? Do you exude an aura of confidence and belief that attracts success, or do people treat you as if your opinions carry little weight and pleasing you is optional?

When I started my sales career, I noticed my results were hit-and-miss. I found some people easy to sell to, while others intimidated me. As I thought back to those meetings at the end of each day, I started to see that the people I had success with were the ones who were most like me. Similar age, common background, the sort of people I could see myself having as friends. The ones I blew it with were the ones who were very different in age, wealth, culture, and bearing. I felt like a kid in their presence. And I realized I didn't talk to them as easily as I talked with my other customers.

My language was stilted because I was trying so hard to impress them I got tongue-tied and stumbled over "umms," "errs," and "maybes." This lack of confidence and almost apologetic demeanor meant I didn't look them in the eye as much as I should have, instead averting my gaze to look at the pages of my presentation, which I flipped through in robotic fashion. When I asked for anything with these people, I sounded like a wolf in my own ears, but I'm sure they heard me bleat like a sheep.

My sales manager at the time told me the best way to overcome fear was to learn more about the subject that intimidated me. He challenged me to learn all I could about these customers. So I went to work researching them.

When I'd learned all I could, my manager then challenged me to spend two weeks asking everyone I met for something. I asked, "Like what?" and he said it didn't matter.

If a restaurant brought me a sandwich with too much fat on the bacon, I should send it back to the kitchen and ask them to trim it. If I was buying something in a retail store, I should ask for a free item or a discount every time. If I saw a pretty girl at a club, I should go suggest she should buy me a drink.

His ideas sounded preposterous. But he had a way of asking me to do things as if he fully expected me to say yes. So I did. And in doing it, I learned why he gave me this counsel.

The more I asked for things in my private life, the more I got. And this translated to my customer calls.

In future meetings I found I was able to hold an intelligent conversation about their business, not just hide behind my presentation kit. The amount of time I looked them in the eyes increased. My confidence to ask for their business went up, and so did my bank account.

That was a quarter of a century ago, and it's proved to be good policy ever since. Ask and ye shall receive. I challenge you to spend two weeks asking everyone you meet for the things you want, in a voice that sounds like you fully expect them to say yes. Don't worry about sounding overbearing—you can always dial it back after the experiment is done. Those who try this find it works. You will too.

CLOSING TECHNIQUES

So as top sellers are sitting across the table from customers and need to ask for the business, what works best? They're quick to tell us that it's not what they do here that matters most. It's how well they navigated the sale up to this point that decides if they win or lose. In fact, by scoring the opportunity on the Snapshot at regular intervals and making frequent course corrections to close their gaps, most have a decent sense that they've already won the sale by now and that the close is just a formality. This type of certainty comes with experience and by following a sound sales process.

For this reason, star salespeople say closing is more about the whole conversation you've been having with the customer than it is about anything you do in a final meeting. However, they have some favorite phrases to cap the sale. Here are three:

The Trilogy

This is where you summarize in three ways what you will deliver, such as (1) your product, (2) your benefits, and (3) what your solution will mean to the customer:

- "Do we agree my solution is (1) the best fit to your criteria, (2) easier to implement, and (3) more reliable than other units you've tested? Okay then, unless you know of a reason we shouldn't proceed . . ."
- "Our office layouts are (1) made with carbon-neutral materials that meet your environmental policy, (2) more ergonomically designed, which helps people conserve energy as they work, especially relevant since half your workforce is over 40, and (3) prefitted with power and communications cabling so each work desk can be set up 20 percent faster."

The Trilogy Close works through the principle of triples, where three things together act as a set of hammer blows to drive the message home.

You probably already use the Trilogy instinctively in daily life. "Let's go for (1) dinner, (2) a movie, and (3) see where the night takes us." Or parents might relate to: "If you eat your vegetables, you'll (1) grow up strong, (2) see in the dark, and (3) get ice cream for dessert."

Three benefits are always more memorable than one.

The Alternative

A classic. This is where you offer two or three choices, knowing that any answer the buyer gives will be a commitment to you. Don't offer too many alternatives, or you'll confuse them.

If you're offering three choices, put your preferred one in the middle so it's not the first one they hear nor the last one. People defer to the middle ground more often. If you're offering two choices, give

293

a slight nod and smile when you mention the option you want them to take. People tend to follow such body language:

- "Would you prefer your executive fleet to be the Gulfstreams or the Learjets? In fact, if I can arrange a special flight next week to go up and sign the order at 20,000 feet, is Tuesday or Thursday better?"
- "Would you like to have this installed during the summer holidays while the office is almost vacant, or after people get back to work?"
- "Do you want us to train all the users together, or do you want us to run different sessions in smaller teams?"

The Alternative works on the assumption that the customer has already decided to buy, and the only question remaining is which of the options you present should be chosen.

Back to the Future

This is where you treat the decision to buy as obvious and self-evident. In fact, you skip asking for the order at all, and you move straight on to the type of questions that would normally follow a commitment being given, such as these:

- "What will your boss say when she sees this installed next month?"
- "I'll come myself when we deliver it, and we'll do a group photo over lunch to mark the occasion. Is Monday afternoon good?"
- "You mentioned that it was important for your engineers to learn the system before anyone else. Who should I talk with to book a date for their session?"

This Back to the Future close removes the tension a customer feels when they face a moment of decision. You simply skip that part by jumping to the future and have the conversation that would follow. When the buyer joins you there and starts talking about that future, it's clear they're along for the ride and have settled into that frame of mind. Now they own it.

While these three phrases ease the customer past the close without hitting it head-on, they really are no substitute to squaring your shoulders, lifting your chin firmly, and fixing your gaze coolly on your target's eyes to say:

> I believe in this solution and the company backing me.
> And based on our discussions, so do you.
> Now I want to be in business with you. Today.

Stay silent. Wait for them to make the next move. Don't blink.

BEYOND THE CLOSE

All through the sales process, you've been making promises for something the customer's stakeholders can't touch, smell, or see. If you're selling a solution to a problem, or an enabler for change, what you're selling is the result, not the product. When companies pay salespeople commissions on these deals, they're rewarding us for making a promise, not for delivering it.

That's not how your counterparts in the customer's organization are rewarded. Their company doesn't hand buyers a bonus for signing a deal. It might, however, reward them for achieving the sought-after results.

So to show that we're truly customer centric is to demonstrate an interest in the customer's welfare well beyond the close of the sale. Progressive-thinking salespeople stay close to their customer even after they've handed the deal along to a customer service team, partner, or other group that takes care of the delivery, installation, education, and support.

As mentioned in the discussion on using case studies in Chapter 13, after winning a deal is where all the notes you took during the sale become gold dust. Dig out all those old F2F Meeting Plans and Solution Maps for each person or department. You'll see metrics recorded here if you asked the right questions during the sale. Some metrics will be for their performance as it is today, and others will reflect their desired state. The same things would be written in your proposal—another resource to refer to.

In the postsale period, it pays to create a document you and the customer can use as a scorecard. Decide who will measure it, what metrics to use, and agree to meet on a monthly or quarterly basis (with the support staff your company assigns to look after this customer). Your task in these Value Track meetings is to stay on top of these numbers.

Where they hit or exceed their goal using your solution: celebrate it. Where they get behind the curve: talk about why. There may be gaps in the way their people are using your solution, which some training from your company could resolve. There may be other issues you need to fix, or there may be problems internal to their organization that aren't deficiencies on your company's part but still need to be aired and resolved.

Along the way as you are seen to be "delivering the promise," ask for referrals to other departments or to companies in your territory with similar needs.

Take in a camera to snap people's photos, and write up testimonials that show their faces and preliminary results. Ask them to approve or modify these. Top sellers collect case studies and reference stories like trophies to be displayed.

At the end of six months and then a year and at key dates thereafter, sales superstars make sure they repeat these meetings, always measuring, always helping to tune the customer's results. Of course, you don't usurp your own customer support team, but you *do* orchestrate their efforts when what's on the line is your reputation. It's just good account management.

As you do this, you will gain insight into new opportunities to add services, extend contracts, and network to other people in the account. Here you are passing the threshold of the Insight junction in the Sales Expansion Loop again. This is the third time you've been here. This time you're *adding* insight to your supporters in the account about what's working in their usage of the last solution you sold them. You're *gaining* insight into changes in their business and the new challenges and opportunities people are talking about on the inside.

This customer intimacy allows you to propose new ideas. Of course you'll need to research these a bit more before proposing anything. But this only brings you back to the start of the Sales Expansion Loop . . . I believe you know your way from here.

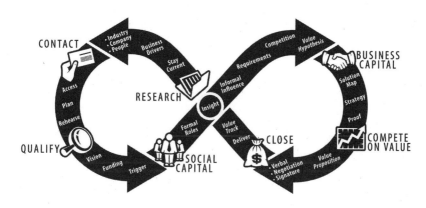

Endnotes

Foreword

1. BRICS is an international political organization of leading emerging economies that comprises Brazil, Russia, India, the People's Republic of China, and South Africa. These are developing or newly industrialized countries distinguished by their large economies and significant influence on regional and global affairs.

Chapter 1

1. Lori Wizdo with Peter Burris and Sophia I. Vargas, *The Lead Nurturing Payoff for the Tech Industry*, Forrester Research, October 21, 2011.

Chapter 2

1. Source: "Rechercher" in the *Merriam-Webster Online Dictionary* and *Wiktionary*.

2. Rudyard Kipling, "The Elephant's Child," *Just So Stories*, Macmillan, New York, 1902.

Chapter 3

1. http://en.wikipedia.org/wiki/Helmuth_von_Moltke_the_Elder.

2. From a speech to the National Defense Executive Reserve Conference in Washington, DC, November 14, 1957. In Public Papers of the Presidents of the United States, Dwight D. Eisenhower, 1957, National Archives and Records Service, Government Printing Office, Washington, DC, p. 818.

3. Eric Heydenberk and Rob Okrzesik, "What Is Instinct and Why Is It So Important?" *The Human Brain: An Owner's Manual*, 2001, http://library.thinkquest.org/C0114820/emotional/instinct/php3.

4. Reporters Committee for Freedom of the Press (U.S.), "Reporter's Recording Guide: A State-by-State Guide to Taping Phone Calls and In-Person Conversation," researched and written by McCormick Legal Fellow Kristen Rasmussen, Ethics and Excellence in Journalism Legal Fellow Jack Komperda, and legal intern Raymond Baldino, http://www.rcfp.org/reporters-recording-guide. See also Karen Holden, Senior Partner, A City Law Firm LLP (U.K.), "The Legal Ramifications of Recording Conversations," August 2009, http://www.newbusiness.co.uk/articles/legal-advice/the-legal-ramifications-recording-conversations; and John Elliott, David Landy, and Clayton Utz, "Australia: Recording a Meeting?" September 2010, http://www.mondaq.com/australia/article.asp?articleid=110488.

5. According to *The Free Dictionary* by Farlex (www.thefreedictionary.com), a *primer* is described as a cap or tube containing a small amount of explosive used to detonate the main explosive charge of a firearm or mine, or it is an undercoat of paint applied to prepare a surface for painting, or it is a segment of DNA or RNA that is complementary to a given DNA sequence and that is needed to initiate replication by DNA polymerase. For our purposes in explaining social capital as a primer for business capital, all three definitions apply as appropriate metaphors.

6. Aron Rolston, *Between a Rock and a Hard Place*, Atria Books, New York, 2004, was adapted into Danny Boyle's film *127 Hours* starring James Franco (Fox Searchlight, 2010).

Chapter 4

1. A. D. McNaught and the International Union of Pure and Applied Chemistry, *Compendium of Chemical Terminology*, 2d ed., Oxford, UK, Blackwell Science, 1997.

Chapter 5

1. Sun-tzu, *The Art of War*, edited by James Clavell, Delacort Press, 1983.

2. The statistic of a 2.3-million-member military is from the article by Christopher Bodeen of the Associated Press, "China's Military Launches Diplomatic Charm Offensive Amid Concerns over Rapid Expansion," *Washington Post*, October 21, 2011. According to the U.S. Central Intelligence Agency's *CIA World Factbook 2011*, the true number of men and women aged 16 to 49 *available* for military service in China is 750 million.

3. Carol Millett, editor, "Huawei Clinches Everything Everywhere Network Upgrade Deal," *Mobile Today*, May 9, 2011.

4. Harriet Alexander, "China's New Silk Road into Europe," *The Telegraph*, July 4, 2010.

5. Peter Gorenstein, "China Ends America's Century Old Manufacturing Dominance," *Daily Ticker* on Yahoo! Finance.com, March 14, 2011; and Peter Marsh, "China Noses Ahead as Top Goods Producer," *Financial Times*, March 13, 2011.

6. Trevor Royle, "Why China Is Ready to Bail Out Eurozone," *Herald Scotland*, October 30, 2011.

7. Max Hastings, "Europe Is Cosying Up to the Chinese Dragon at Its Peril," *Daily Mail*, October 30, 2011.

Chapter 6

1. Dr. Stephen R. Wenn of Laurier University, "Riding into the Sunset: Richard Pound, Dick Ebersol, and Long-Term Olympic Television Contracts," a paper presented at the Fifth International Symposium for Olympic Research, September 8–10, 2000. See also Sally Jenkins, "Peacock Power," *Sports Illustrated*, December 25, 1995.

Chapter 7

1. Matt Phillips, "Malcolm Gladwell on Culture, Cockpit Communication and Plane Crashes," in *Wall Street Journal's Middleseat* blog, December 4, 2008.

2. Sae Park, "The Danger of Outliers," *Asiance* magazine, December 2008, http://www.asiancemagazine.com/dec_2008/the_danger_of_outliers.

Chapter 8

1. Robert D. Putnam, *Bowling Alone: The Collapse and Revival of American Community*, Simon & Schuster, New York, 2000.

2. Nan Lin, *Social Capital: A Theory of Social Structure and Action*, Cambridge University Press, Cambridge, U.K., 2001; and Jens Eklinder-Frick, Lars Torsten Eriksson, and Lars Hallén, "Bridging and Bonding Forms of Social Capital in a Regional Strategic Framework," *Industrial Marketing Management*, vol. 40, no. 6, August 2011, pp. 994–1003.

3. Jonathan Davis, "Buffett on Bridge," www.buffettcup.com.

4. Peter Ostrow, "Sales Forecasting: How Top Performers Leverage the Past, Visualize the Present, and Improve Their Future Revenue," Aberdeen Group, Boston, July 2011, and Peter Ostrow, "Sales Forecasting: Analytics to the Rescue!" Aberdeen Group, Boston, June 30, 2010.

Chapter 10

1. Adapted from Dr. A. J. Schuler, "Overcoming Resistance to Change: Top Ten Reasons for Change Resistance," 2003, www.schulersolutions.com/resistance_to_change.html. To find out more about Dr. Schuler's programs and services, visit www.SchulerSolutions.com.

2. Facebook "People Talking About" rankings on December 21, 2011. *The Dark Knight Rises* (film): 12,337; *The Girl with the Dragon Tattoo* (novel): 10,457; *Endworlds* (novel): 8,534; *Indiana Jones* (film): 4,776; *The Walking Dead* (novel): 4,044. *Star Wars The Clone Wars* (television): 1,572. Michael Crichton's *Micro* (novel): 1,024. Stephen King's *11/22/63* (novel): 542.

3. Ibid.

Chapter 11

1. Warren E. Buffett, Chairman's Letter, Berkshire Hathaway, Inc., 1990 Annual Report, http://www.berkshirehathaway.com/letters/1990.html.

2. The term *classical conditioning* (also called a *Pavlovian response*) comes from an experiment where the 1904 Nobel Prize–winning physiologist Ivan Pavlov observed that when a bell was rung just before food was presented to a dog, the dog would salivate in anticipation of the meal. Through repetition as the dog came to associate the ringing of the bell with the presentation of food, it would salivate when the bell rang even when no food was present. Fields as diverse as sports training, the military, and advertising agencies have since applied this concept to make people respond to specific stimuli with a range of predetermined learned reflexes. The more an act is repeated, the easier a subject performs the act. See Ivan Pavlov (translated by G. V. Anrep), *Conditioned Reflexes: An Investigation of the Physiological Activity of the Cerebral Cortex*, Oxford University Press, London, 1927; and Robert F. Schmidt and Gerhard Thews (translated by Marguerite A. Biederman-Thorson), "Behavior Memory (Learning by Conditioning)," *Human Physiology*, Springer, New York, 1989, pp. 155–156.

3. "Richard Bandler," *Wikipedia*, http://en.wikipedia.org/wiki/Richard_Bandler.

Chapter 12

1. "EMC Corporation Q2 2011 Earnings Call Transcript," *Morningstar*, July 20, 2011.

2. "New Pricelist 2012," January 19, 2011, Airbus.com.

3. Seth Stevenson, "The Cocktail Creationist," *New York Magazine*, May 21, 2005.

Chapter 14

1. Sara Reisatd-Long, "The Best Time of Day for Superior Brain Power," *Mind Power News*, October 14, 2010; and Lee Gerdes and Sung Lee, MD, "Your Brainwaves on Sleep," *Brain World*, March 18, 2011.

2. C. L. Asplund, J. J. Todd, A. P. Snyder, and R. Marois, "A Central Role for the Lateral Prefrontal Cortex in Goal-Directed and Stimulus-Driven Attention," *Nature Neuroscience*, vol. 13, 2010, 507–512.

3. Dr. Hannu Verkasalo, Zokem Technologies, "Mobile Web and Application Usage Goes Up," December 31, 2010. Zokem Mobile Insights statistics are based on patented nonparametric measurements that take place directly in smartphones. In the study, Zokem analyzed a data set of more than 10,000 smartphone users, including 6.5 million distinct smartphone application usage sessions in 16 countries between 2009 and 2010.

4. K. Parham, "The Best Time to Give a Presentation at Work," August 2011, www.realsimple.com; and A. Bradbury, *Successful Presentation Skills,* Kogan Page, Philadelphia, March 2010.

5. Dan Zarrella, Social Media Marketing Scientist, "New Data: Emails Sent on Saturdays Have Higher CTRs and Lower Unsub Rates," *Hubspot,* February 1, 2011; "The Science of Email Marketing," webinar, *Hubspot;* Bob Nunn, "10 Charts on the Best Time of Day/Week for Social Media Marketing," *Brand Mechanics,* January 18, 2011; and Matt McNeill, "When Is the Best Time to Send My Email Marketing Campaign?" *Knowledge Base,* September 2, 2010, www.Sign-Up.to.

6. Ken Moley, "The Results Are In: Best Times for a Webinar," *Marketing Watchdog Journal,* no. 51, May 2008.

7. Accountemps, "Study: Tuesday Most Productive Day of Work Week," *Boston Business Journal,* February 7, 2008.

8. Greg Miller, "The Emotional Brain Weighs Its Options," *Science,* vol. 313, no. 5787, August 4, 2006.

9. "Penn & Teller: BS," S01E07, Showtime, March 7, 2003.

10. Roger Dawson, "Never Make a Concession When You're Negotiating Unless You Ask for Something in Return," a blog by Roger Dawson, www.rdawson.com/articles/trading-off.html. Also see Roger Dawson's book, *Secrets of Power Negotiating,* Career Press, 2000.

Chapter 15

1. *Building Resiliency: The New Business Imperative,* Human Performance Institute, April 2010, and *Engagement Is the Keystone of Employee Productivity,* Human Performance Institute, June 2010. See https://www.hpinstitute.com/research-press/research-and-white-papers.

Index

About the Author

Nic Read is a former executive director at Ernst & Young where he was global cochair of the firm's revenue growth consulting practice. His research and opinions on growth and sales governance have been covered by *Forbes*, FOX and ABC television, *USAToday*, *SellingPower*, *Thinksales*, and other international magazines, webcasts, and television and radio shows.

Winner of the gold International Business Award in 2005 and 2007, he is coauthor to the chart-topping *Selling to the C-Suite* (McGraw-Hill, 2009). He is also founder of the consulting and training firm SalesLabs, where he is a lead designer of workshops, consulting methodologies, and sales simulations taught at selected business schools and to clients in over 40 countries.

His early career was in sales and management, dialing the numbers, chasing the leads, hitting the bricks, and bringing home the bacon. He now advises clients that range from Fortune 100 companies to entrepreneurial start-ups in media, entertainment, telecommunications, computer hardware, software, banking, financial and professional services, energy, pharmaceuticals, manufacturing, biotech, logistics, and aerospace.

By design, his career has been nomadic, dropping him into the hotspots of globalization, deregulation, and other shifts in business dynamics for which understanding is best gained on the ground. He was in Germany soon after the fall of the Berlin Wall helping companies break into virgin East European markets; he relocated to Shanghai after China's entry to the World Trade Organization and rise as a financial power; and he was in New York as the global financial crisis sent shockwaves around the world. He is currently based in London where he is watching the cultural, monetary, and political changes in the Eurozone, Africa, and Middle East with great interest.